Firecrest
Round the World

FIRECREST ROUND THE WORLD

Alain Gerbault

Two Complete Books

The Fight of the Firecrest
&
In Quest of the Sun

DAVID McKAY COMPANY, INC.
New York

First Dual U. S. Edition, 1981
Firecrest Round the World

ISBN 0-679-50978-X

Manufactured in the United States of America

THE FIGHT OF THE FIRECREST

by

ALAIN GERBAULT

The Record of a Lone-Hand Cruise from East to West across the Atlantic

CONTENTS

ILLUSTRATIONS

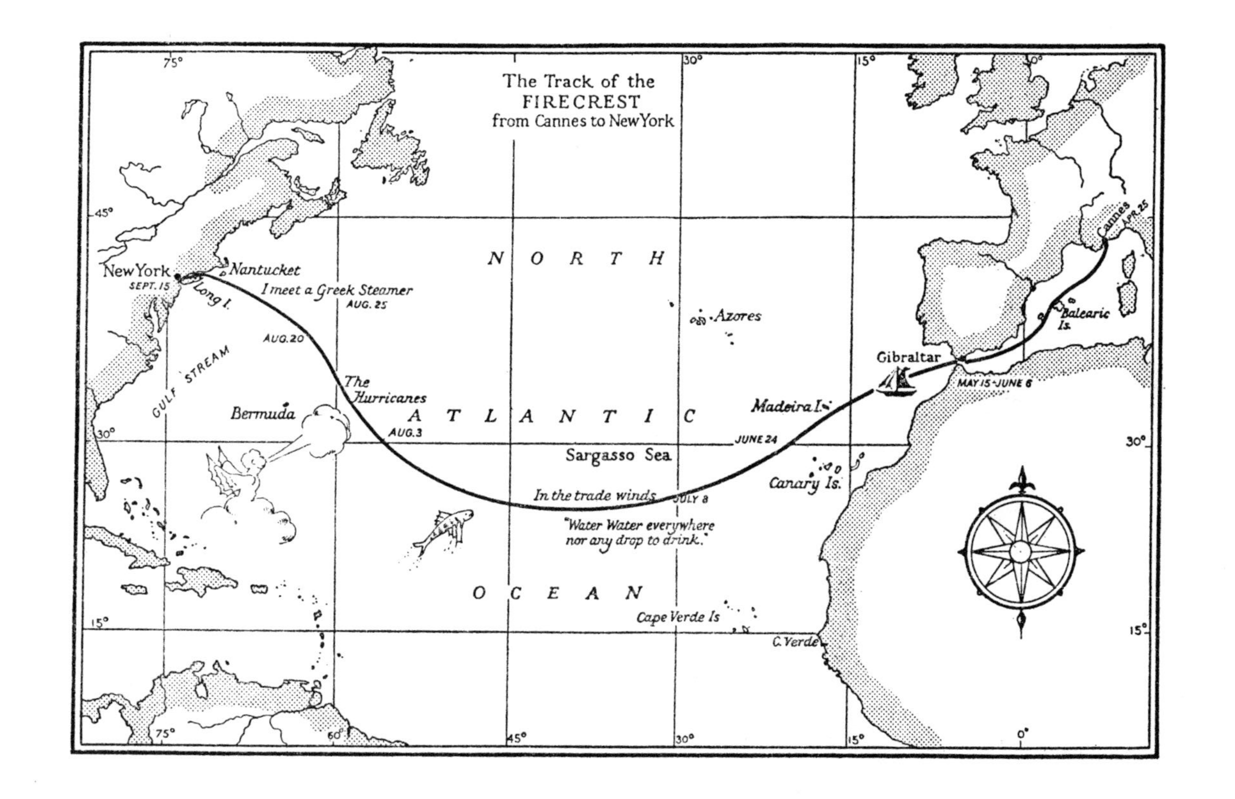
The Track of the
FIRECREST
from Cannes to New York
NORTH ATLANTIC OCEAN
New York
SEPT. 15
Nantucket
Long I.
I meet a Greek Steamer
AUG. 25
AUG. 20
GULF STREAM
The Hurricanes
Bermuda
AUG. 3
Azores
Sargasso Sea
In the trade winds
JULY 8
"Water Water everywhere
nor any drop to drink."
Cape Verde Is
C. Verde
Canary Is.
JUNE 24
Madeira I.
Gibraltar
MAY 15-JUNE 6
Balearic Is.
Cannes
APR. 25
75°
60°
45°
30°
15°
0°

CHAPTER ONE

WHICH IS REALLY THE PREFACE

It is in a country house near New York, and on a wonderfully quiet evening, that I am wondering whether the adventures of the past months are real. Glancing out through the window I can see Long Island Sound, and the mast of my little *Firecrest* a few hundred yards away as she lies alongside Fort Totten pier.

But it is not a dream. I have crossed the Atlantic alone, and am now in the United States. Less than a month ago I was tossing like a cork on the crest of the waves, and fighting for life against hurricanes that buried my little boat under tons of green water and tore her sails to ribbons.

Near me is the log book that I never failed to keep, even in the worst weather. Turning the leaves, still moistened with salt water, my eyes fall on this interesting day of my cruise:

"Aboard the *Firecrest*, the 14th of August, at sea, 34 degrees 45 minutes of north latitude, and 56 degrees 10 minutes of west longitude.

"Strong westerly gales. The motion of the boat

has been fierce all night, and seas are breaking aboard every minute. At four o'clock in the morning a jib sheet broke under the strain, and I had to splice it at once. The deck is all the time under water. Keeping all the hatches shut down does not prevent getting everything soaked down below. Cooking my breakfast is a very difficult task, and it is only after two hours of tossing about in the narrow galley, and after having my head bumped many times against the panels of the forecastle, that I am able to absorb a cup of tea and some bacon rashers.

"At nine a.m. the reef lacing of my staysail breaks. The motion of the boat is now so violent, and the wind so strong, that I cannot repair it. All my cups and glasses are broken into small pieces.

"At noon a huge wave breaks aboard and carries away my sail locker hatch. The waves are increasing in size, the sea is now tremendous. It blows so hard that my sails cannot stand the strain. A big hole appears in my staysail, and my mainsail rips down the centre seam, leaving a three-yard-long slit. I have to lower both to save them: a very difficult and risky job to do in such a wind, and with such a sea.

"Can hardly stand on the wet and slippery deck, and it requires one full hour to accomplish the task. I am tempted to set my storm trysail, but the wind is still increasing. It is now a real hurricane.

In such weather no sail can stand. The humming of the steel shrouds now gives exactly the same note one hears in a fast express train. It means that the wind has attained a velocity of more than sixty miles an hour.

"It is necessary now or never to use my sea-anchor. Have made one end of a forty-fathom line fast to the sea-anchor, and the other end fast to my anchor chain. Have dropped the steel-hooped bag overboard, attaching to it a small buoy as a float. The line has stiffened, and, very slowly, the boat's head has come into the wind.

"The motion is not now so bad, although I am badly pounded by the seas. I have lashed some old sails on the top of my sail locker to prevent the water from rushing in. I am feeling absolutely dead tired, but have still more work to do. Have taken down below my tattered sails, and, closing behind me all the openings, have spent all the evening and the greater part of the night with palm and needle.

"It is now raining hard. In the saloon the water is at the floor level. Trying to pump the water out I have made the annoying discovery that my pump is out of order. It is now raining harder; am soaked to the skin; there is not a single dry place in the boat, and I cannot find a way to prevent the rain water leaking through many places around the skylight and hatchways."

This was but an ordinary day during the month of gales encountered towards the middle of the cruise. But what a life it was! Although it is only a few days since I landed I am longing to heave up anchor again and live again on the open seas.

And here, too, I start dreaming. "How did I become a sailor? How did the love of the open sea come to me?"

I spent the greater part of my youth at Dinard, near the old fortified town of St. Malo, the home of the famous French corsairs who were the glory of the French navy three hundred years ago.

When my father, who spent a good part of the summer on his yacht, was not taking me with him on long cruises, I was always trying to ship with the hardy Breton fishermen for a day, and making fishermen's sons my companions. Even then my absorbing ambition was to own a little craft of my own.

Once my brother and I saved money enough to buy a boat, but another bought her before we were ready. I envied the Breton fishermen their independent life, and was thrilled by the tales of their daring and hardihood.

It was at Dinard and St. Malo that I learned to love the sea, the waves and the boisterous winds. Books of adventure were my favourites. Many of them were describing the adventures of gold-hunters in Klondike and Alaska. The name Eldorado exercised great fascination for me. I used to think when I became a man I should try to discover Eldorado.

When quite a little boy Joseph Conrad put his finger one day on an unexplored part of a chart of Central Africa, and said, "When I grow up I will go there." He fulfilled his dream. I shall never fulfil my boyhood's dream, but shall probably share the fate of Edgar Allan Poe's hero.

After a happy youth by the seaside at Dinard, I was sent to Paris to study and become a boarder in the Stanislas College. There, shut between high walls, longing to escape, to see the world, dreaming of adventure, I spent the most unhappy years of my life. But I had to study to graduate as a civil engineer.

When the war came I enlisted in 1914 in the Flying Corps, and after the dull life at college it was a glorious adventure.

A young American, an aviator in my squadron, the 31st French, lent me some of Jack London's books. It was in reading "The Cruise of the *Shark*" that I first learned that it was possible to cross the ocean in a small boat.

I decided at once that it was going to be my life, if I was lucky enough to get through the war. Later I was able to include two of my friends in my schemes, and to decide to buy a boat, and sail round the world after adventure. But these two friends were killed fighting in the air, and I was left alone at the armistice.

After the war I could neither work in a city nor lead the dull life of a business man. I wanted freedom, open air, adventure. I found it on the sea.

Putting aside my future as a civil engineer, I searched for a year in all the French ports for a boat I could handle alone, and it was only in 1921, while visiting my friend Ralph Stock, the author of "The Cruise of the *Dream Ship*," aboard his yacht, that I found, lying near his boat at Southampton, a nice little craft. It was the *Firecrest*.

CHAPTER TWO

THE *FIRECREST*

THE *Firecrest* is a racing cruiser, designed by the late Dixon Kemp, and built by P. T. Harris at Rowhedge, Essex, in 1892. It speaks well for the designer that a boat built under the length and sail area rule has crossed the Atlantic and shown herself a splendid cruising boat.

She is a typical English cutter, narrow and deep for a length of 39 feet over all, and 30 feet on the water-line. Her greatest beam is 8 feet 6 inches. A 7-feet draught is exceptionally deep for her size. This draught, and the three tons and a half of lead she carries on her keel, added to the three tons of inside ballast, makes it practically impossible for her to capsize. Her deck is flush, unbroken save for one companion-way and a hatch forward, two skylights and the sail locker hatch, and she has the strength to resist the pressure of tons of green water breaking over her bow. She is cutter rigged, and here I can hear the great army of theoretical yachtsmen exclaim, "A cutter or sloop is not fit for cruising in alone. Why not a ketch or a schooner?" It is a matter of taste. Personally I prefer to reef sails rather than take them in. In any case I have found that the cutter is the best cruising rig for a small boat because it gives the maximum speed with the minimum sail area.

There is not enough room on deck to carry a real lifeboat. But as a concession to the conventions, and to permit of going ashore when lying in harbour, I carry a six-foot dinghy made of canvas. It is a Berthon of the type used in France aboard submarines. It is collapsible, and once folded it takes no room at all alongside the skylights.

The *Firecrest* is very strongly built of old English oak and teak. Although thirty-two years old she is absolutely sound, and a poem would be needed to sing her staunchness. But better that I refrain, and, instead, describe the inside of my floating home.

This home comprises three compartments, separated by doors and bulkheads. Astern lies my sleeping-cabin with two bunks, and lockers under them. A wash-basin receives the water of a fifteen-gallon tank fixed under the deck. The cabin is panelled with mahogany and bird's-eye maple. On each side racks are filled with books. Forward of the sleeping-room, and amidships, is a saloon likewise panelled with mahogany and maple. On each side are two cupboards with good accommodation. In the centre is a folding table. In the bow is the "fo'c'sle," with two folding cots and a galley. Here I cook my meals on a Swedish

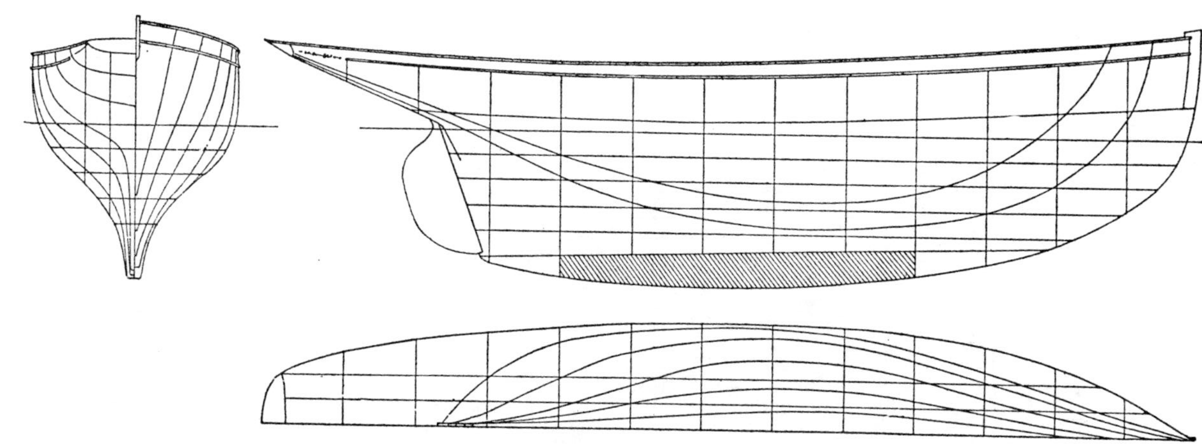

The lines of the *Firecrest*, a typical Dixon Kemp Cutter, built in 1892.
Overall length 39 feet; beam 8 feet 6 inches.

kerosene stove, which is hung on gimbals to keep it vertical when the boat is rolling. On either side are numerous lockers filled with provisions: ship's biscuits, rice and potatoes. On the port side is a pump communicating with two tanks of fresh water. For light I have a kerosene lamp and candles hung on gimbals.

This boat is my only home, and she carries aboard all my possessions. What do I care, therefore, if there is no wind? I am in no hurry. I am at home with my best friends—my books. There is not much room aboard, but I can carry fourteen feet of literature, which measurement means about two hundred books, and they are all books of adventure or poems. Loti, Farrère, Conrad, Stevenson, Jack London, James Connolly, Shakespeare and Kipling are in the place of honour with Poe, Verhaeren, Plato, Shelley, François Villon, Lord Tennyson and John Masefield.

I like them so much that it is difficult to rank them in order of preference, but of all the books which range themselves along my little cabin shelves those which have to do with the sea take first place.

I have always thought Edgar Allan Poe to be the greatest poet, for to the perfection of rhythm he adds nobleness of thought.

But I am also very fond of Jack London, a master of the short story, whose life exercised a

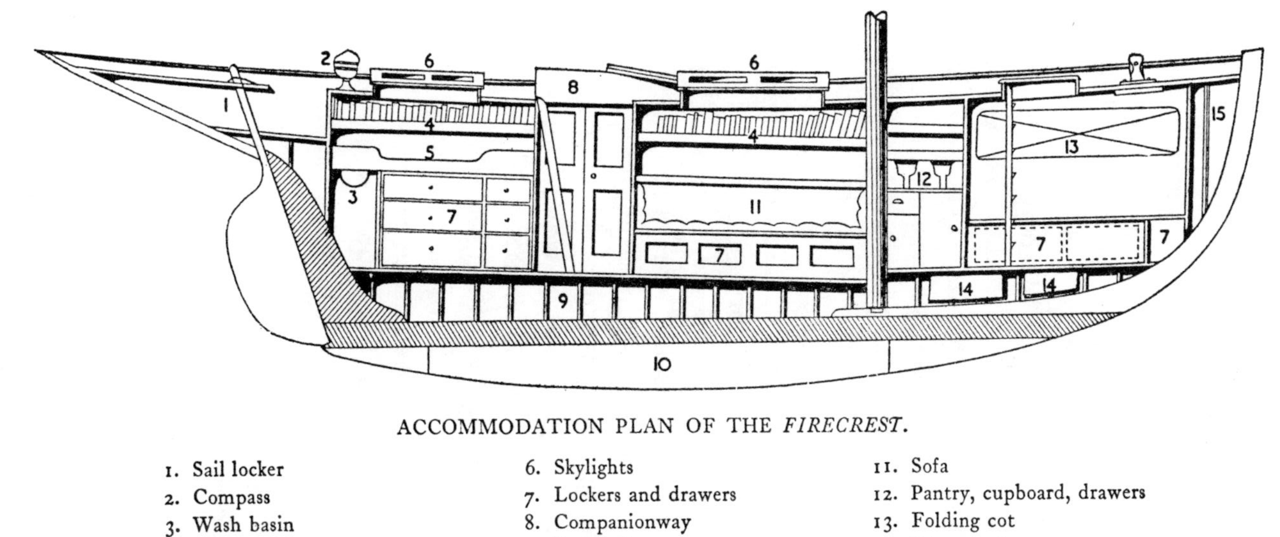

ACCOMMODATION PLAN OF THE *FIRECREST*.

1. Sail locker
2. Compass
3. Wash basin
4. Bookshelves
5. Bunk
6. Skylights
7. Lockers and drawers
8. Companionway
9. Iron ballast
10. Lead keel
11. Sofa
12. Pantry, cupboard, drawers
13. Folding cot
14. Water tanks
15. Cupboard

great fascination for me. He always wrote with power and yet simplicity. Although he shipped very young aboard a three-masted schooner, one senses that he was never a sailor at heart, though he stayed always a lover of open air and adventure.

I remember that one day, after a storm, I threw overboard some books by Oscar Wilde, whose lack of sincerity jarred upon a temperament rendered simple by contact with the sea. Out of the lot I kept only "The Ballad of Reading Gaol."

Stevenson evidently had in common with London a great love for open air and adventure. He, too, seems never to have been a sailor at heart, unless one excepts his fine poem "Christmas at Sea," for he never described that which is beautiful about the life and hardships of sailors.

Victor Hugo has often wonderful descriptions of storms. That of the tempest in "The Man Who Laughs" is to my mind magnificent. It is a pity, however, that the technical terms are all wrong. The cyclone revolves in the opposite direction to that exacted by Nature. But then some paintings are often wonderful although they disregard all the laws of perspective.

Shakespeare describes the sailor as a ruffian without describing anything that is beautiful in him. His descriptions are fine, and the technical errors very few, although he makes ships start from Bohemian ports: an error similar to the one in Kipling's famous poem, "The Road to Mandalay." Kipling is probably one of the greatest sea-writers, and certainly a very great poet. Amongst my favourites by him is "The Last Chantey."

James Connolly described wonderfully the life and hardships of American fishermen.

Pierre Loti ranks high in my esteem. "Pêcheur d'Islande" and "Mon Frère Yves" are in the place of honour, although he often got his inspiration from the navigating bridge and not from the fore-castle.

Herman Melville is also in my library, and I am never tired of reading "Moby Dick" and "Typee."

Conrad, that great writer of the sea, and describer, with true art, of tempests and typhoons, is not my favourite author. I suppose it is because the psychology of his heroes is far too complicated for me.

Although he is not such a great writer, Bill Adams holds in my esteem, as a lover of the sea, a higher place than Conrad. Some of his short stories seem to be well-nigh perfect, and evidently he was one of the few writers to see that which is beautiful in the rough life of sailors. He loves the sea and, for that reason, is nearer me than any other writer.

And last of all, in a shelf near my bunk, are my

very favourite books. They are all either poems or ballads. For somehow I feel that the ballad is the aptest poetical form with which to describe the roving life of sailormen.

For this reason John Masefield is next to my bunk, for he is the poet I like best with his salt-water ballads, and of all these "Sea Fever" and the haunting "Cape Horn Gospel." How wonderfully he describes life aboard sailing-ships and understands the beauty of a sailor's life; but we must not forget that many centuries before him Antiphilos of Byzantium had written, "Oh! Give me my berth in the worst corner of the boat. The joy to hear the leather panels sound under the pounding of the flying spray.

"Give! Take! Games and yarns of sailormen—I had all this happiness—I who am of plain tastes."

CHAPTER THREE

WESTWARD TO GIBRALTAR

HAVING bought my boat I took it at once to the south of France, leaving England at the time that Shackleton started on his last trip. My boat withstood very well the gales of the Bay of Biscay, and having survived them I could not imagine worse weather to stop the *Firecrest*.

During more than a year I cruised about the south coast of France with a young English boy, and incidentally played in lawn-tennis tournaments on the French Riviera. Lawn tennis had been for a long time my favourite sport, but after living aboard and cruising about for more than two years, all the things which happened on land became of minor importance once I had started.

It was only for the fun of the thing and to prove to myself that I could do it all alone that I started on my trip to America. During more than a year I trained physically, cruising in all sorts of weather, learning to handle my sails alone. Only when I felt myself ready, when I knew that I could stand the mental and physical strain, did I start on my cruise.

At last came the glorious day of departure. The

gay harbour of Cannes lay basking in the spring sunshine. On one side the old town and two great square towers dominate the harbour. On the other side were about fifty white yachts tied up to the quays. Next to my boat is *Perlette*, a small 15-foot boat owned by two young girls, who are its only crew. Their boldness is very much admired by all the fishermen and the land lubbers along the quay, who stop to watch them flying about barefoot up the rigging.

A little farther on the *Lavengro*, a 120-ton ketch, is preparing to sail for the same destination as mine, Gibraltar. Although I have only a small chance of defeating a boat ten times bigger than mine and manned by a crew of seven, I do not want to be beaten at the start. I manage to weigh anchor first, and get under way under all canvas. The light breeze is freshening and I must take in my topsail, even as I pass between the moles. There I wave a last good-bye to the two little French girl sailors and to the French-Breton crew of the yacht *Eblis*, who are waving their handkerchiefs to me from the pier.

Outside the harbour the wind is freshening again and I have to change my jib, reef my mainsail and do it quickly, for I can see the *Lavengro* now leaving the harbour and racing after me. We are both tacking against a strong head wind, and although not sailing as fast as the *Lavengro*, I can keep the better wind. We are rushing towards the open sea and leaving the beautiful golden island of Lerins on the lee. Outside the sheltered bay waves and wind increase. My lee rail is deeply buried in the water. Spray is splashing above. It is an oilskin job to steer.

But my heart is light, and as the *Firecrest's* bow cuts the waves I am singing a complaint of Breton fishermen.

> "La bonne sainte lui a répondu: Il vente;
> C'est le vent de la mer qui nous tourmente."
>
> "The blessed lady answered: It blows;
> It is the wind of the sea that torments us."

The glass is falling and black clouds appear ahead. Land is becoming scarcely visible. At four-thirty o'clock I am crossing *Lavengro's* bow, close-hauled on the other tack, when a strong squall strikes us. In haste I lower my mainsail and take in my jib. As the task is finished I catch a last glimpse of the *Lavengro* running before the gale in the opposite direction.

I am now so tired from the exertions of the day that I stay hove to for the night under storm jib and close reefed mainsail, and leaving my boat to take care of herself, I go below and turn in.

Here are some extracts from my log:

"*26th April.*—At two in the morning the wind shifts to north-west and I am able to run before the wind under *square-sail.* My boat is making at this time the best speed she will ever make during this cruise. My log records thirty miles in three hours. The glass is falling. A strong gale is still blowing. At six in the evening the wind increases again. It is very difficult to keep the boat on her course. Soon it becomes quite dangerous to run before the wind. I am going almost as fast as the following sea; so when a wave breaks aboard, the green seas stay on the deck a dangerously long time.

"The operation of taking in my squaresail is very dangerous. The squaresail yard, twenty feet long, is twice as long as my boat's beam. As I take it in my boat now runs under bare poles and rolls violently in the trough of the sea. The lee-end of the yard drags in a wave and I nearly go overboard. Only after fully an hour's dangerous work do I have the yard-arm and sail safely and snugly stowed alongside the deck. I decided to use it no more, and very tired after sixteen hours at the tiller, I hove the boat to for the night.

"27*th.*—All night very hard rain and gale. Seas breaking aboard all night. The glass is still falling and I stay hove to all day. In the morning I discover that my rolling-gear gooseneck is broken. I am not surprised, because it had been made smaller than my specifications.

"28*th*.—At four a.m. I am able to get under way again.

"Towards noon ran into a dead calm. I repair a broken topping lift. At ten-forty p.m. a very strong blow (mistral) compels me to lower my mainsail. In a few minutes the wind turns to a storm. The sea becomes tremendous. I am dead tired, leave my boat hove to and turn in, sleeping until seven the next morning. The seas pound the boat all night and about every fifteen minutes a big wave comes crashing aboard.

"29*th*.—Very heavy sea. North-east gales that shift to west towards evening. I am very tired. At noon get under way again under stormsail and staysail, but the wind is too strong and I am making little headway against it. My jib halyard breaks and my jib tumbles into the sea. At the risk of my life, with towering green seas breaking over me, I rescue it.

"30*th*.—End of gale. The glass rose afterwards and for twenty days I had hardly any wind."

The 1st of May, sixth day out from Cannes, was a very exciting one. After some days between sea and sky, when observations and calculations tell one land is near, it is always a source of breathless wonder to discover land exactly where it ought to be.

In going aloft at noon I was able to discern a

small cone rise from the water. That was land exactly where it ought to be. I felt proud of my navigation, although the navigator's work is nothing compared with the sailor's work. Soon many other cones appeared on my port bow. To the eyes of an inexperienced sailor they would have seemed to be many different islands, but I knew they were peaks a thousand to three thousand feet high whose bases were joined under the horizon. There, at least forty miles away, was Minorca, the second in size of the Balearic Islands.

The next day many more peaks appeared, this time ahead, and towards evening the whole island of Majorca rose from the sea. Then the wind became a very little breeze, and on the morrow I was able to distinguish smoke from chimneys on land and the houses. For some days I followed Majorca's northern shore, tacking against a head wind.

I shall always remember the wonderful vision I had one morning of a small estuary between peaks over four thousand feet high covered with snow. Sailing near the land I suddenly discovered the little old village of Port Soler on the flank of the mountain overlooking the river, and found myself in the midst of a fishing fleet of small sailing-boats putting out to sea.

The fishermen were seemingly very surprised

to see among them a small white yacht flying the French flag, but I went about, turning towards the open sea and carrying with me the wonderful vision of those old houses on the flank of the rugged and arid mountain. Villages, towns, are no more to us sailors than are houses to the ordinary traveller seen at the corner of a road. We pass and carry with us a souvenir.

During the numerous days of calm which followed I glided slowly between those islands of beauty—Dragonera, Iviza, Formentera—blessing that light breeze which permitted me to sail slowly in sight of their marvels. So faint was the breeze that I was not averaging more than fifteen miles a day.

At last one morning, the 15th day of May, I saw towering out from the mist a monstrous rock presenting geometrical lines. It was Gibraltar's eastern side, which one cannot contemplate from the sea without a sentiment of awe, so much has man's work altered nature.

Towards noon I rounded Europa Point, and entered the naval harbour as a gale off the Levant was rising. I dropped anchor gaily near Vanderbilt's fine three-masted schooner, which in 1905 won a famous transatlantic yacht race. I had completed the first part of my cruise.

I was boarded at once by the police, the port's doctor and the naval authorities. Everybody was very much surprised to discover that I was alone and had come from France.

Less interesting was an army of ship chandlers who tried to board me with their small launches. To rid myself of their importunities, I had to explain to them that I was a mere sailor and that I had no money.

I was surprised to see very few warships to represent the glory of England on the seas—only two destroyers and a depot ship bearing the once famous name, *Cormorant*. I would have liked to have seen Gibraltar in Nelson's day, when the warships were beautiful frigates with white sails, when the seamen were real sailors. Nowadays, the modern seaman is more or less a mechanic, driving a train on the water. The trading-sailing ships are giving place to steamers; only some fishermen and yachtsmen continue the tradition and keep alive the science of handling ropes and sails on the open seas.

During the two weeks I spent at Gibraltar I worked hard fitting out for my long passage. The British authorities were very kind to me; I was allowed to enter the Royal Naval Dockyard and use its workers. In the evenings I used to walk in the wonderful public gardens of Alameda between the green-flowered narcissi, which can be seen nowhere else in the world, and look towards the sea and the North African shore.

At last I was ready. Before weighing anchor I sent to some friends the following postcard:

80 gallons of fresh water
80 pounds of salt beef
60 pounds of ship's biscuit
30 pounds of butter
20 pounds of bacon
24 pots of jam
50 pounds of potatoes

with a small arrow pointed towards a mysterious destination and the indication of four thousand five hundred miles.

I wanted nobody to know what I was attempting, should I not be successful. Many friends knew that I was starting for a long cruise, but two only knew that I was trying to cross the Atlantic without landing between Gibraltar and New York.

CHAPTER FOUR

THE ATLANTIC

It was the 6th of June at twelve that I left Gibraltar singing gaily—Hurrah, I am outward bound. The great adventure was only beginning.

Before leaving France I had purchased a wind chart. This purported to show the direction of the prevailing winds on the Atlantic. It indicated that a boat sailing south-west from the Strait of Gibraltar would soon strike the north-east trade winds, which would carry him with fair winds south of the Tropic of Cancer, which is at the twenty-third parallel and south of the Sargasso Sea. Thence he would have to sail west, and wait to be south of Bermuda before going north towards New York.

Although that course would carry me far to the south of a direct course to New York, and add many hundreds of miles to the distance to be sailed, I determined to follow it rather than to try to beat my way straight across the Atlantic against prevalent head winds. A straight line is the shortest distance for a steamer, but not the fastest course for a sailing-boat.

A boat sailing from New York towards Gibraltar will meet westerly winds most of the way, and will have to cover just a little over three thousand miles. From Gibraltar to New York one has to sail at least four thousand five hundred miles. This explains the difficulty of the passage from east to west. Joshua Slocum, in 1895, and Blackburne, in 1902, crossed the Atlantic single-handed, from west to east, stopping at the Azores. The longest distance, covered without landing, was two thousand miles.

Nobody had ever attempted to cross the North Atlantic alone from east to west. Slocum had accomplished a remarkable feat in staying seventy-two days alone at sea in the Indian Ocean. I always had a great admiration for this famous navigator. I knew that my passage would last much longer than any of his, but I was happy at the thought of the difficulties to be overcome.

Aboard a sailing-boat you never know when you will arrive, and it was this reason that made me carry four months' food. The winds eventually proved anything but fair, so that many times during the passage I congratulated myself on my foresight.

I left Gibraltar on the 6th of June, and it was an auspicious start, for the day was beautiful. When leaving the harbour the wind was very light, and I lay on deck basking in the sun, and dreaming of the days that were to come—of the joys, and possible hardships, that lay ahead.

I had unbounded faith in my gallant boat, and a good deal of confidence in my navigation. I felt supremely fit, absolutely without anxiety, and with pleasant anticipation of a sunny run down the trade winds to the tropics, where I would find abundant sunshine, flying fish and possibly adventure.

So I took a last glimpse of the land, and of the noble rock of Gibraltar shining in the spring sun.

The light wind increased, so I trimmed in the sheets and laid my course from Algeciras Bay towards the Strait and the North African coast, and soon I was in the Strait rounding Carnero Point.

The fish were so plentiful that they seemed to be making the water boil. Porpoises gambolled about the boat, and sea-gulls dived in the midst of their schools. I should have been glad to have hooked a fish, but was sailing too fast to make the attempt worth while.

That evening, at six o'clock, the *Firecrest*, running before an east wind, passed Monoqui, an old Moorish fort, the last promontory of the European coast. Here I fell into company with two large, three-masted schooners, and was delighted to find that the *Firecrest* could hold her own with them.

As night fell the wind increased, until it blew half a gale. A little later I could see the Tangier light. By ten o'clock it was blowing a full gale. The wind then suddenly veered to the south-west —dead ahead—and my first jib was blown to pieces. Then came a heavy downpour of rain. It being the first day of the cruise, I soon tired. I determined, therefore, to have a good night's sleep, come what might. So I hove to under close-reefed mainsail and staysail, went below and turned in.

It was blowing hard, but the *Firecrest* was behaving beautifully in the confused seas of the Strait, heeling to the blast when her sails filled and then, rounding to, she would shake most of the wind from her canvas. So she backed and filled all night, while I slept below, certain that whatever the night or morrow held in store my cutter would be equal to it.

On the second day out we encountered a strong south-westerly wind, dead ahead. At times it rained hard, and I could carry only close-reefed mainsail and storm jib.

I had had the patent rolling gear for reefing the mainsail repaired at Gibraltar after damaging it in the Mediterranean, but the *Firecrest's* jumps in the heavy seas soon broke off more of the teeth of the storm-wheel. For the rest of the voyage, therefore, it was necessary to lower the mainsail all the way, and to roll the boom by hand when reefing was necessary. The old mainsail then started to rip along the seams and I had to lower and repair it, otherwise it would have torn from luff to leech.

The next day was fine, so I set the repaired mainsail, second jib and the little gaff topsail. At noon I took the sun, and found I had logged fifty miles in the first two days.

At two p.m. that day I finally lost sight of Cape Spartel on the African coast. I was now clear of all land and on the open ocean. The world of water was wholly mine.

It was on the third day from Gibraltar that I met the trade winds. These were light at first, but increased very quickly to a gale, which lasted for a full week and then blew out.

I had been waiting eagerly for the first sight of a flying fish, and was delighted when, on the 10th of June, a small silver streak shot out of the water and flew nearly a hundred yards before it disappeared.

When running before the wind the *Firecrest* could not steer herself under whole canvas. In this I was less lucky than Captain Slocum, who could, aboard the *Spray*, run many days before the wind without having to touch the tiller. The consequence was that during those first days of trade winds, and after steering in daylight for twelve hours continuously, being all the time careful to avoid jibbing, I became tired. I knew, too, that I must conserve my strength for longer battles with the elements that were to come. Therefore I heaved the boat to, shut the companion-way and went to sleep, but was out of my bunk promptly by five o'clock every morning to cook breakfast. This invariably consisted of porridge made from oatmeal, bacon, ship's biscuits, butter and tea with condensed milk.

I was not long at sea before I discovered that I had been swindled by the ship chandlers at Gibraltar, where I had laid in most of my supplies. The salt beef was good at the top of the barrel, but farther down it was largely made up of bones and fat.

I had ordered a well-known brand of tea, but I did not get it. This taught me a lesson, and in future I determined to inspect very carefully all the food taken aboard.

The cooking was done on an oil-stove in the narrow forecastle. It stood on the starboard locker, swinging in gimbals so that, theoretically, the top would always be level no matter how the boat heeled or pitched. In practice, however, it sometimes failed.

The roll or list of the *Firecrest* was sometimes so great that the frying-pan would frequently fall from the stove, which often meant a burnt bare leg. It may be imagined, therefore, that during a storm cooking was difficult.

In such a narrow place—so limited that a fat man could hardly turn round—it was difficult to move, and many times one was thrown with violence against the boat's sides.

Usually at six o'clock I went on deck, rolled out the reef from my mainsail, cast off the tiller-lashing and gathered way again. Twelve hours of unbroken steering followed, during which from fifty to ninety miles was covered—a good average for a small boat.

Although it is very monotonous to steer twelve hours in succession, after the first day or two I never felt wearied. But it was necessary to be constantly watchful against jibbing in this strong wind, lest part of the rigging or even the mast was carried away.

The time passed very quickly at the tiller, for I was always admiring that thing of beauty, the *Firecrest*, as she flew before the strong breeze.

Her clean bow was cutting the water like a knife, whilst a long frill of snowy foam lengthening astern marked her wake. I could often see the log I was towing, far astern, rise to the top of a wave.

If the wind was not too strong I was usually reading one of my favourite books, and soon the end of the day came. If I could not read I was dreaming; thinking of the beautiful poems of the sea, thinking of the artificial life in civilized countries, but always feeling happy and my own master.

The long daily task was soon over. Just before

sunset I called it a day, hove the boat to, went below and prepared supper. This usually consisted of salt beef, rice and potatoes. I cooked my "spuds" in salt water to save my store of fresh, and found that the tang of the ocean gave them a delicious flavour.

The sea breeze was sharpening the appetite, and, of course, I could not lodge a complaint about anybody else in relation to the cooking. Supper over, I was soon in my bunk, and slept while the boat pitched to the seas.

Some extracts from the log book will give a general idea of life during those first days of trade winds.

"*Monday, 11th June.*—Strong north-east wind, cloudy, rough sea. Twelve-thirty, take a reef in foresail. Roll two turns in mainsail—in second jib, up storm jib. At noon, ninety miles by log in twenty-four hours. Strong wind has become a whole gale. Hove to at seven-thirty p.m.

"*Tuesday, 12th June, seven a.m.*—Course south-west, strong north wind, by log at noon seventy-six miles. Very high sea. Hove to at seven p.m.

"*Wednesday, 13th June.*—Hove to all night. Six a.m., course west-south-west; strong wind north-west; met a steamer rolling violently.

"*Thursday, 14th June.*—Strong breeze north;

by log at noon fifty-four miles; latitude by sun sight 34 degrees 21 minutes.

"*Friday*, 15*th June.*—Fresh wind, blue sky, by log at noon sixty-eight miles. At one p.m., the bobstay breaks. Had difficult task repairing it." (The bobstay is a wire rope that fastens to the stem just under the water line and runs to the end of the bowsprit.)

"To repair it had to cling to end of the bowsprit." (That is one of the worst places on board a small craft when the seas are running high. One is likely to be washed off as the boat dips her bowsprit deep into the green seas and lifts it again.)

"Had to work with both hands and cling on with legs. Several times the *Firecrest* dipped me under completely." (What did I care! The ocean was not cold, and I had no clothes on to bother me.)

(I recall to mind an account I once read of a small boat discovered in the English Channel, after a gale, with nobody on board. In the log was written: 'Have to go to the end of the bowsprit to make repairs. Shall I come back?')

"*Saturday*, 16*th June.*—Very fresh wind. By log at noon seventy-two miles. Two p.m., the foot of the mainsail rips. Have to take it in and hoist the trysail.

"*Sunday*, 17*th June.*—Very fresh wind north. Course, south-east, at noon there is a whole gale.

After observations find am six hundred and twenty miles from Gibraltar and forty miles south-west of Madeira, which I can't sight.

"This afternoon have run out of the trades. The gale has died, and the *Firecrest* wallows in an oily sea and a dead calm. Therefore, all the wet clothes and bedding are brought up on deck to dry.

"*Monday*, 18*th June*.—Calm and oily sea. Am busy with palm and needle repairing sails." (After such rough weather there is always a lot of work aboard.) "There is a rope to splice, a sheet to change. For this work is more important even than the navigator's. Had I not known navigation I might have been able to cross the Atlantic. But, had I been inexperienced in the repairing of sails and ropes, I fancy I should have made no other harbour than that of all the missing ships. Astronomical knowledge would then have been of small value."

CHAPTER FIVE

ALARMING DISCOVERIES

When well within the area of trade winds I was making very good runs, but on the 18th the breeze became very light and its direction changed.

Here, too, I met a large proportion of south-west winds, which are quite exceptional in this part of the Atlantic at this period of the year.

My wind chart showed that thousands of observations have been taken there in June and July, and that a south-west wind had never been observed. It is curious, therefore, that I encountered eight head winds in succession.

Another curious fact was the total absence of life. No dolphins, no flying fish. Water all round and the *Firecrest* and I alone upon it.

The cruising books I have aboard mention a great number of flying fish north of Madeira. I awaited them eagerly to relieve the monotony of a meat diet. But I was far south of Madeira and only saw one, two days after leaving Gibraltar.

During that period of light winds I made experiments by setting the sails in different ways in an endeavour to get the *Firecrest* to sail herself before the wind. Hauling down the mainsail and setting in its place the trysail—a leg o' mutton sail without boom or gaff—and trimming the jib in flat, I at last found that she would keep her course without a hand on the tiller. For if she broached to under the press of the trysail, the jib would fill and put her back on her course.

This rig, of course, meant reduced speed in knots per hour, as the trysail was much smaller than the mainsail. But I could now let the *Firecrest* sail herself all night, and the twenty-four hours of sailing at reduced speed figured out at about the same as twelve hours of sailing with all the canvas she had been able to carry. From now onwards I could get more rest, and suffered less from strain. I now had more time, too, to repair sails and do more thorough cooking. As a matter of fact, when the weather was fine, time was even found to read favourite authors.

If I had had more luck with the wind I could, had I wanted, have spent the greater part of the trip in the cabin.

I soon got used to sleeping very lightly, and lying in my bunk, with my head against the panels some inches above the water line, I could appreciate the speed of the boat by the noise of the water against her sides.

By the motion of the boat, the proportion of rolling and pitching, I soon could tell at once whether she had changed her course, and jumped on deck to modify the angle of the tiller.

At this date I will quote from my log again.

"22*nd June.*—Good north breeze. Course west-south-west. Cold and cloudy. Am above the great depths (more than 3,500 fathoms). At noon, by log, 80 miles in 24 hours. Position by hour, angle and meridian is latitude 30 degrees 4 minutes north, longitude 21 degrees 3 minutes. Calm all afternoon and night. Spent all afternoon in trying to solve the chess problems in the *Field*.

"23*rd June.*—Very light northerly breeze. Course south-south-west. *Firecrest* has steered herself for last four days. Trysail became chafed by the balloon foresail sheet. Up mainsail, and, steering all afternoon with the feet, repair it.

"Sails are chafing so badly and needing so frequently to be repaired fear twine will not hold out. But what do I care! Shall use my blankets. By log at noon thirty-seven miles.

"24th *June.*—Calm night. Light north-westerly. Went aloft to replace a topping lift block. Busy Sunday coiling ropes and making everything ship-shape aboard. Have pumped the boat dry and found little water in her. Shaved with cream without using soap and water. The first warm day since Gibraltar. Spent a very pleasant Sunday working on deck without clothes and bathing in the warm June sun.

"25*th June.*—Light northerly breeze. Course west-south-west. Sight some 'Portuguese men-of-war,' a sort of flat jellyfish showing a long blue fan as a sail. There have been many discussions by mariners about them. Some say they can only drift to leeward, while others have maintained they can actually work to windward like a vessel. From own observations of the shape and angles of their sail-like fans I conclude they are hove to and drift slowly to leeward.

"It is interesting to watch them capsize and right themselves again. Some are nearly a foot long. Remained on deck all day, bathing in the sun and reading. Am now thirteen days from Gibraltar and have covered about one-quarter of the distance to New York.

"26*th June.*—Light north-easterly breeze. Use my balloon foresail as a spinnaker, and steer all day. At noon the sun is nearly overhead. Towards evening feel giddy and head aches. By log at noon sixty-two miles.

"27*th June.*—Light north-easterly breeze. Calm afternoon. The *Firecrest* makes very slow progress, but do not care. Life is good lying on deck under the tropical sun.

"28*th June.*—Light easterly breeze. Sight for the first time three big fishes in the wake of the boat. They are the *Coryphenæ hippuris* of the scientist, called dorado by the Portuguese and wrongly dolphins by English fishermen. I admire their flashing colours, changing from electric blue to green. At night get latitude from Polar Star and longitude from Altair.

"*1st, 2nd and 3rd July.*—Strong southerly winds, rain, frequent squalls. Sea very rough and confused. Am steering south, again trying to find the trade winds. Notice that regardless of the barometer and the wind chart, I meet mostly head winds and get rough weather on Sundays.

"It is odd that the seas run so short here, in mid-Atlantic, where I expected to find the long ocean swell of which I have heard so much. I know well the choppy seas of the Bay of Biscay and the Gulf of Lyons; but here in mid-ocean the seas run shorter and choppier than any I have ever encountered. There are four or five waves to the length of my boat."

A very important event occurred on July 4th. For the first time two flying fishes landed on deck. They were little chaps, the biggest one five inches long, and the other a regular minnow only an inch and a half long.

They were fresh food; I hastened to fry them, and found them of a most delicate flavour and a toothsome morsel.

It later breezed up to a strong gale, and the seas were constantly breaking on deck. I had to roll three turns in the mainsail. The wind also nearly blew my staysail to ribbons before I could get it in, and I had to put canvas covers on the skylights to keep the water out. The boat jumped viciously, and there was a heavy strain on the bowsprit. At last the starboard wire masthead-runner broke, and I had to replace it with good old manila rope, which I like a good deal better than wire.

It seemed just like a western monsoon, but who ever heard of such a thing farther north than Cape Verde? However, as I have said, everything seemed unusual when on board the *Firecrest*.

I ran into the trade winds again on July 6th and began to make better time, logging sixty-one miles that day. I noted, too, that I was on the edge of the Sargasso Sea, for I saw some of the weeds which collect so solidly in that great eddy in mid-ocean.

The boat was now one month out from Gibraltar and in longitude 31 west. All conditions were favourable and I had begun to feel gratified at my progress when, suddenly, I made an alarming discovery. Most of my supply of fresh water had spoiled.

Before leaving Gibraltar I had laid in a store of eighty gallons. About thirty gallons of this were in galvanized tanks beneath the floor of the forecastle, from which I could pump it to the galley. The remaining fifty gallons were in two water-casks, one of which was lashed on deck, and the other stowed in a corner of the forecastle.

These two casks were new, and had been purchased in Gibraltar. It was their contents that had gone bad, for when I drew from both I found the water had turned red, and that it tasted too sour to use.

This disaster meant only fifteen gallons of good water with some two thousand five hundred miles yet to sail, and the prospect of being at sea for at least another month.

I therefore carefully estimated the probable number of days still required to reach port, based on the average speed thus far and the distance yet to sail, and I came to the conclusion that one small glass of water a day would henceforward be my portion; so I put myself on that short ration.

It was evident that the discoloration of the water was caused by the oak with which my casks were constructed. After some speculation I concluded that the cause was tannic acid, and that the casks had not been sufficiently soaked before being filled.

I carried a small apparatus to condense sea water, but needed all my fuel to cook. The sun at noon was nearly at the zenith. Every part of the boat was hot and dry, and nowhere more than the inside of my throat, and I should have liked to have drunk all day long at this stage of the trip.

Daily and anxiously I scanned the horizon for clouds presaging the coming of rain. How welcome some of the rain squalls and rainstorms I had sailed through would have been; but the skies remained clear, and the tropic sun pelted its rays upon me without mercy. I had now to do all my cooking in sea-water, and this only added to my thirst.

Although I had not killed the ill-fated albatross, I was haunted by the Rime of the Ancient Mariner:

> "Water, water everywhere,
> Nor any drop to drink."

On the 7th of July I shaved and cut my hair, also repaired the mainsail, which was constantly ripping. One of the topping lifts broke in a strong north-east squall. Next day my topsail was blown into ribbons, and without that headsail the *Firecrest* would not steer herself so well.

The Sargasso weeds were more numerous and clung to my log. Flying fish had disappeared. It was warm, much too warm. My thirst increased. I began to suffer from fever, and my throat swelled. From the salt beef cask came a very bad odour. Was I going to run short of meat too?

CHAPTER SIX

IN THE TRADE WINDS

It meant this, then, that on July 6th I had two thousand four hundred miles of ocean yet to sail, and when I discovered that I had only fifteen gallons of water left, I had been averaging about fifty miles a day, the consequence being that, even with fair winds, I faced the probability that it would require at least one month more to complete the voyage, and the possibility that it might take much longer. As a matter of fact, it was not till sixty-nine days later that I came finally to anchor.

It seemed a long time before rain fell in sufficient quantities to enable the refilling of the empty water-casks. I had had to adhere to the minute ration of a cup of water a day, for I dared not always reckon on rain, and I did not, if I could help it, want to make a landing of any sort before reaching the American coast.

Meanwhile, there was plenty of work to be done, water or no water. The seams of the mainsail were constantly ripping when there was anything like a strong sailing breeze. There was now not a single seam in it which I had not sewn together once, and there were many that had been resewn several times, almost clear across the breadth of the sail.

July 7th stands as an example of a fairly busy day.

My log reads:

"Wind north-east, good breeze. Course of *Firecrest* west by compass. Shaved and tried to cut my hair. Cleaned the fo'c'sle and put everything shipshape. Boat steers self under trysail and headsails. At noon find I have logged forty miles in twenty-four hours. One p.m., repaired mainsail. Spliced port topping lift (rope that supports the main boom when the mainsail is lowered). At four p.m. wind hauls to east. Boat suddenly jibs while I am enjoying a little tea in the saloon. Altered course to south-west. Sargasso weeds more numerous."

Next day my jib topsail was blown into small ribbons and I had to go to the end of the bowsprit to recover what was left of it—mostly bolt ropes with a few rags hanging to them.

The *Firecrest* was now running before a strong easterly wind, and, by noon of July 9th, had reeled off seventy-two miles in the twenty-four hours. Though that was an average of only three miles an hour I was satisfied, for the boat was steering herself most of the time, though she did not do it so well after I had lost my jib topsail. It was the headsails trimmed in flat that kept her on her course.

I logged seventy-seven miles from noon on the 9th to noon on the 10th, and that night I moved into the forecastle to sleep there for a change, and try the folding cots. But I was wakened during the night by a cold douche in the face. Part of a wave had come down through the hatch, which I had left open.

I was still, and at intervals, trying experiments with the sails to discover the best way by which to get the *Firecrest* to steer herself without hand or foot on the tiller. With a following wind I winged her out with the mainsail to starboard one side, and the balloon forestaysail to port as a spinnaker. She ran well under that rig, but I had to watch her all the time. At night I took the mainsail in and altered the course a little, letting her follow her bowsprit under forestaysail and jib.

Whenever the wind rose to a moderate gale something would give way. While I was mending the balloon forestaysail, the port steel wire runner, which steadies the masthead when on the starboard tack, parted and I had to stop sail-mending to put good rope in place of steel wire. While I was at work on the new runner, the jib sheet pennants broke. Next day the bobstay parted again and I had to splice it. If I took in the mainsail to repair it I had to hoist the trysail in its place. Then, no sooner had I finished repairing the mainsail than the trysail would give way, and I had to be busy again with palm and needle.

I am not given to superstition, but Friday, July 13th, was exceptionally bad. The *Firecrest* rolled horribly, the seas ran very high and things had been breaking aboard since dawn. Early that morning a big hole appeared in the forestaysail. I took it in and was letting the boat steer herself before the wind with the balloon foresail boomed out when the spinnaker boom broke, and fell overboard.

Walking out on the bowsprit to try to recover it, I put my feet on the cross-tree (or whiskers) which spreads the bowsprit shrouds. It broke under me and I fell into the water, but I caught hold of the bobstay and managed to crawl back on board ship. All this time the boat was steering herself, and doing more than three knots. Had I missed the forestay I should have stayed alone in mid-ocean. After that the narrow deck seemed particularly comfortable!

That day I found my position as latitude 27 degrees north, longitude 38.15 west. I therefore decided that I had made enough southing and altered course from south-west to west. Taking into consideration all probabilities, and if my wind charts could be believed, I should have a fair wind till 32 degrees of northern latitude.

Having survived the calamities of Friday the 13th, I felt ready to face anything the next day, which was also France's national day. So I dressed the ship as best I could by running up the French colours, the flags of the Yacht Club of France and the boat's private burgee.

But by ten o'clock the *Firecrest* was tearing along before a gale from east-north-east, and a strong squall hit her. I had, therefore, to take in the balloon forestaysail to save it, and set the smaller staysail instead.

Waves which seemed at least twenty feet high came roaring over the starboard quarter, and swept the deck from stem to stern. It was hard work to keep the deck without being washed overboard, and by night I was tired out.

Under headsails only the *Firecrest* was steering herself, so I went below and let the gale rage. Things were in a terrible mess below decks, for I had had no chance to clean up there for two days; but things were put in order before turning in. The boat rolled terribly all that night, and had I not tested her beforehand and found her well worthy of confidence, I should have thought that at times she was about to capsize. It was difficult to hang to the bunk, and I had to brace myself to keep from being thrown on the floor. Nevertheless, being fagged out, I found ways of sleeping somehow.

When I went on deck the next morning I found the honest little craft holding as truly to her course as though a hand had been at the tiller. Yet landsmen wonder why a sailor learns to love his boat, and thinks of her as a personality.

I also found some flying fish on deck, so I breakfasted sumptuously on fresh food for the first time for many days. The next day there were more of them. Only a man who has lived on smelly salt beef and ship's biscuit can truly appreciate the delicious flavour of a flying fish.

All the following day we scudded before the gale, and on the morning of the 16th it abated to an extent which enabled me to proceed to the repair of sails. The staysail was torn and the sea was still running high, the consequence being that it was hard to ply the needle on the leaping deck. There was more water than usual, too, to pump out that day; for a good chunk of one of the big seas had come in through a half-open hatch.

From this point a period of variable winds, calms and squalls, followed, and I was kept busy changing and repairing sails, particularly the balloon staysail, which had been badly torn in the heavy weather. This took three days to repair, steering with the foot while I sewed.

CHAPTER SEVEN

THIRST AND THE DORADOS

IT was always very hot, and I was always thirsty whilst the sun beat down, but I had to get along on that one cup of water a day, not a drop more. It was more than two weeks after I had found that I was short of drinking water before I managed to catch rain water in my sails, and on the night of July 17th a rain squall blew up, enabling me to collect about two more pints of water to add to the small supply. I sat naked in the rain, and enjoyed its refreshing coolness. I also found relief during the day in the form of frequent baths on deck by dousing myself with sea water from a canvas bucket. It was refreshing, but unluckily the effect soon passed, and I would be as hot and thirsty as ever.

I had just finished repairing the forestaysail when the mainsail ripped for fifteen feet along a seam. There was therefore nothing to do but haul it down, get to repairing and set the trysail in its place. This meant twenty-four hours' work with needle and twine. To make matters worse, I now began to develop a sore throat, and by the following day it was so badly swollen that I could swallow nothing but a little condensed milk and water. For four days this continued. By July 28th I was so weak from fever that I lowered all but the headsails, and went below and turned in, leaving the *Firecrest* to take care of herself.

Flying fish occasionally landed on deck, but I could take but little interest in them, for my throat was too sore to allow of eating anything solid. The tropical light, too, began to dazzle me. Many times, on looking towards the horizon, it seemed that land was ahead, but the delusion never lasted very long.

Sometimes, towards evening, small clouds would appear and take the fallacious appearance of white sails: whilst the inflammation of my throat seemed to sharpen thirst till it became hard to keep within the allowance of one cup of water a day.

By the morning of the 29th of July I was feeling a little better, but extremely weak after four days of milk diet. The handling of the sails in consequence took four times as long. I, however, steered due west all that day, and at night got a restful sleep, for the wind had died down and the sea was smooth again. This calm weather lasted for a week, and it seemed as though the *Firecrest* had been caught in the doldrums. One calm and blistering day succeeded another, until it seemed as though the very brain was burning in the scorching heat of the tropic sun.

My conditions at this stage were anything but enviable. Rotten sails which required constant sewing and patching; a little bad water; fever and no wind. It gave no joyful feeling, but a certain sense of satisfaction in meeting and surmounting these obstacles. Perhaps I was over confident, but I knew that before I reached the American coast I would get wind enough—an anticipation which was more than abundantly fulfilled. An entry in my log at that time reads:

"Very hot, terribly thirsty. Should like to take a swim, but throat still so sore had better not.

"Have certainly lost the trade winds. This is the second time wind chart has lied. It promises fair winds to the 34th degree of north latitude. Only at the 29th degree and *Firecrest* lolling about in a greasy swell; sails idly flapping when set to catch the vagrant airs. If it had not been for the false promises of the wind chart would have gone farther south, and probably caught south-east winds."

However, everything seemed unusual on this cruise. And, anyway, very few forecasts are ever fulfilled.

"Have had to throw overboard that cask of salt beef. The tropics are too hot for it, and I can no longer stand either the taste or smell."

Playing around my boat were great numbers of small fish, the name of which I did not know. They had big heads in comparison with their bodies; in fact, were nearly all head with a small, beak-like mouth. I tried in vain to hook them, but they would not bite. I managed to spear one of them, but found he contained almost no eatable flesh.

On the 1st of August my throat was well enough to make it safe to take a swim. The depths overside were clear and cool as any lake, and the *Firecrest* lay rolling idly to a long undulation from the west. So I plunged over the rail and enjoyed the refreshing coolness of mid-ocean.

It had been calm all day, and the sunset was glorious. Some faint streamers of cloud spread fanwise out from the west, far up towards the zenith, in fleecy rolls and balls of vapour such as the seamen call "mares' tails," while others were in the form of a fish's scales. As the fiery sun dipped into the ocean, its rays first touched it with crimson until the whole western horizon was aglow with the brilliance of it.

I watched this glorious sight until night came down and Venus hung over the horizon.

Above blazed the brilliant Vega, and more to the west was Altair, whilst in the south was Antares, meshed in the long legs of the Scorpion. It was well worth coming three thousand miles to witness.

Then for two days came a strong northerly wind in which I could barely lay my course due west. The rotten sails again began to rip, and once more I was forced to bring out my twine, needle and palm and set to work.

But despite the heading winds I was slowly making my westing, and by August 2nd—fifty-four days out—I was in west longitude 53.44 and north latitude 29.50. This position figured out at about one thousand seven hundred miles from New York. I had shaped my course to pass far south of the Bermuda Islands, but in this strong heading wind and rough sea the *Firecrest* made little headway. Rain fell in torrents that day, but it was impossible to catch and store any of it in my water-tanks, for the spray was flying over the *Firecrest* in clouds, and all the water I caught would have been brackish from it.

There was no time for idling now. I was constantly busy with needle, twine and marlin-spike, repairing damages.

The *Firecrest* carried a double topping lift, but despite the two ropes to support the main boom one or the other frequently broke, and had to be spliced, or new ones rove off. The main gaff had to be hoisted between them, and, as they were only about eight inches apart, this was a fussy and aggravating job, especially as the boat was thrashing about in a rough sea with the gaff swinging. The place for the crew in hoisting the mainsail is near the mast, but when hoisting I had constantly to run aft and guide the end of the gaff between the topping lifts.

Again there came warm and pleasant weather. The boat steered herself, and I would constantly lie on deck peering over the rail, lazily trying to pierce the depths, some three thousand fathoms down. It was then that I noticed, for the first time, three dim shapes following my boat. Swimming several feet under the surface in the *Firecrest's* shadow, were a trio of dorados, a species of mackerel, but attaining a length of nearly five feet.

More than two weeks before, I had thrown away the salt beef, and I had not tasted fresh meat since leaving Gibraltar. The flying fish had constituted my only change of diet. And there, swimming just beneath, were many pounds of good fresh fish. My mouth watered in anticipation of a horse-mackerel steak, an idea more exciting than any gale.

Getting out a hook and line I tried to catch one, using a small flying fish as bait; but they paid not the slightest attention to it. And this despite the fact that right ahead of the boat the flying fish were flying, and the bonitos jumping high after them. The big ones were as swift as lightning, and the flying fish had but little chance of escaping them. And even if they do, the sea crow and albatross are waiting for them in the air.

So I asked myself, If the dorados feed on flying fish, why will they not bite at mine? This extreme shyness of the dorados for a covered hook was noted by my friend Ralph Stock, in his "Cruise of the *Dream Ship*," and by William Washburn Nutting when crossing the Atlantic in his *Typhoon*.

But I wanted those fish, and, somehow, I had to get one. But how? I tried shooting them with a rifle and managed to hit one, but he sank so quickly that, even if the boat had not been moving. I could not have caught him by diving. I tried to spear one with my granes—a sort of harpoon with three prongs—but they kept well out of reach.

In despair I gave up, and sat on the rail dipping my bare feet in the water, and it was then that the unexpected happened. Three dorados made a simultaneous dash for my toes. They were mighty quick, but luckily I was quicker. My harpoon transfixed one, and soon I had him, a three-foot fish, gasping and jumping on deck.

Here, at last, was fresh food in plenty, and, what was more, I now knew the way to catch more.

For it simply meant that dorados were curious, and to catch one you had to attract its attention.

But soon they got used to seeing sunburnt feet trailing alongside, and I had to invent a fresh lure. First I tried trailing a white enamelled plate in the water. This succeeded in stirring their curiosity anew, and very soon I had more of them than I could eat.

The colours of these fish as they lay dying on the deck of the *Firecrest* were amazing. Their electric-blue bodies, with long golden tails, passed through all the hues of the rainbow, finally becoming fixed green with gold spots. It was one of the many marvels of the sea of which I had read but had never before seen.

Next day I had bonito boiled for breakfast, fried for lunch and boiled for supper. This meant by far the largest part of a three-foot fish. Next day I caught more of them, but many escaped my harpoon. They followed the boat, however, and through the clear water I could see plainly the wounds I had made in them, which gave me an uncomfortable feeling, for I had marred without attaining my object.

They are excellent food, but they have not the delicious flavour of the flying fish, upon which they feed. I found in the stomach of one at least a score of flying fishes' wings.

That day also I discovered a curious kind of

marine growth on the side of the boat. It looked like black and white flowers held to the hull by a long, rubber-like neck. It was for this reason that many fish were following the *Firecrest*. They like a boat with a fouled bottom.

I now had an abundance to eat, but little to drink, and as I had to filter all the water I drank through a cloth, it tasted infernally bad.

CHAPTER EIGHT

STORMY DAYS

THEN the blessed rains came. I can hardly describe how welcome they were. I dreaded to drink even the scant allowance of water I permitted myself, for it was getting dangerously foul from the heat and long storage in a tank.

Black clouds gathered on the western horizon on the night of the 4th of August. In the gathering dusk they rose mightily from the sea, like huge mountains of pitch frowning down upon the little boat as though bent on engulfing her in some awful disaster. But I could laugh in their faces, for I knew the sturdiness and seaworthiness of the *Firecrest*. So I thought, "Let them come on, and I hope they will bring rain." Forked lightning zigzagged across the piled-up mass, and the towering peaks of utter blackness that reared themselves above it, lighting the glassy ocean with a ghastly, blinding glare.

I sat on deck, admiring the display of natural forces gathering for an outburst of wrath. Though it was impressive to a sailor, and might have been even alarming to a landsman, I had little fear of what was to come. Clearly I was in for a summer squall, and after the long, torrid days and sweltering nights, the prospect of a change was a pleasant anticipation.

That vast curtain of cloud rolled up over the heavens, blotting out star after star as though to hide a tragedy about to be staged in that remote part of the world, where the *Firecrest* and I awaited the onset. There was practically nothing to do but shorten sail and prepare to catch any rain that might be coming.

Very soon I heard the comforting patter of raindrops on the deck and in the sea, and I was reminded of the sailorman's saying:

> "When rain comes before the wind,
> Topsail sheets and halyards mind."

The *Firecrest* was soon made all snug, and when the squall came she reeled under it, but when the first fierce onslaught had passed I was able, by lowering the gaff and lifting the boom, to transform my mainsail into a sort of big pocket to collect and drain the water into the cask at the foot of the mast.

These rain squalls continued all night, so that I managed to catch and store ten gallons: a much more important asset to me even than the catch of fish, for I now felt assured that I should not lack either food or water, for the sea brought one and the heavens the other.

I was therefore now quite contented, even

happy, and in no hurry to get to New York; in fact, feeling quite at home on the high seas.

The wind was still west, and dead ahead, which meant slow progress, but pace was not a consideration. It was now more than three weeks since I had had a fair wind, despite the promising arrow on the wind charts. But I had plenty of fish, and water enough for present needs, besides which, black clouds encircled the horizon, giving promise of more rain.

It soon seemed to be evident that I had eaten a little too much fish during the last few days, for my head and legs ached, and I was presumably suffering from fish poisoning. The *Firecrest* was now thrashing heavily into a choppy head-sea, and making hardly any headway.

That night, the 7th of August, I became quite ill. Body and legs ached so much that I could hardly sleep. Next morning the wind increased, and a very rough sea was running; but at noon I had logged off sixty-six miles in twenty-four hours —a fairly good showing against wind and sea.

I also noticed clouds high above moving against the wind, so concluded I was in for a spell of bad weather. The lacing which held the mainsail to the gaff now broke in several places, and the thimble at the clew of the jib pulled out of the grummet. More repairs!

Two months had now elapsed since I had left

Gibraltar, and thus far the cruise had been all that I had anticipated. From day to day I looked forward to new adventure, and such hardships as I had so far encountered had been only those which any seaman on old sailing ships would have expected as part of the day's work.

It had been definitely proved that the *Firecrest* could be easily handled alone, and that if I fell ill she could look after herself—given the proper sails. We were good companions. She did her part of the work and I did mine, the consequences being that I felt an increasing fondness for her. She was surely a gallant little craft and fulfilled every expectation.

It was true that I had some one thousand five hundred miles yet to sail before I could drop anchor in New York harbour, but when one had sailed some three thousand miles, another one thousand five hundred, with plenty of food and water, held no terrors; in fact, only a pleasant prospect.

But I did not know what kind of weather to expect as I headed more northward towards the north Atlantic coast, and felt perhaps unwarrantably confident that whatever came, the *Firecrest* would be equal to it. But I hardly anticipated the gales and hurricanes that were to lie in my course, as if waiting for the oncoming of the staunch little cutter and her rotted and ragged suit of aged canvas. As it proved, the worst was yet to come, and I sailed confidently and in blissful ignorance to meet it.

The navigation of the boat was, of course, an important part of such a deep-sea cruise, but it was actually the least exacting of all the many tasks that came to hand. I found it a great deal more important to acquire good seamanship "before the mast"—in other words, to be able to repair sails and splice ropes—than to find the boat's latitude and longitude. As a matter of fact, I believe a man who did not know how to figure his latitude and longitude at all could cross the Atlantic alone provided he knew how to handle his boat. Steering west by his compass he could not very well miss the broadside of America; he would have to hit land somewhere, unless his compass played him tricks.

Apropos of this, the late Frank Norris gave, in his book "Shanghaied," a very curious description of a boat's navigation. He shows us Moran of *The Lady Letty* lying on her back on deck to bring a star to the horizon, then rushing down below and spending all night covering the four sides of the log-table with figures. "In the morning," he says, "she had found her position, and rated the chronometer." Surely Frank Norris would never have written such stuff had he been a sailor.

When taking an observation the navigator of a

small craft must stand as high as possible above deck to decrease the error of observation. Instead of looking towards the sun or star, one looks through the telescope of the sextant towards the horizon, and sees the reflection in the mirror of the celestial object: and once the observation is taken, not more than a few minutes are required to find the position.

The difficulty is when taking an observation in a gale and rough sea, when the deck is heaving underfoot and the boat reeling and pitching. Then the lone navigator has to cling to something with his bare feet, and it's handy to have the feet bare for that purpose, for both hands are of course needed to handle the sextant.

Assume that one is ready, instrument in hand. Where is the horizon? A tall wave rears its head across one's vision and the horizon as viewed from the deck seems high in the air. Only when one is on the top of a wave can one see the real horizon. But one usually has time to get its sight before a big wave breaks aboard to bury self and sextant in spray.

But the sight has been got before one's balance is lost, and a clutch is made at anything to save one from pitching overboard. When the observation is taken, one hurries off below to take the Greenwich time from the chronometer.

Now comes the navigation table, but I found

that a well-trained mathematical mind was very badly needed to calculate at all while the boat jumped and tossed upon the surges.

In any case, I found that if one could locate oneself within ten miles of one's actual position, it was good approximation on a small boat.

CHAPTER NINE

NIGHTS AT THE TILLER

Two months ago I had left Gibraltar on the four thousand five hundred mile voyage alone across the Atlantic by this long southern route. For two months I had neither seen, nor spoken to, a living soul. My readers may imagine that this long period of loneliness might be depressing, but I did not find it so. The fact that there was no one to talk to never seemed to make the least difference. I suppose I was accustomed to my own companionship, and, very likely, such contentment was in a large measure due to the tremendous fascination the ocean held for me.

Most of the time was fully occupied in repairing the ravages the wind made in the aged suit of sails the *Firecrest* displayed to it. These were constantly ripping out at the seams, the consequence being that I was kept at work on them for hours at a time on a slippery, sloping deck, and engaged half the time in bracing myself to meet the heel of the cutter.

A whole new suit of sails could have been made for the *Firecrest* with much less effort had I carried the spare canvas, but, as it was, I had barely enough to make patches. My stock of needles also was getting low, and I feared that my twine would not last until I reached port.

Owing to the bad condition of the sails I had often to shift them. To make and take in sail to suit the varying conditions of calm, light breezes or gales was quite enough, but, in addition, I had frequently to haul down one sail to repair it and set another in its place.

Besides this work there were two meals a day to cook, so that little time was found for reading, though the library shelves were well stocked with tales of sea adventures. When night arrived, too, I was over-tired to read, and fell in my bunk half asleep. Sleep had to be very light, however, for when the wind shifted I had to jump on deck to modify the tiller's angle.

I had strange dreams, too. Sometimes the incidents of my dreams were land happenings, but the idea of reaching my aim never deserted my sleeping mind. I would often be engaged in a dream-argument with myself. "If I am on land I have not crossed the Atlantic. Then why have I not started?" Then I would find, to my joy, that I was aboard the *Firecrest*. A glance on deck would follow to see that everything was well, and off to sleep again with the satisfied feeling that the boat was getting nearer its destination.

Very often during a calm day I took my sleep,

and if, towards evening, the wind strengthened, I passed all the night at the tiller. It is always difficult to fight against sleep, but I never felt bodily weary during those long hours.

The *Firecrest* was, under such conditions, sailing slowly, leaving astern a phosphorescent wake, and I was occupied in steering by a star. At such a time, alone upon the sea, gazing at the celestial dome, I often pondered on the smallness of man, the imperfect theory of evolution, of the Newton and Einstein theories, of the various histories of the world which claim that the earth is getting gradually colder and that man started from a very low level to progress to his present high state of civilization. All these theories and systems seemed, out in mid-ocean, only hypotheses emitted by men because they explained better than others the phenomena which our poor powers allow us to register during our era.

Often the different incidents of my own life passed before my memory during those quiet hours, with all the details which have cropped up to modify my conception of life, and which had actually influenced the present-day situation by which I found myself at the tiller of my little boat on the wide, night-shrouded ocean.

A great sensibility and the deceptive ideas of a youth fond of ideals obliged me early to be my own companion; then came the sad life for such of a boarder at school, the war and my mother's death, which broke up the ordinary outlook on life. The war memories are still before me. Fighting high above the clouds; the incendiary bullets which pierced my wings; the hostile machine brought down in flames; the temporary joy of triumph. But back on earth I am nothing but a child who has lost a mother.

Time somehow did not fill the emptiness. One after the other my best friends had died in the air. The armistice came, but I was thinking of those dead flying pals some of us forget too easily; of the vanity of the survivors who wear rather ostentatiously the medals celebrating a victory which really belongs to the dead. For when one has not given his life for his country one has not given everything.

Many other incidents in life passed before my memory. Some apparently of no importance, but which, in these surroundings, left a deep impression. Nor do I know why I was once suddenly brought to an incident three years ago.

I was in a train de luxe, going towards Madrid, when, glancing through the window, I saw a young beggar. He was running barefoot alongside the rails. His brown skin was shining between the rags which covered him. He was more beautiful than the young beggar painted by Murillo, more realistic than the club-footed child of Ribeira. He was begging as they do in Spain, for he seemed to grant a favour instead of asking for one. He was a prince of life, this dirty and ragged beggar, running free in the sunlight, and far happier than the travellers the train was carrying in its luxurious interior.

I felt I should have liked to have been in his place, and to have started my life again fifteen years ago—I who am always roving in quest of youth.

At any rate, I felt I was master aboard my own boat, and could go on roving round the world looking for the open air, the great spaces and adventure; leading the plain life of a seaman, and bathing in the sun a body and mind not content to inhabit the houses of men.

So now, happy to have found my *métier* and to have nearly fulfilled my dream, I recited at the tiller my favourite sea-poem.

The night thus passed quickly. One after the other the stars faded. The grey dawn broke in the east and I was again able to distinguish the shape and lines of the *Firecrest*.

CHAPTER TEN

FIERCE GALES IN THE HURRICANE ZONE

THE 9th of August, sixty-four days out from Gibraltar, found the *Firecrest* about five hundred miles east of the Bermuda Islands and approximately one thousand two hundred miles from New York, my port. So, judging by experience thus far, I reckoned that it would require about one month more to complete the voyage; but, at the same time, I knew the past was no guide to what there might be to come.

I felt sure that strong westerly gales lay between my present position and the American coast, a forecast that was amply and fully realized. In fact, I had a taste of what was coming on that very day.

There had been rain-squalls and a very confused sea all night. The wind was westerly, very strong and dead ahead. I had shaped my course to pass south of Bermuda, and cut the Gulf Stream so far south as to get the benefit of its north-easterly current in carrying me up to New York; so I laid the *Firecrest* on the starboard tack and headed her south-west.

During the forenoon she lay practically hove to under forestaysail while I repaired several rips in the mainsail, but by the afternoon, when I was ready to set it again, the wind had increased to a gale.

The seas were running high and broke on board frequently throughout the afternoon. The deck seemed constantly under water. The narrow little cutter lay heeled over before the blast as she drove into the seas, burying her lee rail at times several feet under water.

The deck sloped like the roof of a house, and I had to be careful in moving about. One slip and I should have gone overboard to leeward, and the cutter, with no one on board, would have gone on her way leaving me food for sharks and bonitos.

The deck was so badly awash that I had to keep the skylights and hatchways closed. This made it hot and uncomfortable below decks. Cooking under such conditions was a difficult task. My forecastle was just wide enough to stand in, between the stove on the starboard side and the water-casks and the galley on the other.

If, in a thoughtless moment, I set down a cup or dish, it was likely to be hurled spinning across the forecastle on to the opposite locker or the floor. My stove, too, had a habit of tossing a kettle of water, or a dishful of hot food, on my bare legs and feet: so I had to watch it carefully when the cutter was pitching about.

That day a huge whale swam swiftly across the bow of the *Firecrest*, making the spray fly in a turmoil. The monster was making approximately ten knots, and was very likely running before the sword fish, his natural enemies.

The gale continued throughout the night. I had put the *Firecrest* on the other tack, heading north-north-west, and, after trimming the sails so that she would hold to that course, let her take care of herself while I got what sleep I could in a bunk that seemed to be trying to leap from under me.

I was up at four o'clock the next morning, and got on deck just in time to get the mainsail down before a heavy gust that whipped the sea into flying scud, and would surely have stripped the *Firecrest* of her canvas.

It was dirty weather. A vicious wind was driving before it huge waves with high curling crests like Kipling's white horses, and which bore down upon my lonely little craft as though bent on her destruction. When she plunged into them she buried her bow under a smother of frosty green water that raced along the deck and flew in a sheet of spray into the sails.

A great canopy of dull, leaden clouds hid the heavens from horizon to horizon, and battalions of stray storm clouds scurried past at lower altitudes, whilst gusts of rain pelted my face with stinging force.

I was drenched; washed alternately with spray and rain; but it was warm and I wore little clothing. In fact, clothing was of little use under such conditions, for it would only have served to keep me constantly wet. Without it I quickly dried off.

But there was nothing to lament over. This was the kind of weather I had expected; the kind that puts to the test a seaman's skill and endurance and the staunchness of his craft. Far from being either distressed or awed by the majesty of the ocean in a wrathy mood, I felt thrilled to the sense of combat. Here was something to fight, a worthy foeman, and I found myself singing snatches of all the sea songs I could remember.

> "O for a soft and gentle breeze,
> I heard a fair one cry.
> But give to me the snoring breeze
> And white waves heaving high,
> And white waves heaving high, my boy!"

The *Firecrest* was plunging as though bent on becoming a submarine, and heeling heavily to the gusts. The gale was blowing straight from the direction I wanted to sail, and she had to fight for every inch she gained against it.

She was not making too bad weather of it, except for the strain on the bowsprit. She was constantly burying it deep into the sea and prising it out again. As she flung it clear of the water I could feel the whole rigging, mast, bowsprit and sails jump and the cutter shake from the sudden release from tension. My faith in the bobstay was weak, and if it gave way in one of those jumps the bowsprit might go by the board.

The waves were running so high that it was difficult to take an observation. Only when the cutter topped the crest of a sea could I get a glimpse of the distant horizon, even when the flying cloudwrack above opened to give me a chance to shoot the sun. However, I satisfied myself that I was in latitude 32.54, and longitude 56.30.

Going below, I discovered that the *Firecrest* was shipping a considerable amount of water. Yet the skylight covers were closed as tight as I could get them, and all openings shut. But the covers lifted enough when the seas broke over them to let a little water in each time. The result was that everything below decks was becoming saturated.

The gale veered to the south-west in the afternoon, but showed no signs of diminishing. At seven o'clock I set about reefing the staysail, but it got loose and was ripping from foot to leech. It was difficult to make and take in sail or do anything on deck with the boat leaping about and so often raked with the seas; but I managed to get the staysail below and roll the boom so as to show less mainsail.

Tired and soaked as I was, I could not afford to rest while the staysail was split. It was too necessary; so I stayed up nearly all night sewing it together again, and it was two o'clock next morning before I turned in. There was a succession of squalls throughout the night, so I let the cutter lie hove to, riding as easily as possible, but making no headway.

Next day the gale blew itself out, leaving a rough sea running. From now, and for about twenty-four hours, I had moderate weather, and took advantage of it to ply my needle, repairing staysail, mainsail and trysail by turns.

On Monday, August 13th, my observation showed that I had logged only about forty-five miles in twenty-four hours. I could not make much westing against these gales which were carrying me north of my course.

By the afternoon of that day the *Firecrest* was tossing in another fierce wind and rough sea. She laboured and pounded and buried her bowsprit in the solid green seas, putting a great strain on that stick and bobstay.

I was convinced by this time that a long bowsprit, such as the *Firecrest* carried, and the main gaff (boom across the upper part of the mainsail) were a couple of nuisances for a man sailing single-handed. I determined, therefore, to get rid of the gaff once I reached New York, and to carry instead a Marconi, or leg-o'-mutton mainsail, which should be balanced by a shorter bowsprit.

At last I gave up trying to repair one of the staysails, as it seemed likely to take all my twine.

Fierce seas broke over the cutter all that night. Next morning everything in the forecastle was wet from the water that had been driven in round the hatchway. On deck at four o'clock I found the *Firecrest* plunging into a strong head sea and trying to make what headway she could against the strong westerly gale. There was a good deal of water on deck most of the time, as the seas still broke over her.

The barometer was very low, indicating that conditions were going to be worse. Throughout the forenoon the gale kept increasing, until at eleven a.m. its force was tremendous, and things were in sad disorder below decks owing to the battering the little boat was receiving.

I had had difficulty in cooking breakfast, and was vainly attempting to boil rice for lunch when a green sea broke aboard and the kettle of hot water was tossed from the stove on to my knees. Going on deck to see what damage had been done, I discovered that the wave had carried away the hatch cover of my sail locker, a compartment in the extreme after part of the boat.

Holes were beginning to show in the mainsail and staysail, so I had to take them in. This seemed a good opportunity to try out my sea-anchor, so I let her ride to it, with a spitfire jib to steady her. I found, however, that there was little difference in the boat's action, and that she could do nearly as well without it.

Many seamen claim that a sea-anchor is a great help in heavy weather when the winds are so high that it is impossible to carry any canvas to hold the vessel's head to the wind, but I did not find it so with my type of boat.

My experience appears to have been the opposite of nearly all that has been written about boats in heavy seas. In any case, I think the so-called danger of being caught in the trough of the seas does not apply to such a small boat as the *Firecrest*, for I found it didn't matter much whether she was head, side or stern to the wind and seas when she had no way on. If she could carry any canvas at all, I gave her a reefed trysail and a spitfire jib and found the motion easier.

It was necessary to cover that sail locker hatchway with something to keep the water out, so I plugged it with old sails in the best way I could.

While attempting to cook supper that night, the air pump on my stove, which forces the oil through a small hole in the burner, broke, and I had to give up cooking. Also, although dead tired, I spent nearly the whole night repairing the staysail.

The storm clouds cleared away next morning, August 15th, and the gale moderated a little. I had been letting the *Firecrest* ride to the sea-anchor while repairing the sails, but, just before noon, I hauled in the anchor with tripping line, got the mainsail and jib on her and by noon was under way again, steering north-west.

This was the last occasion on which I used that sea-anchor. It had proved of no real use; so why bother with it?

Within twenty minutes after getting under way a squall struck the cutter and tore to ribbons the staysail that I had been working on for ten solid hours. It was gone in a twinkling.

The joke was certainly on me, and I was obliged to smile at the thought of all the hours spent sewing those rags together only to have them whipped away in that fashion. Then I hoisted a jib in place of them.

By this time I had been without sleep for thirty hours. The *Firecrest* was taking care of herself, so I turned in and got a two-hour nap. Next day, in more moderate weather, I put things shipshape down below, throwing overboard the things I had found useless. This always gives considerable pleasure, for it is one of the joys of the sea that you are not obliged to keep with you things you dislike.

Dorados were still trailing the boat, but they were

now too shy to be lured within reach of my harpoon. On the following day, however, I managed to coax one near enough to spear him. He was a foot and a half long. I thought of my actual superiority, but I thought, too, that some stormy day these voracious fish might have their turn in reward for their tenacity in following me.

The *Firecrest* was logging some fifty to sixty miles a day in the variable weather that now followed. Frequent squalls, often with heavy rain, kept me busy handling sails.

On August 18th the gales came on again; my sails began to rip; parts of the rigging broke under press of sail and the leaping of the cutter added to my discomfort. The pump got out of order, too. The seas were also running high, and by nighttime I was cold, wet and tired, so took some quinine to ward off a chill.

The irony of it all was that after having been on short rations of water for a month I was now getting so much that I could not get rid of it. It was also impossible to keep the heavy rains and spray from coming through the sails with which I had plugged the sail-locker hatch.

The water had now risen to the level of the cabin floor, and, when the *Firecrest* listed, it splashed around in the lockers and bunks, wetting and spoiling everything.

On deck it was blowing a regular hurricane.

The sky was entirely obscured with thick clouds, hanging so low and thick that it seemed like night. I had to reef the mainsail down until nothing was showing but its peak, the jaws of the boom and gaff being only four or five feet apart. The seas became so high, and the boat laboured so heavily, that it seemed at times as though she would jump the mast out of her. The rain, too, came in slanting torrents, driven before a stinging blast and almost blinding me. Facing it I could hardly open my eyes, and when I did I could hardly have seen from one end of the boat to the other.

For several days now I had been exposed to drenching rain and spray, the consequence being the skin of my hands had become so soft that it was very painful to pull on the ropes.

CHAPTER ELEVEN

THE TEST

NEITHER the baffling gales that ripped the sails and set the lockers awash, nor exposure to drenching seas and cutting rains were sufficient to burn the sea-fever out of my veins. A man crossing the ocean alone must expect some distressing times. Sailormen of ancient times who rounded the Capes of Good Hope and Horn, had to fight for their lives and suffered more from cold and exposure. I had a feeling, too, that there was a pretty good chance that some day the *Firecrest* and I would encounter a storm that we should not weather.

The gale continued throughout the night of the 19th of August. Sea after sea swept over the little cutter, and she shook and reeled under them. I was awakened often by the shock of the seas and the heavy listing of the boat.

It was a dirty-looking morning on the 20th, and the climax of all the gales that had gone before. It was the day, too, when the *Firecrest* came near to making the port of missing ships. As far as the eye could see there was nothing but an angry welter of water, overhung with a low-lying canopy of leaden, scurrying clouds, driving before the gale.

By ten o'clock the wind had increased to hurricane force. The seas ran short and viciously. Their curling crests racing before the thrust of the wind seemed to be torn into little whirlpools before they broke into a lather of soapy foam. These great seas bore down on the little cutter as though they were finally bent on her destruction. But she rose to them and fought her way through them in a way that made me want to sing a poem in her praise.

Then, in a moment, I seemed engulfed in disaster. The incident occurred just after noon. The *Firecrest* was sailing full and by, under a bit of her mainsail, and jib. Suddenly I saw, towering on my limited horizon, a huge wave rearing its curling, snowy crest so high that it dwarfed all others I had ever seen. I could hardly believe my eyes. It was a thing of beauty as well as of awe as it came roaring down upon us.

Knowing that if I stayed on deck I would meet death by being washed overboard, I had just time to climb into the rigging, and was about half-way to the masthead when it burst upon the *Firecrest* in fury, burying her from my sight under tons of solid water and a lather of foam. The gallant little boat staggered and reeled under the blow, until I began to wonder anxiously whether she was going to founder or fight her way back to the surface.

Slowly she came out of the smother of it, and the great wave roared away to leeward. I slid down from my perch in the rigging to discover that it had broken off the outboard part of the bowsprit. Held by the jibstay, it lay in a maze of rigging and sail under the lee rail, where every sea used it as a battering ram against the planking, threatening, at every blow, to stave a hole in the hull.

The mast was also swaying dangerously as the *Firecrest* rolled. Somehow the shrouds had become loose at the masthead. There was now a fair prospect that the cutter would roll the mast out of her, even if the broken bowsprit failed to stave the hole it seemed trying for. The wind cut my face with stinging force, and the deck was, most of the time, awash with breaking seas.

But I was obliged to jump to work to save both boat and life. First I had to get the mainsail off her, and, in trying to do so, found the hurricane held the sail so hard against the lee topping lift that I had to rig a purchase to haul it down with the downhaul; but I finally managed to get it stowed.

It proved a tremendous job to haul the wreckage aboard. The deck was like a slide, and the gale so violent that I had to crouch down in order to keep from being wrenched off the deck and hurled bodily into the sea. I clung desperately to the shrouds at intervals. The broken part of the bowsprit was terrifically heavy, and I had to lash a rope round it while it was tossing about and buffeting the side. Several times it nearly jerked me overboard.

At last I had the jib in, and the bowsprit safely lashed on deck; but it was nearly dusk and I felt worn out. That whipping mast had, however, to be reckoned with, and I could take no rest till at least an attempt had been made to get it tight. So, going aloft on the shaking stick, and clinging to it as it swung from side to side, I speedily discovered that the racking which held the port shrouds in a sort of eye had given way.

Twice I was swung clear of the ship, still clinging to a rope, to be dashed back against the mast with a bang. After nearly losing my hold more than once I found that I was too exhausted to make repairs that night, so slid down to deck to find the whole boat vibrating from the shaking spar.

I feared the deck might soon be opened under the strain of it, so, to steady it, I hoisted a close-reefed trysail, and filled her away on the starboard tack, in order to let the starboard and undamaged shrouds take the strain. I then hauled the clew of the reefed staysail to windward, and hove to.

With this nursing she rode a little easier, and the slatting of the mast was not quite so severe.

It was now nearly dark and the gale seemed to be moderating a little, so I went below to get supper.

But when I tried to start a fire, neither of the two Primus stoves would work: so I had to turn in, hungry, cold, drenched and exhausted, for the first time on the cruise sad, fagged out and fed up.

At this point Bermuda lay only three hundred miles south, but New York at least one thousand miles away. I knew, too, that it would be good judgment to head for the islands, and make repairs there before going on to New York; but I had set my heart on making the voyage from Gibraltar to the American coast without touching at any port, and to abandon that plan was heart-breaking.

So much did I feel upon this point that I think I should not have cared if a wave had swept over us and carried the *Firecrest* to the bottom of the sea. I tried vainly to sleep. The mast was still slatting about so hard that I feared it would either tear up the deck or carry it away. For some hours I stayed in my bunk thinking the problem out with aching head, and then suddenly decided to try the seemingly impossible.

I got up again, and, as I needed food badly, began to work at the stoves. I filed down three sail needles and broke them, one after another, before I could get one small enough to clear the hole through which the kerosene was fed to the vaporising burner. And it was nearly dawn before I got the burner working, but I was then able to cook a breakfast of tea and bacon.

This dispatched, I began to feel ashamed of the indecisions of the night before. I felt ready for the battle again, and I determined to sail through thick and thin to New York, the goal of the trip.

On going on deck again I found that, though the gale had moderated a little, it was still blowing hard, and the sea tremendous.

The mast had to be steadied at all costs, and the damaged rigging repaired. It was hard to climb on the swinging stick, and it was harder to stay on it at all. With legs around the crosstrees I had to work head downwards. In that position it took me more than an hour to put a racking seizing round the two shrouds where they came close together at the masthead. Then, dropping down to the deck, I set the shrouds taut with the turnbuckles just above the rail. The mast was now as safe as I could make it.

But there was still the broken bowsprit to repair, and I found it was a job for the carpenter's saw and axe. With these tools I cut a slot in the broken end of the stick, slid it into position and fastened it there with the iron pin that originally held it in place. This gave me a jury bowsprit eight feet shorter than the original one.

As it proved, however, the hardest part of the job had still to be done, for I had to make a bobstay to hold down the end of the bowsprit. This I did by cutting a piece from the anchor-chain, and shackling it into a ringbolt fixed into the cutter's stem just below the water line. To do this I had to hang head downwards from the bowsprit, near the stem, to reach that ringbolt under water. The consequence being that as her bow rose and fell she alternately dipped me two or three feet under water and brought me out dripping and sputtering, to repeat the dose again and again.

I don't quite know how I managed to complete the job, but it certainly had to be done, and, at the expense of many unwilling drinks of sea water, the shackle was got into place and bolted there.

As though in sullen irony, no sooner was this work finished than the gale suddenly moderated. It was just as though the elements were acknowledging that they were defeated, and were surrendering to the gallant little craft.

Taking advantage of this milder weather I made two observations, and located myself in latitude 36.10 north, and longitude 62.06 west. My position was thus about eight hundred miles from New York as the crow flies, but about one thousand to one thousand two hundred miles of actual sailing distance.

Although utterly exhausted I was sustained by a keen sense of satisfaction. So much so that I went to work repairing the pump, and soon found the cause of the trouble. A bit of a match had stuck in the valve, and this out I got it working again. After two hours of pumping the boat became clear of water, for I could hear the pump sucking dry; always a joy to a seaman's heart.

Going aloft to make sure the standing rigging was secure, I found the stays had chafed against the mast. It would therefore require careful handling to bring the mast into New York whole. Under the shortened bowsprit and reduced headsails the *Firecrest* was badly balanced, so that when I set the mainsail again I had to reef it by four turns of the boom in order to be able to steer at all; the consequence being that when sailing close-hauled she made much leeway.

I had, however, finished the repair work, so, lashing the tiller, I set my course for New York, and then fell exhausted on my bunk.

I had been, in succession, yacht hand, cook, rigger, carpenter, skipper and navigator, and, although absolutely done, was rather pleased with myself in consequence.

CHAPTER TWELVE

GULF STREAM AND A LINER

BUT the gales had not done with us yet, for they lasted another four days, and my log book reads as follows:

"22*nd August.*—Three a.m., rain squall. Five a.m., wind freshening. Seas beating aboard. Eight a.m., seas increasing. Ten a.m., rain squall. Twelve, seas very confused. Port topping lift broke. Spliced it. Mainsail again opening at the seams. Three p.m., strong rain squall. Four p.m., wind increased to a strong gale. Sea very rough. Boat behaves beautifully. Wind west-south-west. Course north-west.

"Running short of potatoes. Had dinner of five potatoes boiled in salt water. Will have to live mainly on rice soon. Seven p.m., hurricane. Wind howling and whistling furiously. Am obliged to heave to. Sky very dark and threatening to windward. Took in working jib. Gale so furious that the jib tore in the operation.

"The sea is getting warmer now. Must be in Gulf Stream."

Next day bad luck gripped me. I spent most of it in repairing sails, but at ten a.m. I lured a five-foot bonito alongside and speared him with my granes. As I hit him he leaped clear of the water and I had to let go my harpoon to avoid going overboard. That meant there would be no more bonito steak for me, and it happened just at a time when I needed all the food I could catch. But I was partly compensated by a flying fish that alighted on deck.

It was now the twentieth day of these gales. I was constantly soaked with rain, and was constantly drugging myself with quinine.

Had another giant wave, like that of the 20th of August, swept over the *Firecrest* whilst she was disabled by the first, she might have been left a dismantled little hulk on a trackless sea, hundreds of miles from the paths of transatlantic liners. But it might have still been possible to have made New York, some months later, by using the boom for a mast, with a short squaresail set.

That huge sea had, however, proved itself a "fair-weather wave," as the seamen say, for it actually marked the height of the storm, and forecast the coming of less boisterous weather.

For twenty successive days now the *Firecrest* had fought against squalls and gales, and finally the hurricane that almost ended her cruise. And the little cutter certainly showed the scars from the battering she had suffered.

Jagged rips, outlined with long rows of stitches,

ran zigzag across her sails. The reefing gear of the main boom had broken long ago. One of her hatches had been washed away, and the jury bowsprit so reduced her headsails as to put her sail plan quite out of balance.

But crippled as she was, I was intensely proud of her!

Designed, built and rigged for racing, she had proved herself a splendid cruiser, sound and able, and as nearly unsinkable as such a craft could be. The marks of my handiwork were on her sails and rigging from the jib tack to mainsail clew. Yet now all looked neat, trim and seaworthy.

Unable to make much westing against the gales and the Gulf Stream, the *Firecrest* had been driven northward several hundred miles from Bermuda, until she was now almost in the latitude of Nantucket Island, but some three hundred and sixty miles east of it.

We were now actually crossing the Gulf Stream, and nearing the course always made by the great liners between New York and European ports; so I began to look expectantly for their clouds of smoke, their towering hulls by day, and the blaze of their lights as they swept past at night. It was also getting cold, by which I realized that I was now out of the Gulf.

My throat was quite sore, and badly swollen, when I turned out at four a.m. on August 25th.

But the never-ending damages to my sails had to be repaired, no matter whether well or ill.

As I was repairing the lacing of the trysail to the mast a vicious rain squall hit the *Firecrest* and ripped the stitches along the luff. So I took it in and made for shelter below decks, leaving the cutter to take care of herself under her head-sails.

Of course a rain squall at sea is a very minor incident provided it does not catch you with too much sail set, and so beat the boat down with the first gust.

By noon I had the trysail repaired, and got my position by sun and chronometer as longitude west 62.07, latitude north 38.18. This showed that I had actually been losing some westing, but I was content to let her head northward in order to get out of the contrary current of the Gulf Stream. There came a strong west wind after the squall, and as the sky cleared it showed patches of the most radiant blue. Under the trysail and head-sails the *Firecrest* was now making splendid weather of it, and continued to do so until late in the afternoon, when the wind moderated and she was able to carry the mainsail again.

Next morning, the 26th, I found two flying fish on deck, and that day I had another feast on their delicious flesh, for the last time. The wind had in the interval shifted to north-west, so I put the cutter about and shaped our course west-south-west, and nearer to the direction of New York. Most of the day was now spent in putting things in order and repairing the mainsail, which ripped again. By night a dead calm had developed.

One of the odd spectacles of the sea, a water-spout, and the first one I had seen on the voyage, was put on, apparently for my benefit, on the following day. A lively squall swept past about a mile distant, carrying a low black cloud. Connecting it with the ocean was a sturdy column of water drawn up in corkscrew fashion as the whirl-pool of wind lashed the sea. I had a splendid view of it, but it was impossible to see where the water ended and the cloud began, and in any case it passed roaring away to leeward.

Although I was now fairly far north, the bonitos still followed the boat, and on August 27th I shot one with a rifle in the hope of retrieving him, but it did no good, for he sank like a stone. The flying fish also had vanished, so with no harpoon to kill bonitos and no flying fish, I was reduced to a diet of cereal, bacon, rice and potatoes.

Next day the wind was fair, and allowed of the balloon forestaysail being rigged out as a spin-naker. I was thus able to make more westing, and by noon I was in west longitude 65.39.

I noticed that the water and fish were of a different colour, and that the seaweed was different.

I must therefore have crossed the Gulf Stream. I also found the patent log to be out of order. It was probably full of salt and needed boiling in fresh water. The land was evidently getting near, for the sea-gulls were from now onward much more numerous.

That night, August 28th, I sighted, for the first time, a steamer passing westward, with all her lights blazing. After months of isolation it was a strange sensation to find other ships on the sea. Evidently the world of water was no more my own, and in consequence I felt a little sad as I watched that liner speed on her way.

I was now actually in the steamship lane, for next morning, August 29th, I spied another steamer, and through the glass I made out her name and her port. I began to feel, therefore, that the *Firecrest* had made a gallant fight and was nearing her home. When the steamship was near enough I started semaphoring with my arms, and this was the message:

"Report yacht *Firecrest*, eighty-four days from Gibraltar."

It was rather difficult to do because there was a heavy swell running, and I had in consequence to cling to the rigging with my legs and feet whilst I waved my arms. But they did not seem to understand my message, so slowed their engines and came nearer.

From the bridge, the captain, using a megaphone, asked me in broken French and English what I wanted. I had no megaphone, but shouted that I did not want them to stop, but only to report me in New York. That I was only out for a sail, perfectly happy and needed nothing. But with a thousand immigrants lining the rails, and all talking at once, I could not make myself understood.

The passengers seemed to be excited and surprised to see a small boat and lone mariner at sea, they consequently kept calling out in Greek. I was sorry then that I had not brought a set of international code signals, for I should have enjoyed a joke at their expense by signalling, "What can I do for you?"

I tried to signal to them to go on their way, but the steamer came nearer, dangerously near. Her great hulk took the wind out of my sails so that I could make no headway, and we promptly drifted together. The *Firecrest* bumped against the steamer's steel side, and her mast barely reached to the lower deck of the big immigrant boat.

This bumping against the liner's side placed my little boat in greater danger of being sunk than by any of the storms she had weathered. They threw me a line and I made it fast to the mast. Then I called out to them to haul the cutter forward so that I could get her out of her present dangerous position, but was horrified to discover that they had started their engines again and were towing her!

In vain I shouted to them to cast away; that I wanted no help to reach New York. But when I drew my knife and started to cut the rope they finally understood and cast off the tow line. I had now some steering way. The cutter's sails filled, and she drew away.

I was just congratulating myself on escaping when I noticed they were lowering a boat, so I hove to and waited. Two young Greek officers, shining with gold braid, came aboard, bringing food, and asking if I needed it. I told them I had plenty of food, but accepted their gift since they were kind enough to bring it.

One of them demanded why I had not steered the *Firecrest* when they were towing her, and undertook to show me how to handle my boat. This rather annoyed me, so I replied as gently as I could that a sailor, and not a mechanic, should know that a sailing boat cannot steer with no wind in her sails!

One of these youths wrote his position on a piece of paper as longitude 62.30 west, latitude 41 north. My own observations had shown my position as longitude 66.39, latitude 41. I was therefore startled to note that there was a difference of some two hundred miles. When I told them of my own observations they at once insisted theirs were correct. It then occurred to me that my chronometer might be wrong, after being tossed about for so many days at sea. In any case I could not be sure that my own was right; I therefore kept the two positions in my log book. Later on I learned that mine was correct, but I shall never know whether the young officer had made a mistake, or whether the liner was in error as to her position.

As my visitors were leaving to go back aboard their ship, I discovered that the food they gave me could be of little use. It consisted of three bottles of brandy and canned fish, which I don't like.

At any rate the steamer went on her way with her immigrants cheering the *Firecrest*, which I answered by dipping my flag.

After this incident the horizon was soon free again, and I was pleased to be alone.

CHAPTER THIRTEEN

THE END OF THE CRUISE

THEN came three days of calm and fog, with the *Firecrest* right in the sea-lane of the transatlantic liners. Nevertheless I managed to sleep peacefully nearly all the afternoon of the first of these days. Towards the evening, however, the siren of a steamer warned me to be on the look-out, and for a time I kept blowing on my fog-horn. The steamer passed close, but was invisible.

At this stage all my fine-weather sails had been blown away. This fact, together with the additional ones that the hull was covered with seaweed, and that I was under shortened sail resulting from the broken bowsprit, meant that little headway was being made.

I was in a real danger, too, in the dense blinding mist which was now blanketing the face of the ocean, and I have no words to describe the melancholy of those days, which were little different from the nights.

So thick was the fog that I could not see the mast from the stern. The steamships' sirens came wailing out of the fog like a plaint, and my own fog-horn seemed to be a sort of death-knell. But despite it all I was most of the time sleeping and gathering strength after those shrewd days of continuous gales.

On the third day of the fog-spell the situation got on my nerves, and I began to think, for a little while, that eventually one of the liners must run me down. I could hear one siren approaching apparently straight at the cutter from astern, whilst all this time the *Firecrest* had practically no steerage-way by which to get her out of the steamer's course. There was nothing to do, therefore, but to keep the fog-horn going in the hope that the look-out man would hear it: and for a few minutes it seemed likely that I might share the supposed fate of Captain Slocum, the famous single-hander, whose small boat was believed to have been sunk in a fog.

Fortunately my horn was heard, and the liner signalled that she would pass to starboard.

That day I took an observation, and found that the *Firecrest* had made twenty miles in the twenty-four hours, and this although there had been no wind at all. It was fairly certain, therefore, that there was a tide setting westward, and that I was getting nearer land.

There were more signs of the nearness of land on the following day, Sunday, September 2nd. The colour of the water had changed, porpoises were plentiful and there were dead butterflies on the water. I knew for certain now that my navigation was correct.

All that day, and the one following, the *Firecrest* sailed slowly westward. Towards three o'clock in the afternoon of Monday, September 3rd, I noticed that the gulls were unusually numerous. The reason soon became evident, for, on the horizon, three miles distant, was a fishing schooner, followed by a regular cloud of gulls.

The wind was very light, and for two hours I sailed towards the schooner, she herself being right on my course. At about four o'clock her dories went back aboard, and she headed towards the *Firecrest*, so I hoisted my flag. The schooner passed near enough for me to read her name, the *Henrietta*, of Boston.

The crew was busy dressing cod and halibut, but the skipper sent a dory to the cutter. A French fisherman from St. Pierre came on board, and quickly showed his astonishment when he learnt that the *Firecrest* and I were coming from France. I was promptly asked to come aboard and partake of their dinner. So, leaving my boat steering herself, close-hauled and on her course, I went a-visiting at sea.

I found the *Henrietta's* deck waist-deep in fish, and as I looked about her cluttered deck and watched the fishermen at work dressing the catch of the day, I was vividly reminded of the descriptions I had read of the sights on board the *We're Here* in Kipling's "Captains Courageous."

The crew all gave me a smiling welcome, and I was glad to be among them, and to listen to their peculiar Boston accent. Somehow I felt far more at home with these fishermen than with the Greeks on the liner, for these were real sailormen.

Down below, where the table was set, I, for the first time in ninety days, tasted fresh bread, butter, fresh meat and pie. As may be imagined, I had never enjoyed a meal so much. They then offered me food for the boat, and I gladly accepted some melons, bread and butter.

The meal over I went on deck and had a yarn with the skipper, Captain Albert Hines, who was at the wheel steering the schooner after the *Firecrest*. It was an odd sensation to see my boat sailing away, and holding her course with nobody on board; so much so that I began to be a little fearful that the *Henrietta's* engine might stop: for close-hauled in a light wind I scarcely think the fishing schooner could have overhauled the cutter.

Skipper Hines proved a fine old sea-dog, and it was a keen pleasure to meet a man like him, knowing as he did the sea and his boat. He gave me a chart of Georges Bank, the great fishing ground east of Cape Cod and Nantucket Island over which we were sailing—and a ball of twine to repair my sails. I also confirmed from him, to my satisfaction, that my position, as obtained from my own observations, was absolutely correct.

By this time the fog had commenced to shut down again, and at times it hid the *Firecrest* from my sight. This being so, I felt anxious to get back on board her before I lost her altogether. So a couple of the fishermen rowed me over, and I gave them the bottles of brandy the officers of the steamer had given me. They then rowed back to the *Henrietta*, when we exchanged some farewell blasts on the fog-horn, and as we were doing so the schooner faded out of sight in the mist. This visit to the *Henrietta* had been a pleasant break in the voyage.

If the *Firecrest* had now had any wind I should have been sailing up Long Island Sound within a few days, for it lies only about two hundred miles from Georges Bank, but the days that ensued were generally calm, with catspaws, now and then, to fan her along for an hour or two, and then leave her rolling in an oily calm.

The tide, too, ran strongly over the shoal, carrying the *Firecrest* backwards and forwards like a shuttlecock, and whilst this game was being played I filled the time by repairing my staysail and mainsail, and, most of the time, I was in sight of some fishing schooner or other.

Using the chart Captain Hines had given me, and sounding constantly with the lead line, I gradually worked my way through Nantucket shoals. Passing over these I one day sighted a couple of small whales, little chaps no bigger than the *Firecrest*.

It was on the morning of the 10th of September that I sighted land, Nantucket, for the first time since leaving the African coast, a few days out from Gibraltar. But I cannot say that I gave a cheery cry of "land-ho." On the contrary, I felt a little sad, for I realized that it stood out there forecasting the end of my cruise; that it meant that all the happy and strenuous days I had spent on the open seas would soon be over, and that I should be obliged to stay ashore for several months. No longer would I be king of all I surveyed, but amongst human beings and a sharer in civilization once more.

On the following day I sighted the Island of No Man's Land, and sailed through a fleet of innumerable small motor fishing boats. On Wednesday, the 12th of September, I had the pleasure of meeting at sea part of the United States' naval fleet manœuvring off Newport. It was a wonderful sight, and I watched with the keenest interest the swift destroyers moving in line at a speed of more than thirty knots.

I had decided to approach New York through Long Island Sound, as I did not want to pass through the Hudson River.

For the first time in three weeks I found a good sailing breeze off Block Island, and by evening had entered the Sound, passing through the Race. So I sadly bade good-bye to the old ocean.

There were plenty of passing steamers now. The Sound liners, all ablaze with lighted windows, and electric lamps on deck, tore past all night, often with strains of music that came to me sweetly across the star-lit waters. After a lone cruise such as this had been these lighted steamers at night possessed a certain fascination.

No longer could I allow the *Firecrest* a free helm to steer herself with at night. We were too near land, and I had a course marked by buoys and lights to follow. So near the goal, I was afraid to fail.

From now onward for two days I sailed along the beautiful north shore of Long Island, admiring the stately country houses and their green lawns. Then the Sound shores come closer together, and I was opposite the mouth of the East River.

So, at two o'clock on the morning of September 15th, I dropped anchor off Fort Totten. I had neither left the tiller, nor slept, for the last seventy-two hours, but the cruise of the *Firecrest* was ended, and just one hundred and one days after she had sailed out of Gibraltar harbour.

CHAPTER FOURTEEN

FIRST DAYS ON LAND

I HAD dropped anchor before an American fort, and at daybreak soldiers helped me to lay the *Firecrest* alongside a wharf. At once a crowd of curious camera-men and reporters came aboard. They were all surprised to learn that I had come from France. The Greek steamer had reported me, but everybody had believed it to be the joke of a French fisherman lost on the banks. Many actually thought that I was a bootlegger.

I had not spoken to a human being for three months, but was now obliged to answer the endless questions of the newspapermen during a whole day. I also had to face the camera-men, and, though I had not slept for three days, was obliged to climb up the mast several times to please them.

The privacy of my floating home was soon and constantly invaded by a crowd of visitors. I had to obey the tyranny of far Western civilization. And in this connection I well remember that it was painful to start the wearing of shoes again.

But I had lived too long in a world of dreams to be able to put up for long with the routine of daily life in a big city, and was constantly thinking of the happy days at sea. So strongly did these thoughts recur that, soon after landing, I was dreaming of putting to sea again.

But I still have many charming souvenirs of my stay in New York, nor will words tell what I owe to a certain captain and his wife, my first visitors aboard, who made my stay at Fort Totten a joy and a delight.

The American yachtsmen treated me like a brother. Bill Nutting, the hero of a famous passage across the Atlantic, became one of my best friends. Nor shall I ever forget a lecture I gave at West Point, when two cadets came and told me of their intention to leave the army and sail round the world in a small boat.

The American newspapers had been describing the cruise, but it was humorous, and even painful, to read the extraordinary accounts about it. Every newspaper seemed to want to print something new and startling, whether accurate or not, and in one I was surprised to read that I had on one occasion been unconscious for two days.

I was unknown when I landed, but on the morrow I found I had achieved a sort of bubble fame. Letters and telegrams began to arrive from everywhere, and were so numerous that an army of stenographers would have been necessary to deal with them.

Numerous, too, were the letters of friends, sincere friends, who were really pleased with the success of the cruise. But more numerous were the letters of strangers desirous to join me on my next cruise.

They were all sorts, eccentrics who wanted to become famous, and boys and men sincerely attracted by the lure of adventure.

Very uncommon was the letter of the Californian girl, who wrote:

"I am apt to do everything which is uncommon. When I read about your daring exploit I felt that I ought to do something myself. You know that a man is supposed to have more courage than a woman. I am merely a woman, being only twenty years old, and I have just completed a hike from Los Angeles to Milwaukee, having walked alone two thousand miles. The darker the night the better I like to be alone. I enjoy hearing coyotes howling when I am all alone. . . . I don't know what it is to be afraid. One day I hope to go to Africa. I don't know what I shall do there, but I'll do what other people are afraid to do. . . ."

She concluded by saying that the job of cabin-boy would fulfil her dearest dreams.

Another American girl had certainly a curious idea of life aboard, for, having demonstrated that I could not again start alone, she claimed that she was very adaptable and that any job aboard from cabin-boy to "social secretary" would suit her.

Very keen seemed to be the young girl who wrote:

"I have wasted the first twenty-five years of my life regretting I have been born a girl and not a boy. Now I am going to act just as if I was a boy. To be a sailor, and sail out to the South Sea Islands, has always been my dream. Of course I know that sailing alone with you will not seem very *comme il faut*, but why should we pay any attention to the conventions if we do what we think is right? If you have no sense of humour you will think I am mad, if you have some you will perhaps think the same."

Charming was the letter of a young French girl, who wrote to me from a restaurant, and wanted to sail with me to cook my meals and sew my sails.

From Australia I received a letter written by an old French sailor, which contained a single five-thousand-word sentence filling sixteen pages, with numerous additions between the lines. I was never able to read the letter entirely. The poor lunatic wrote that he had been persecuted by the French consul, and that it was a great pity that the Channel Islands, which were so near the French coast, did not belong to the French. He suggested that I write to the King of England about it and that, after my exploit, he would be obliged to grant my demand. He added that he was writing at the same time to Sir Thomas Lipton to place before him one of his inventions for increasing the course and velocity of yachts, which would permit them to get back the America Cup to Great Britain.

Another inventor proposed to use in place of sails a windmill-like propeller that he had designed.

Curious, too, is a letter from Geneva.

"I am no more a young man, but I am still very strong. I am forty-eight years old, mineralogist, know all Nature's laws, and I would like to explore unknown countries. As I saw in the newspapers that you are going to visit some virgin islands, I am your man."

The letter is signed—"A Good Swiss."

All these letters, however, were not letters from volunteers. Many children sent their congratulations, and these letters are very touching. They are, too, those one keeps and which give one the feeling that something useful has been done to raise the ideals of youth.

An eight-year-old child advised me not to sail towards the Pacific Ocean, which he knew to be dangerous. He was seemingly terribly anxious about me.

Another young American schoolboy wrote that he thought of me when seeing an aeroplane pass above his window. Also, "I am going to work very hard to make a lot of money, buy a boat like yours, and wander round the world; but I must leave you and finish learning my lessons."

A professor in transcendental sciences wanted to predict everything that was going to happen during my next cruise, but I could not accept his offer, for it would eliminate all the unforeseen—adventure's greatest attraction.

All these curious letters are but a few among the many. But most of those I received were quite serious, and from people really attracted by adventure; people willing to give up their jobs to run risks; letters from people belonging to different classes of society; letters from sailormen, mechanics, students and wealthy people. They seemingly wanted to give up everything, and to ask nothing in return. These letters were the hardest of all to answer.

A French officer in command of a destroyer wanted to give up the navy to serve under me. I naturally could not accept the suggestion, but felt very proud of the honour.

A commander in the Russian Navy wanted to ship as one of the crew.

Very brief and business-like was the following letter:

"I am an old sea-dog, born on the northern coast of Norway, fifty years old, active as a young boy. Can do two things well. Sail a boat and cook. Can you use me?"

A volunteer I could have done very well without was one who thought he was qualified because he was very unhappy and tired of life. In fact, he wanted to join me on a dangerous cruise, hoping to lose his life.

The twenty-year-old mechanic had a high opinion of himself who wrote:

"I am afraid of nothing, and I have exceptional nerves. You can dispose of my life as you choose. Consider my proposition. It is worth it."

There was also the seventeen-year-old ex-schoolboy who gave of himself a long and complete description.

"For many years I have been attracted by adventure. When I was still young I was dreaming of travels and wrecks. I gave up my studies, for I did not like the idea of working in a town. I am studying English and mathematics while I am waiting for an occasion to satisfy my savage tastes. I adore the sea, the pampas adventure and the unforeseen. Unluckily I can't give you a fortune for your expedition, but I will give you my instruction, my willingness and my friendship."

I have many times tried to figure out the mentality of the young man who wrote:

"I have for you the greatest admiration. The reason is very simple—your character is exactly mine."

There was also a wonderful polyglot sailor-waiter in a Duval restaurant, who knew navigation, could repair sails and was prepared to speak fluently French, English, German, Italian, Spanish, Norwegian, Danish, Swedish and American.

Perhaps the plumber would have been a good companion, who had no knowledge of maritime matters, but was fond of running, and a keen cyclist. He offered me all he owned, two thousand francs, and good health.

Another volunteer seemed to possess a rare gift for scribbling which would help me to write my books. I have, too, often thought of the big things I could have done together with an old sea-dog who had been at sea for fifteen years, did not want any wages and would follow me to death.

Another seaman, a volunteer of thirty, who had crossed the line twelve times aboard three-masted square-riggers—he gave descriptions of the dangers of the Pacific and of a typhoon in the Tonga Islands—wanted to follow me, and would not hold me responsible whatever happened.

I liked very much the letter of an American boy who sent me his photo at the wheel of a Gloucester schooner, and wrote:

"I should like to go with you. I have been at sea aboard steamers, and I worked aboard a schooner for two months. Of course, I have papers to prove it. I am eighteen years old, five foot ten inches in height, and my weight is one hundred and fifty pounds. I am young, willing, and I am not afraid of work. If you need money I think I shall be able to raise some, but of course a boy of my age cannot be expected to be very rich yet."

Of what wonderful value in new surroundings would have been the quartermaster who had been at sea since he was ten years old, and had been four times round the Horn. He wrote:

"Take me with you. I am afraid of nothing. I shall always obey you. Back home we should be able to teach the French to love the sea. If you want it, I am yours body and soul for this great task."

An English boy, a salesman in a great motor-car firm, wanted to give up his job to follow me. He would have been, I think, a splendid companion.

"Although I have a good position I am wasting my life when the sea and adventure are calling me louder and louder every day. During the war I served in the navy aboard boats hardly bigger than yours, cruising on the northern coast of Scotland. I am longing for adventure, and to see the very islands to which you are sailing. Can you take me with you? I am prepared to face any hardship for the love of the enterprise. If I had money I would give you everything I own."

I was especially sorry to have to disappoint the thirteen-year-old Irish volunteer, who wrote:

"You will find me very useful when things have to be done in a hurry. I should prefer no wages."

The letter is signed—"Respectively yours."

When I re-read all these letters—letters which I shall always keep with me—I cannot help thinking of the great drawing power the sea has when so many strong and energetic men are ready to throw up everything for adventure upon it.

But if I actually took anybody with me it would be as a companion, for I should prefer to do all the work myself.

It was really sad to have to disappoint so many who evidently had a real fondness for the sea, and perhaps this letter from a French sailor was the most difficult to reply to in the negative. He wrote:

"I am longing for the sea. I should like to wander again on the immensity of the ocean. I should like to live again a sailor's life, with its sufferings and its pains. I pray you to take me with you. I shall face without complaining the worst storms. I should like to be with you, sharing your life and those days without a morrow. I ask nothing. I shall bring nothing with me. I don't want to bring back anything. I implore you to take me with you."

It was, in any case, the most pathetic letter I received, and has been placed between my favourite books—John Masefield's ballads and Bill Adams' short stories. It was a letter written by a real sailor, and one able to tell of his great passion for the sea.

The spirit of adventure to-day is anything but dead if one may judge by these few extracts.

CHAPTER FIFTEEN

THE CALL OF THE SEÀ

NEARLY a year has passed since I landed in New York. And now, in a small French town by the sea, I am finishing the writing of this little book. I have just been walking along the seashore, looking out over the open ocean, and a great contentment is about me, for I know that I shall soon be on the sea again.

I have also been thinking once again of the numerous hardships of that last cruise, and am now wondering why I started, and still more why I want to start again.

The life of a single hand aboard a small sailing-boat naturally means a very rough life. He is constantly exposed on deck: the wind cuts the face, rain and spray make the skin so sore that it becomes painful for a time to pull on the ropes. Under the tropical sun he has to suffer from thirst if water runs short. It is true that when the weather is fine he can rest and recuperate, but when many days of gales come in succession, he has neither the time to rest nor often the time to fully repair damage immediately it occurs. In fact his life whilst aboard is often a perpetual struggle of brains and physical strength against disaster.

There is no doubt about it that it is a hard life, and if I were to advise youngsters who might burn to imitate the lone hand, I should say, "Don't do it!" Yet I am going to sea again under such conditions.

Perhaps the comfort and luxury of early youth now ask for the counter-irritant of the plain life of a sailor with all its risks and adventure.

A great love of the sea, and nothing more, was the cause of this, my first long cruise, and those whom I fancy believed that a beaten record or temporary fame was the motive were mistaken. For, as the famous poet Verhaeren wrote:

> "They did not understand the great dream
> That charmed the sea with its voyage;
> For it was not the same lie
> That was taught in their village."

No! I am not happy on land. I am constantly dreaming of the strong smell of tar, of the rough sea-breeze and of the *Firecrest* waiting for me on the other side of the Atlantic.

Nearly three years ago I first went cruising in my little boat, and now the sea has taken hold of me. Whatever happens I shall always go back to the sea like the rover in Masefield's beautiful verses:

THE CALL OF THE SEA

"I must down to the seas again, for the call of the running tide
Is a wild call and a clear call that may not be denied;
And all I ask is a windy day with the white clouds flying,
And the flung spray, and the blown spume, and the sea-gull's
crying."

CHAPTER SIXTEEN

THE REJUVENATED *FIRECREST*

THIS is a sort of appendix for yachtsmen, telling of past experience with the boat and of the alterations which have been carried out on the *Firecrest* before starting on a longer voyage I am about to make, or upon which I shall have started when this little book is published.

I shall not try to pretend that the *Firecrest* is a perfect boat. In fact, there is not such a thing as a perfect boat. Each type, each form of hull, each rig has its advantages and disadvantages. The good sailor is one who knows his ship's good points and faults, who understands her behaviour in a storm, her reactions to the tiller. There are many good ships. Good sailors are not so easy to find, and often one could appropriately quote Kipling's verse:

> "The game is bigger than the player;
> The ship is greater than the crew."

I was able to get from the builders, in England, the lines of the *Firecrest*. Designed by Dixon Kemp under the length and sail area rule, she is rather narrow and deep for her length. The three and a half tons of lead she carries on her keel make her practically uncapsizable, but the strain on the mast and hull is certainly greater than it would be if she had more beam and not so much depth. Her general dimensions are: L.w.l., 39 feet 7 inches; w.l., 31 feet 6 inches; beam, 8 feet 6 inches; draught, 6 feet 3 inches; displacement, 12 tons.

She sails easily to windward even against rough seas and gales. She heaves to very well, working to windward a little more than she drifts. She is certainly difficult to steer before the wind when she is near her speed limit, which is about eight knots, although once in a gale my log registered thirty miles in three hours under a big squaresail.

The chief sources of trouble during my passage were the following: I could not buy new sails, the ones I was using were more than ten years old, and I had to repair them constantly. My bronze roller reefing gear was too small, and made of bad metal; it broke the second day out from Gibraltar. The bowsprit was too long; the bobstay broke many times. The fresh water kept very badly in the oak casks. The gaff mainsail was difficult to hoist and lower in a gale. The solid boom was very heavy. Since her arrival at New York the *Firecrest* has been laid up on City Island, and much work has been done to put her in the best condition possible. A new teak rail has replaced the one which was broken against the pier at Fort

Totten in the gale which wrecked the *Harpoon* last October. The rudder stock has been renewed, and she has been copper sheathed against the destructive worms of the tropical seas.

I have adopted the Bermudan, or jib-headed rig, which will allow me to use a new nine-foot bowsprit, three feet shorter than the old one, which was broken at sea in a hurricane. Instead of a bobstay, there are two bronze rods to keep the bowsprit rigid and suppress the strain on the mast-head when she is dipping into a wave. The total length of the mast above the deck is forty-six feet. The topmast is hollow, twelve feet long, funnelled into the solid one, which is of Oregon pine, thirty-four feet long above the deck, and of a diameter of six and a half inches at the foot. The boom is hollow. Both hollow spars were made by McGruer, in England, of five pieces of wood cemented together. The boom is seven inches in diameter and twenty-seven feet in length. I am still using a roller reefing gear, but this time of galvanized iron; the genuine Channel pilot-boat type made by John Beara, Appledore, Devon. The standing rigging is all new, of plough-steel wire, and G. N. Buckle, who came over here three years ago from England on the *Shamrock*, made a beautiful job of it. The shrouds have individual splices this time, for I have not forgotten that day in August last year when the seizing parted and I nearly lost my mast. The forestay goes to the stem-head, and topmaststay to the bowsprit end. I am using three-quarter inch galvanized iron turnbuckles. I like them better than dead-eyes and lanyards, which do not last very long in the tropics. There seems to be no more reason nowadays for using lanyards than rope shrouds.

The sails are all new, made of twelve-ounce cotton by Burrows, Inc., who took a great interest

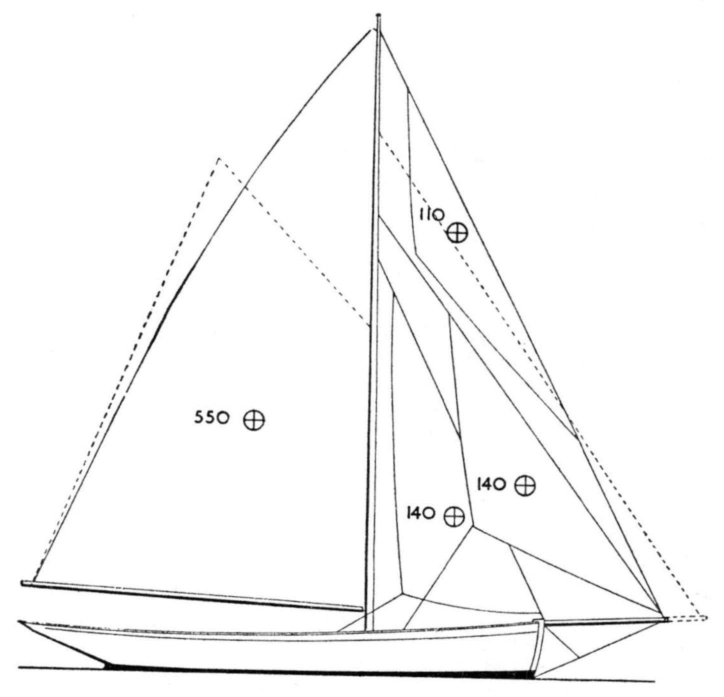

Present Rig of the *Firecrest.*

in them. The seams of mainsail and staysail run up and down with straight stitching. The mainsail is laced to a wooden batten on the boom, and has hoops under the spreader, and hooks on a wire jackstay above. The wire jackstay passes through the hoops and is spliced to an iron turnbuckle on the gooseneck mast-band. The luff rope is manila. I am carrying one spare forestaysail, as it is the most useful sail on a cutter, with hanks on the forestay, three rows of reef points, port and starboard sheets, no boom and no traveller. The jib is set flying on a ring travelling on the bowsprit. The first, second and third jibs are made of flax, with two jib-sheet pennants, and port and starboard sheets belaying near the tiller. I am carrying a light jib topsail to use in the doldrums and variables, and hooking on to the topmaststay. There is a balloon forestaysail, which is a very useful sail, and a storm trysail, in case I should lose my boom, made of slightly stronger canvas.

All the running rigging is rope. It was intended to be of Irish flax, which is stronger for the same diameter than iron wire. As I cannot get in time, from Ireland, all the rope I need, I shall sail with the old rope and get all new Irish flax running rigging in Bermuda. I am using now Irish flax for the jib-sheet pennants and forestaysail sheets. There is one halyard and one purchase for the mainsail, and one halyard and one purchase for the jib, made of two-inch rope. The mainsheet is of two-inch manila and is rove through a double block on a swivel-band on the boom's after end.

It is my first experience with a Marconi rig, but I have great confidence in it. It was very difficult when hoisting my mainsail before to make the gaff pass between the two topping lifts. The wind pressure keeping the gaff against the lee lift made the operation of lowering the mainsail very difficult. When I wanted to set the trysail I had to get the boom on deck—one of the most difficult tasks on a single-hander. The hollow boom and jib-headed mainsail will suppress all those troubles. The boat will not roll so much before the wind, and will be easier to steer with a hollow spar. She could not steer herself before under mainsail with the wind on the quarter, but she could under the try-sail with the jib hauled flat. Now she should steer herself with a jib-headed sail and a hollow boom. I have also invented a new device to keep her on her course in any wind, and I am going to experiment with it between New York and Bermuda.

Now that I am publishing the lines of *Firecrest*, I suppose all the theorists will start arguing about her and try to prove that she is or is not a good boat. Well, I could have sold her last year and had a boat built in France for what I would ask for her, but I like the dear old girl, and I shall sail on her as long as she lasts. She is as good as any boat of her size. I have very good accommodation below, and enough room to carry not only food and gear, but also all of my belongings; for she is my only home.

The water will be carried in galvanized iron tanks. I have had a new one built holding sixty gallons. I still dislike canned food and will only carry with me bacon, rice, potatoes, butter, milk, hard tack, jam, porridge and tea. For cooking I have a Tilley kerosene stove (which works like the Primus under pressure, but requires no prickers), hung on gimbals for cooking at sea, and a Clyde cooker to use in harbour.

To navigate, I carry a patent log, a three-inch radius micrometer sextant, the small navigation tables made by Lieutenant Johnson, R.N., which permit of very quick calculations and give an approximation less than the error of observation on a small boat, two deck watches, which stand rough treatment better than a chronometer hung in gimbals. A compass with card downwards (tell-tale) now swings above my bunk, and when resting a glance will tell me how she is heading.

I am carrying with me a bow and arrows to spear fish on the high seas, some rifles and a small motion-picture camera with a mile of film in small tin boxes, and a new metallic camera especially made for the tropics.

You will ask me where I intend to go and what are my plans. Well, it is nearly impossible for me to tell. I am a-roving—and a rover has no definite plans; it would spoil the fun of the thing. On a sail-boat one has to reckon with the wind. Why go against the wind towards certain islands if there are some equally beautiful ones to leeward? All I know is that I am going to sail to Bermuda, then through the Panama Canal towards the South Sea Islands, and cruise among them where fancy, inspiration and the spirit of adventure take me. I am in no hurry, for I am travelling with my home. I hope I shall be able to carry on always. Maybe some day I shall reach Australia, South Africa or South America. Who knows? I do not want to know, for I like the unexpected.

As I am writing these lines in the *Firecrest's* saloon I am surrounded by beautiful things. The teak and bird's-eye maple panels are shining, and the new blue leather cushions are very comfortable. On the shelves are some two hundred beautifully bound books which strike an artistic note. All are sea books; some of them are over two hundred years old, and tell of the lives of the most famous sailors. Here are John Masefield, Conrad, Stevenson, London, Loti, Farrère and all my favourite sea books: "Slocum," "The Track of the

Typhoon," "75,000 Miles in a Ketch," by Rollier du Baty, "The Cruise of the *Falcon*," the "Travels of Cook" and "Marco Polo."

I have been ashore nearly a year. I have had many difficulties to overcome, but I have won, and I am ready to sail again. Now, every minute of the day, I am thinking of departure, and of the great joy called living, when I shall be again alone on the sea.

IN QUEST OF THE SUN

by

ALAIN GERBAULT

The Journal of the *Firecrest*

CONTENTS

CONTENTS

MAPS

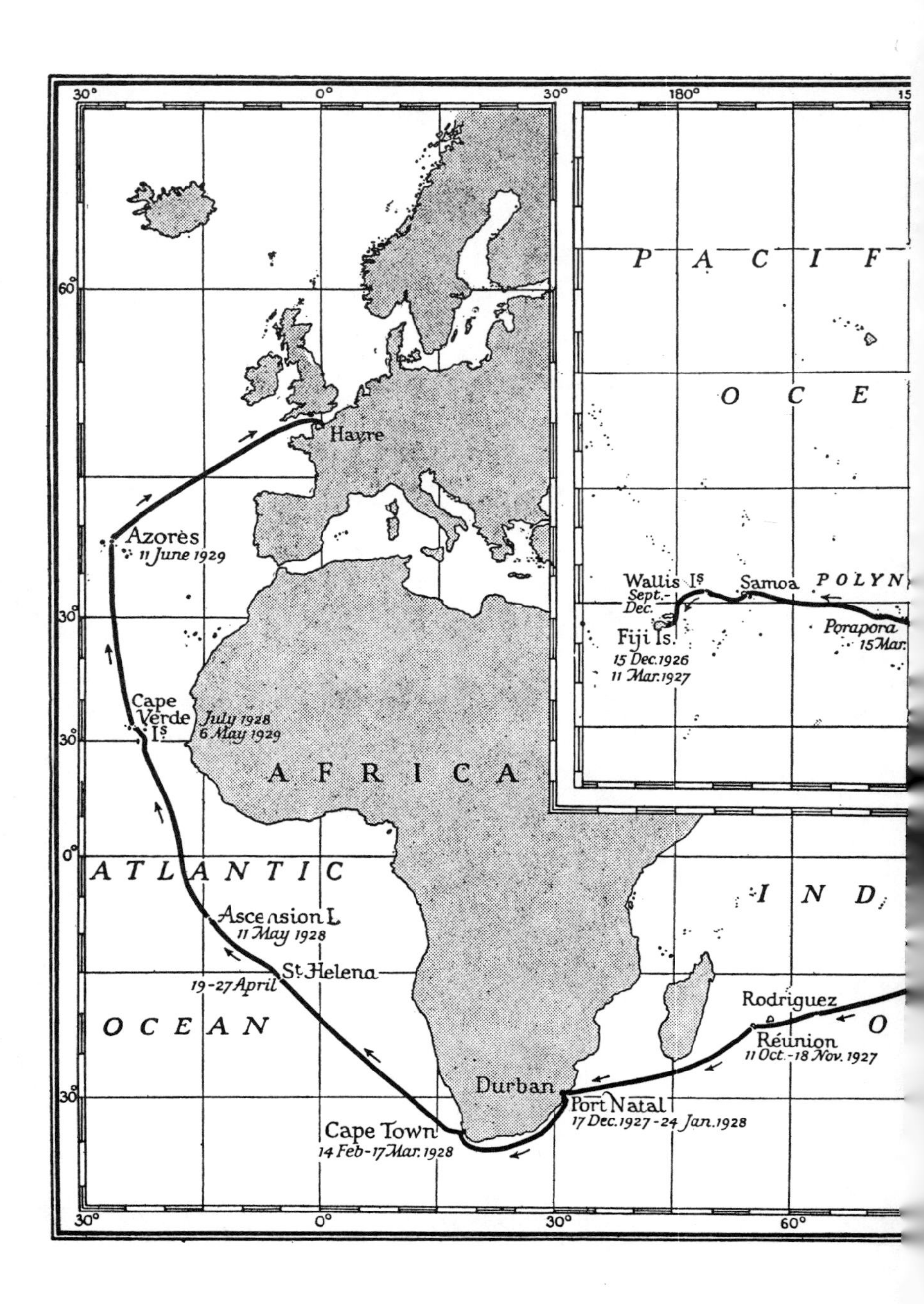

30°
0°
30°
180°
60°
30°
0°
Havre
Azores
11 June 1929
Cape Verde Is
July 1928
6 May 1929
A F R I C A
A T L A N T I C
O C E A N
Ascension I.
11 May 1928
St Helena
19-27 April
Cape Town
14 Feb-17 Mar. 1928
Durban
Port Natal
17 Dec. 1927 - 24 Jan. 1928
Rodriguez
Réunion
11 Oct.-18 Nov. 1927
I N D
O
P A C I F
O C E
Wallis Is
Sept.-Dec.
Samoa
P O L Y N
Fiji Is.
15 Dec. 1926
11 Mar. 1927
Porapora
15 Mar.
60°

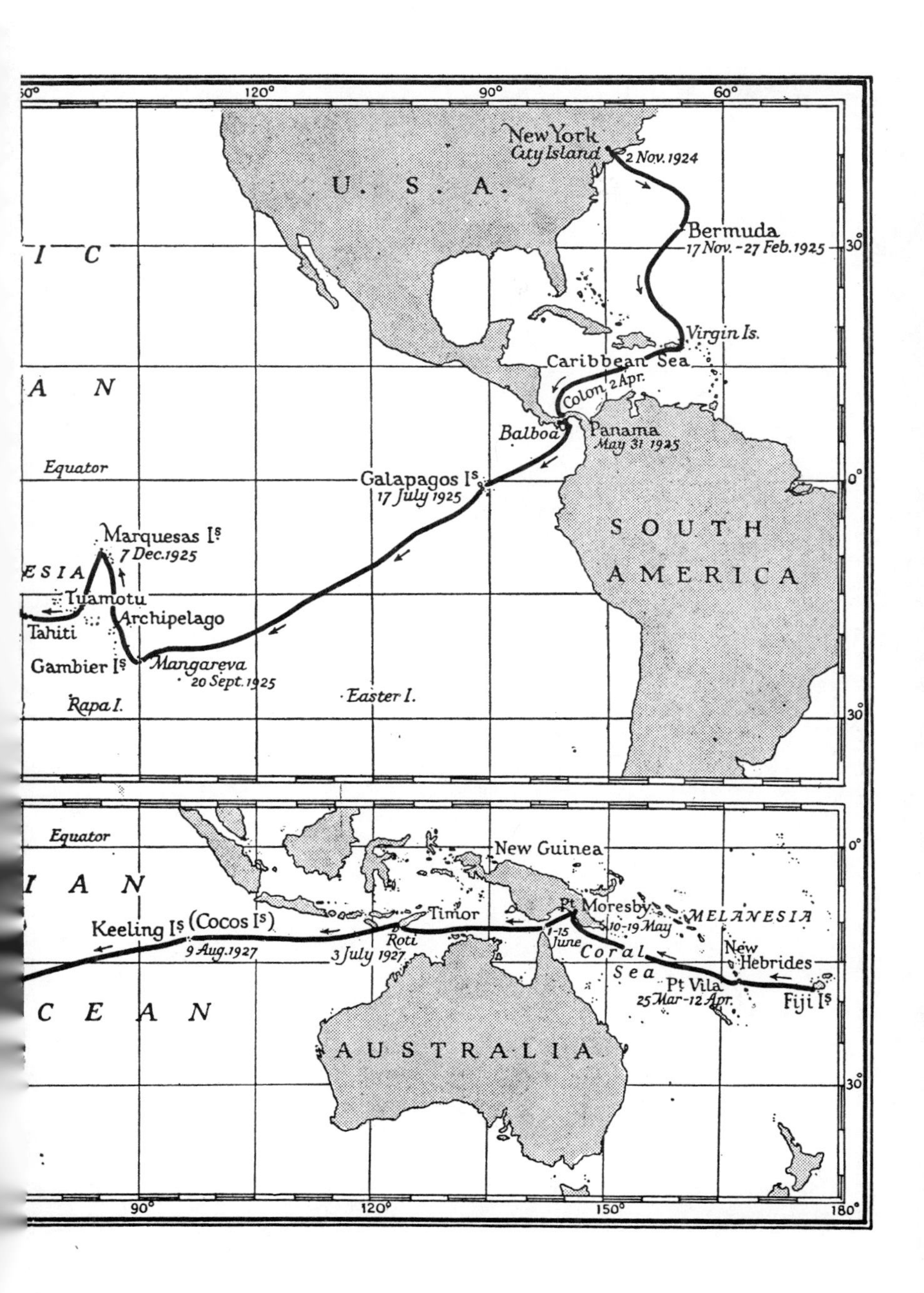

120°
90°
60°
New York
City Island
2 Nov. 1924
U. S. A.
Bermuda
17 Nov. - 27 Feb. 1925
Virgin Is.
Caribbean Sea
Colon 2 Apr.
Balboa
Panama
May 31 1925
Equator
Galapagos Is
17 July 1925
SOUTH
AMERICA
Marquesas Is
7 Dec. 1925
Tuamotu
Archipelago
Tahiti
Gambier Is
Mangareva
20 Sept. 1925
Easter I.
Rapa I.
I C
A N
ESIA
30°
0°
Equator
New Guinea
Pt Moresby
10-19 May
MELANESIA
Keeling Is (Cocos Is)
9 Aug. 1927
Timor
Roti
3 July 1927
1-15 June
Coral Sea
Pt Vila
25 Mar-12 Apr.
New Hebrides
Fiji Is
I A N
C E A N
AUSTRALIA
90°
120°
150°
180°

CHAPTER I

FITTING OUT

On board the Firecrest, *City Island, October 8th,* 1924.
From a letter to my friend P.A.

As soon as I landed from the *Paris,* August 16th, 1924, I hurried to City Island to look at the *Firecrest.* I found her riding at anchor off the shipyard, just where I had left her eight months before. Stripped of rigging she looked smaller than ever, and the paint on her hull presented a lamentable appearance. My delight at seeing her soon yielded to dismay at the enormous amount of work that would have to be done before she would be ready for sea again.

First of all I had a fortnight's hard work in getting the gear I had brought with me through the customs. I claimed exemption for goods in transit, but notwithstanding the support of the agent of the French Line I found myself faced with inflexible rules. Finally, when a high customs official told me that I might have bought everything I wanted in America, I understood and paid up. I even paid duty on my chronometers, and on some English books for my own use on the *Firecrest*; but in the end I obtained possession of the hollow boom and the other things I had brought with me.

I then set to work on various tasks; designing and calculating sails and rigging, ordering a new mast, steel-wire stays, canvas, and supervising every job and replacing whatever was not stout enough to stand the voyage. I found New York by no means an ideal port for getting all I needed for a long cruise. The shipyards are not accustomed to meet the demands of bad weather and high seas, for the yachts they build seldom sail beyond the narrow sheltered waters of Long Island. For this reason a fishing harbour such as Boston or Gloucester would have been better suited for my purpose. I was always having to sign cheques and I simply dared not think of the thousands of dollars it was going to cost me to get my boat seaworthy. Sometimes, when I felt more discouraged than usual, I used to take a walk along the quays. The greatest port in the world in point of view of tonnage, it might well be expected that the quays of New York, with their innumerable craft, would charm the eyes of a seaman. Alas, long rows of numbered sheds hide the ships and jetties from view, and the quays resemble nothing so much as the façade of an immense railway station.

My predilections, indeed, are certainly towards smaller seaports where there are still sailing craft to please the eye—Saint Malo, with its Newfoundland trawlers; La Rochelle, or even the Ladies Dock in London where old clippers with their white sails are still to be seen sometimes. At Battery Place, however, near the Aquarium, I discovered a charming corner whence I could look across to New Jersey and the mouth of the river. Seated on a bench I gazed enviously at boats going down the Hudson and passing the Statue of Liberty on their way to the open sea. Sometimes, too, I had the joy of seeing three- or four-masted schooners, which are, perhaps, the most graceful boats ever launched from American slips.

One day, in a little basin near the Aquarium, I found a rival to my own craft. A number of idlers were watching a decked cutter called the *Carcharias* (the Greek word for shark), which was being exhibited for a fee by its gold-uniformed owner, and on board of which he proposed to get to Piraeus and sail round the world single-handed. One glance was enough for me. The great roof and the general lines of the craft betrayed total inexperience of anything to do with the sea, and I was not at all surprised to hear that he gave up his project about a fortnight later.

In any case the weather that summer was not propitious for yachtsmen. The ketch *Shanghai*, famous for her long voyage from China to Denmark, was wrecked on the coast of Nova Scotia, after having crossed the North Atlantic with her new American owner and a crew of three. I was, unhappily, also without news of my friend William Nutting. Four years previously, on a twenty-ton yacht, he had crossed the Atlantic from Nova Scotia to Cowes in twenty-one days, making a record for a vessel of that size. The same year he had made the more difficult crossing from East to West in seventy days, notwithstanding a violent storm in which one of his crew was washed overboard. On my arrival at New York a year ago, Bill welcomed me as a brother and we became friends. I admired his courage and loyalty, as well as his enthusiasm for the various yachts he had owned. Starting from Bergen the previous June on a Norwegian pilot-boat with three friends, he intended to follow the course of ancient Vikings such as Leif Ericson, son of Red Eric, who had been the first to cross the ocean and land on Labrador, and whose name he had given to his craft. After his departure from Rejkjavik in Iceland, on August 9th, nothing more had been heard of Nutting, and in spite of my absolute confidence in his seamanship I felt very uneasy. It was a bitter disappointment to have to sail from New York without seeing him.

. . . . .

After two months of incessant work the *Firecrest* is ready to sail. I feel very confident of her, for she is in perfect condition. The new mast is of Oregon pine, with a total length of forty-two feet. A new bowsprit, also of Oregon pine, replaces the one that was snapped in a hurricane; the standing rigging, of galvanized steel wire, will bear a strain of ten tons without breaking. The sails are new and sewn in a special way. A new water-tank to hold forty-four gallons keeps the drinking water fresher than oaken barrels do. The bobstays of the bowsprit and the roller for the boom, which had been broken in my passage across, are replaced by a bronze bobstay and a much stronger galvanized iron roller reefing-gear. The new triangular mainsail and the hollow boom should make sailing much easier.

The *Firecrest* is ready to sail. For more than a year I have been on land. At last all my difficulties have been overcome and I shall soon be able to start again. I am writing these lines in the cabin, with the teak and maple fittings glistening around me. Two hundred new volumes are in my bookshelves, and a few beautiful bindings lend an artistic note. These are "The

Lives of the Most Famous French Sailors," in the edition of 1750, which was presented to me by my friends of the Railway Club; and an account of my own voyage, a unique example on Imperial Japan paper, illustrated by Pierre Leconte, and presented by the Yacht Club of France. There are also all my old shipmates, with bindings ruined by salt water—the Jack Londons, Lotis, Conrads and Stevensons, which crossed the Atlantic with me.

Eight bells, midnight, is struck by my polished bronze marine clock. Soon I hope it will be marking the hours in Southern Seas!

CHAPTER II

DEPARTURE FROM NEW YORK

A ROUGH PASSAGE

St. George, Bermuda. Extract from the log

WITHOUT having had a chance of trying my new sails, which were not ready until the last moment, I left the dockyard and dropped anchor off the Morris Yacht Club, Pelham Bay. On Saturday, November 1st, I filled the tanks with fresh water and tied up alongside the Yacht Club pier to embark all my provisions, which had only arrived the previous evening. There were potatoes, rice, sugar, soap, condensed milk, butter, jam, lime-juice, as a preventative from scurvy; in all enough to last me for two months. There was also oil for lighting and cooking. A great number of gifts had been sent by friends, and the whole lot, together with all sorts of gear I had ordered at the last moment, was piled on the deck and soon encumbered it. There were rugs, rifles, cartridges, books, a bow and arrows for fishing on the high seas, a mile and a half of cinematograph film in air-tight boxes, innumerable charts and nautical instructions. I had to stow all this below deck, talking the while to friends who had come to say good-bye, and to numerous members of the Explorers' Club and Cruising Club of America. Despite the secrecy I had tried to preserve concerning my departure, there were also a number of photographers and reporters there.

At last Mrs. Nutting arrived, at two o'clock in the afternoon, bringing some boxes of biscuits which the contractor had not supplied in time. She told me that the American destroyer *Trenton* had gone to search for her husband. Mrs. Nutting came on board the *Firecrest* with W. P. Stephens, editor of Lloyd's Yacht Register, well known in English and American yachting circles.

We got under way almost at once, for we wanted to take

advantage of the tide to descend East River. I cast off from the pier, towed by Bob Schultz in his motor yacht as well as by the commodore of the Morris Yacht Club in his motor yacht. The Yacht Club fired three guns by way of salute, I answered by dipping the French flag. Such was my ceremonious public departure, which was duly recorded by the picture people. How different from the times I left Cannes and Gibraltar. I looked back on them with a sort of melancholy regret, as on things that once had been and were never to return. However, I was full of joy at getting under way again, and delighted to leave behind all the difficulties of life ashore, and to turn my prow to distant isles where no publicity had preceded me. I soon slipped by Fort Totten, across Long Island Sound, where I had landed after my voyage across the Atlantic. Adventure was starting from the same spot it had stopped at.

EXTRACT FROM MY LOG

At 3 p.m. we left Long Island Sound to enter East River. Clearing the dangerous eddies of Hell Gate we passed under the Brooklyn Bridge and off Manhattan and its skyscrapers. My last sight of New York leaves me with the impression of a monstrous and titanic town. Darkness fell as we passed near the Statue of Liberty, and off Coney Island the police boat took my passengers on board and sheered off. I dropped anchor in Sheepshead Bay and went on shore to buy various galley utensils that I lacked, and spent part of the night and the following morning in stowing my stores carefully.

At 11 a.m. I leave Sheepshead Bay, still towed by the *We Two*. The glass has dropped very low during the night and morning and I am expecting bad weather. The sea is rough and squally and towing is a painful job. At noon the tow-rope breaks, so my friends wave me farewell as they put about, for they want to make harbour before the storm breaks upon them.

I am now alone, absolutely alone. I send all my canvas aloft and set a south-easterly course. The sea is rough, the breeze fresh, and the glass low. At five o'clock in the evening

I am south of the Ambrose lightship, when the Sandy Hook coastguard ship signals to me the approach of bad weather. The sunset is of an ominous grey, and huge black clouds pile up in the west. The wind rises and to my great regret, for I know that it is going to pull my new sail out of shape, I have to roll seven turns of the boom, lower the jib and staysail and heave to for the night. The work is lengthy, for the rigging is new and parts of it do not run easily; however, I am pleased to find that my new roller works well. The wind blows up in a gale, the waves are high, but under her shortened mainsail the *Firecrest* lies to excellently, and wearied by the hard work I have just had, I sleep soundly until daybreak.

Monday, November 3rd.—The barometer is rising slightly when I again take up my south-easterly course, at 6.30. Towards 1 p.m. I hoist the staysail and, as the wind blows harder, lower the mainsail and let the *Firecrest* run before it under the fore canvas only. I find the new triangular mainsail very easy to take in, but observe that there are many little details that will need alterations. About 11 p.m. the wind blows a gale from the north-west, but the *Firecrest* speeds on towards the Bermudas by herself, while I turn in and sleep.

Tuesday, November 4th.—The glass keeps on falling. About 8 a.m. the storm increases in violence. We ship great seas that keep the deck awash, and, as it was badly caulked in New York, the water penetrates into the cabin. The wind is howling, gulls pass me, carried by the gale and vainly trying to beat up against it. I stay at the helm until 4 p.m., drenched by the spray and the seas that sweep across the deck, then I leave the *Firecrest* to steer herself and fly before the wind towards the Bermudas under her fore canvas. Towards evening the weather improves and the barometer begins to rise. At noon I was 120 miles from New York.

Wednesday, November 5th.—About 1 a.m. I notice that my red port light is out. I carry the lamp below to light it, but I take my time, for I have not sighted another boat for forty-eight hours. I seize the opportunity of being below to prepare a meal. I am filling the lamp and lighting it when suddenly the *Firecrest* reels under a terrific blow. I rush on deck and in the blackness of the night see the innumerable lights of a steamer fast receding into the gloom. It is my bowsprit that has received the shock. The bronze bobstay is twisted; the bits have been shorn clean away from the deck, and have wrenched it up, leaving a great hole. The forestay and jibstays are adrift and the mast, having no support forward, is bending in a very threatening way.

There is no use whatever in trying to attract the attention of the steamer, which probably never saw me in the darkness of the night; there is no time to be lost if I am going to save the mast. By means of block and tackle I haul the stays taut and lash the bowsprit as firmly as possible to the splintered deck forward. Not until my mast stands firm can I congratulate myself on my escape. When daylight comes I make a closer inspection of the damage and overhaul the repairs I did so hastily in the darkness. I fill the hole in the deck with cotton-waste. At noon I find I have made fifty miles in twenty-four hours. There is an easterly wind, and my course is south-south-east. I hoist the mainsail with two turns only. I am in 72° W. longitude, and 38° 30′ N. latitude.

Thursday, November 6th.—A slight breeze is blowing from the west. I get up the mainsail, but I can only set a small jib on the damaged bowsprit. Great masses of seaweeds are round the boat. Towards evening I sight a sperm whale that disappears in the west. I lower the mainsail and leave the *Firecrest* to steer herself through the night under her fore canvas.

Friday, November 7th.—My boat is still steering herself, the sky is cloudy, at noon I work out that I have made seventy miles in the last twenty-four hours. The Sargasso weeds are very thick, but I expected this, as the Sargasso Sea drifts westward in the winter.

Saturday, November 8th.—At 7 a.m. I sight a steamer eastward bound. The deck of the *Firecrest* is letting in water and I have to keep pumping continually. Numbers of flying-fish dart around the boat. My observations indicate that the Gulf Stream has carried me a long way eastward. The barometer continues to fall and I seize the opportunity to hoist my trysail, which I have not yet tried. The sun sets in a leaden sky that bodes no good. The wind shifts to the north-east and squalls succeed one another during the night.

Sunday, November 9th.—At 2 a.m. the wind veers suddenly. At six o'clock I am awakened by a siren hooting, and thrust my head out of the hatchway to see the steamer *Paget*, of Portsmouth, which has slowed down alongside the *Firecrest*, quite overwhelming her by its enormous bulk. The captain thinks I am in distress and shouts down : "Are you all right?" I assure him that all is well, and the steamer swings off on her course to the north-east, which she had left to come over to me. The sky is darkened by heavy clouds. The sea is rough and the wind is rising and soon the blow comes from the north-east, with squalls and rain. Numbers of dolphins, who love rough weather, leap around the *Firecrest* as she races along on a southerly course. The waves are not exceptionally high, but the sea is very rough, for the waves are coming from two different directions and constantly break on board. The deck leaks continually and my books, clothes and rugs are soaked. Towards noon, wind and sea increase. I am drenched and wearied, but I stay at the helm all night. It is cold, although the water of the Gulf Stream is really quite warm. The rain becomes torrential. I hoist the trysail with two reefs, and the *Firecrest* steers herself. I find that a fish has bitten my mechanical log clean out of order.

Monday, November 10th.—The wind shifts to south-south-east. Not wishing to beat windward against a strong wind and rough sea I lie to, close reefed. I have to keep at the pump all the time, everywhere is damp and I have not a dry stitch to put on me. Towards 1 p.m. the sky clears and the wind drops almost instantly, but the glass is still falling and I know that the storm will come again worse than ever. I take advantage of the calm to dry some of my blankets. About 8 p.m. the wind blows again from the east-south-east and by 10 p.m. has got very squally. I have to roll my mainsail again, green seas are constantly being shipped and the water works its way through the holes in the deck and even puts out my cooking stove. The glass is still falling.

Tuesday, November 11th.—About noon there is a gust of wind from east-south-east which soon veers to the east. I take five turns on my mainsail and two reefs in the trysail. Great waves sweep on board and the water washes in at the broken deck. At 8 a.m. the waves are over thirty feet high. At noon the bowsprit, in spite of all my repairs, will scarce hold and I decide to lie to, but the seas coming from two ways break constantly aboard. I am worn out, numbed and hungry, but the sea is too high to let me do any cooking. I try to warm a little porridge, but a larger wave than usual knocks it over on to the deck, so I must continue on my diet of biscuits. Water is washing on board all the time, and I have to be at the pump constantly. The storm jib splits and the starboard shroud breaks, though it was quite new and made of steel wire nearly half an inch in diameter.

Wednesday, November 12th.—As I lie half asleep I think of the defects in the rigging, of the work too quickly done at New York, and of all that will have to be overhauled at Bermuda before I shall be able to carry on my cruise. Above my bunk is an inverted compass, and when the boat is steering herself I have only to open my eyes and glance up to see how she is keeping to her course. Sea water has worked in through the deck and filled the cup of the compass from above; each time that it fills to the brim it swings over and wakes me up with a start as the water falls on my face in a cold douche. Towards 4 a.m. the storm abates a little, and I am able to fix the bowsprit more firmly, hoist the trysail and make a south-easterly course. Towards evening I notice that the jibstay is getting very worn, and am about to repair it when a sudden gust of wind snaps it and the port preventer backstay at the same instant. I am in danger of losing my mast, for the forestay is slack. I get all canvas in and with new tackle rig up a jury stay. Hardly have I done this when darkness falls, accompanied by a deluge of rain. The mast bends beneath the strain, and, stripped of canvas, the boat rolls terribly. Luckily the moon rises soon after and I am able to see better about me, and set taut the fore and jib stays. I hoist the mainsail once more and lie to under shortened sail. Then I turn in and sleep soundly between soaking wet blankets, for I am exhausted.

Thursday, November 13th.—There is a terrific gale, a bit more from the east; I am at the helm all day long and have to lash myself to the tiller, so high has the sea grown. Numerous rainbows appear, but between the patches of cloud the sky is of too pale a blue and I know that the bad weather is not nearly over yet. The sea gets rougher and the glass falls lower and lower. I am very exhausted, but I have to pump hard during part of the night.

Friday, November 14th.—The wind has gone down a little, but the sea is still high. My observations make me a hundred miles from Bermuda. There is a huge rainbow in the sky. The glass is low, but the heavens are clearing up towards the south, where I foretell the fine weather is coming from. Towards evening the wind drops and the glass slowly begins to rise.

Saturday, November 15th.—I hoist my first jib and all my canvas. It is the first fine day I have had since I left New York. At 3 p.m. I pass near the mail-boat *St. George* from Bermuda, bound for New York. They dip their ensign and I answer the salute. Towards evening there is only light head wind. The night is clear and two stellar observations give my position as fifty miles north from Bermuda.

Sunday, November 16th.—All day long I have been tacking against a stiff head wind and I took a number of sextant sights, for the Bermudas are surrounded by coral reefs that stretch out to sea more than fifteen miles from the northern shores and have wrecked many a good vessel. Towards 3 p.m. I sight land off the starboard bow, and when night falls see the flash from St. David's lighthouse. I keep on tacking towards land for some time, then lie to and turn in, utterly worn out with fatigue. At daybreak the following morning land is out of sight and a Sumner line shows me that I have drifted some thirty miles to the south-east. I tack all that day, in a choppy sea, shipping a deal of green water which keeps me constantly at the pump. About 4 a.m. I sight land once again, and in the morning dusk pass close to an American destroyer and enter the harbour of St. George.

Dr. Shelley, a descendant of the poet, comes aboard and gives me a clean bill of health. He tells me that all incoming boats are complaining of bad weather, and that a schooner of two hundred tons took fifteen days to get here from the American coast, and has suffered heavy damage in the voyage.

CHAPTER III

AT BERMUDA

The Firecrest *is made seaworthy again*

By nine o'clock in the morning, after a rough passage lasting sixteen days, I had dropped anchor in St. George's harbour; by ten o'clock I had already found a master caulker, carpenter and blacksmith and had started the repairs. I got leave to moor alongside a little island belonging to the Crown, on which I alone had the right to set foot. To my great delight I discovered that the workmen of Bermuda, though slower than those I had employed in America, were far more thorough. After a fortnight's work the deck was made perfectly watertight and the damage caused by my collision with the steamer thoroughly repaired. The sails had been stretched most curiously in the storms I had met. At New York, although I had been careful to have the mainsail cut nearly a foot too short in each dimension, it had come over eighteen inches too long for the boom and some thirty inches too long for the mast. I was not surprised, for a new sail has to be gradually stretched before it assumes its final shape, and I had met a heavy gale the first day out. So it was necessary to have it recut. Exposed to wind and rain and sea-water for fifteen days, with never a chance to get dry, the canvas was already attacked by mildew. I had the sails thoroughly painted with red ochred linseed oil that, while making them weatherproof, at the same time preserved them from the dampness of the tropics and gave them a deep red tinge.

The hull of the *Firecrest* was still leaking a little and I decided to get her high and dry. Very sportingly the Darrell brothers, who had twice taken part in the New York–Bermuda race in the yawl *Dainty,* offered me the use of their slipway. So I left Port St. George to go to Hamilton, the capital of the islands, on Main Island, at the other extremity of the group.

It was an extremely interesting piece of navigation through the narrow passages between dangerous coral reefs, so dreaded by the mariners of yore that they had bestowed on the group the name of Devil's Islands. As to what their original name was, no one knows. Oveido, who wrote a history of the West Indies, asserts that the Islands were discovered by a Spanish captain named Juan Bermudez, in 1515; but the name of Bermuda was already on the map *Legatio Babylonica*—published by Peter Martyr in 1511. Who will ever know?

About 4 p.m. I cast anchor in Hamilton harbour in the midst of islands covered with luxuriant vegetation and bearing the names of the first colonists from England who arrived there from Plymouth early in the seventeenth century. Not far from me lay the big American schooner *Zodiac*, belonging to Mr. Johnson of the New York Yacht Club, who asked me to tea on his boat.

Hamilton was much more lively than St. George. Every week mail-boats arrive from New York and land crowds of American tourists, who come to combine a holiday from business with a rest from the Prohibition laws. The quays were thronged with people and heaped up with goods. Alongside the wharfs were often some fine schooners, mostly flying the British flag, which were employed in the rum-running trade. They were all of beautiful lines, built for speed, and were manned by excellent crews—often Americans—and it was a constant pleasure to me to look at their rigging. Perhaps the most beautiful of them all was the *Ethel B. Smith*, but there was also the *Marie Celeste* from St. Pierre et Miquelon, flying the French flag, whose superstructure bore the marks of many bullets, evidence of more than one encounter with Prohibition gun-boats.

I spent several pleasant weeks at Hamilton. I was elected an honorary member of the Royal Bermuda Yacht Club, where I received a warm welcome. I went to several race meetings and got some good tennis on the excellent cement courts. During my stay here I was presented—on board an English mail-boat—with the Blue Water Medal for 1923, awarded each year by the American Cruising Club for the best amateur exploit of seamanship.

A curious and highly agreeable characteristic of these fortunate islands was the absence of motor-cars, which are prohibited on account of the restricted area of the islands and the scarcity of roads. On the other hand, the number of bicycles in use was enormous.

I pulled the *Firecrest* high and dry at Inverrurie, and discovered that she leaked at two places. After repairs I returned to St. George on January 2nd. There I met with a delightful welcome from the inhabitants and especially from the officers of the Artillery. One of the hotels at St. George possessed an excellent bathing-pool, where I witnessed several swimming competitions. There were some good swimmers and an excellent water-polo team. I had the pleasure of seeing Gertrude Ederle, Aileen Riggin and Helen Wainwright give exhibitions of diving and modern swimming. During the fête I was introduced to Sir Joseph Asser, the governor of the islands, and Lady Asser, and we talked about le Havre, where they had been living during the War, and where we had many common friends.

The *Firecrest* still continued to leak a little and I decided to get her on shore once more to do in the end what I ought to have done first, by taking off the copper sheathing and recaulking entirely the hull. This time I put her on shore at St. David. In my opinion this was the most beautiful island of the whole group, perhaps because it was the one least frequented by tourists. It was a lengthy job to raise the copper sheathing and six workmen were needed to do it, for each nail had to be drawn separately in order not to rip the metal.

When the copper was taken off, the hull was completely recaulked. But it was discouraging to think that I had already paid for this work at New York while I myself had been in France. For the total sum I spent on this work I could have built an entirely new boat in France. However, after three months' stay I had the joy of being able to weigh the anchor, knowing my old *Firecrest* was sound and in good condition, for I had supervised all the work myself.

The population of St. David interested me very much on account of their simple and naïve habits. They spoke a curious dialect of English, full of old nautical expressions. Unfortunately my sojourn in the island was spoiled by a sad accident to a young half-caste native whom I employed to cook for me while I was working on the boat. He was fatally burned while lighting the oil stove. So I was again confirmed in my decision to stay solitary all the time and never to share the risks of my dangerous cruise with anyone.

At last, on February 27th, I was ready to weigh and several friends followed me out in a motor-launch, taking photographs of my departure. As I had been delayed so long I decided not to put in at the Antilles, but to make direct for the Isthmus of Panama. The breeze continued to get up while the glass fell, and on March 3rd, while I was sailing under shortened canvas, a terrific gust of wind heeled the *Firecrest* right over on her beam ends. The rain fell in torrents and the sea was very choppy. Towards evening the storm had all the appearance of a cyclone, and I hoisted my storm-sails, keeping on the starboard tack to get away from the centre of the depression. Unfortunately the barometer could give me no guide as to what was likely to happen. At Bermuda I had forgotten to take it down from the bulkhead where it was fixed while the deck was being caulked, and the continuous blows had quite put it out of action.

March 5th found the *Firecrest* making a southerly course under storm-sails, jib and trysail, in a choppy sea. I had, as a matter of fact, decided to take the 5,000 Virgins passage between the isles of Saint Thomas and Santa Cruz, and thus avoid the Antilles further westward, where I should have met with a contrary current; but that evening the sunset was very ominous, and at 10 p.m. I was obliged to lie to again. A torrential rain, lightning and squalls succeeded one another all night long. The next morning the sky cleared up and I was able to repair the damage done by the storm, but on the evening of March 7th there was a stiff wind from the north-west; on Sunday morning the sea was raging and the force of the wind was a full storm, so I made a course with my mainsail rolled five turns. On the 9th I was still obliged to lie to, but the *Firecrest* was behaving so well that I began to ask myself whether I was not showing too much caution. But an attempt I made to pick up my course under a fore staysail and storm-sails close reefed showed that the strain on the rigging and hull of the boat was too great. Even under this shortened sail the *Firecrest* reached eight knots, which was her maximum speed.

This was the last of the bad weather, and on March 12th, when I was in 20° N. latitude, I met the trade-winds. From now onwards I could reckon on slower yet pleasanter sailing in the tropical seas. On Friday, March 13th, I ought to have sighted, when night came on, the light of Sombrero, which is situated on a rock in the midst of the Virgin Islands channel, but visibility was bad and I could make out nothing. I followed a zig-zag course which ought to have taken me free from all danger. The day following, a solar observation and a bearing of the island of Santa Cruz, which hove in sight in the morning, showed me that my chronometers were a minute slow on the calculated rate and this had taken me fifteen miles farther than I thought from the light of Sombrero.

The next day I sighted the southernmost headland of Puerto Rico. I steered to south-west towards Panama and in the Antilles Sea made a good stretch before the trade-winds that blew freshly and steadily from the north-east. The passage was marked by absolutely no incidents and I had plenty of leisure time to read. I enjoyed the lives of the buccaneers and the exploits of those extraordinary captains and mariners such as Graaf, Grammont, and du Lussan, who sailed these seas in the seventeenth and eighteenth centuries, before the alliance between France and England brought to an end the constant war of pillage and piracy. But what I liked above all else was to picture myself on these islands when they were inhabited by the simple and generous Caribs, who welcomed Columbus and his companions with open arms, only to be exterminated to the very last man by the implacable white race.

On the evening of April 1st land hove in sight; at 8 p.m. I saw the light on Toro point, and at 1 a.m. entered the harbour of Colon. Between the two breakwaters I was dazzled by the innumerable lights and barely escaped being run down by a steamer going out. I dropped anchor under the shelter of the breakwaters, having covered, in thirty-three days, the 1,800 miles between here and Bermuda.

CHAPTER IV

AT PANAMA

Yacht Firecrest, *Isle of Taboga, Bay of Panama, June 3rd,* 1925

It was on April 2nd, and at 1 a.m., that I dropped anchor in the harbour of Port Colon, behind the western breakwater. At daybreak I hoisted the yellow flag of the International Code. At 7 a.m. a motor-launch ran alongside the *Firecrest*, with the regular customs, health and police officers aboard, and also an official sent to determine the tonnage of my little ship. As in all American ports, there was a meticulous inspection that lasted more than half an hour, in rather marked contrast to the few formalities observed in British ports. Finally I was told that I should be authorized to go through the Panama Canal subject to payment of a sum of 72 cents per ton, which, added to the five dollars mensuration tax, entitled me, for eleven dollars, to use the enormous locks constructed to raise steamers of over 10,000 tons burthen. I should not be allowed to pass through the canal under sail, and so would have to be towed; I should also be obliged to carry an official pilot, whose services were tendered free of charge. All the same, by courtesy, I was allowed to leave my anchorage without a tug and run up to Cristobal, which is the United States quarter of the town and belongs to them, as well as a zone the whole length of the Canal fixed by the Treaty of Hay-Bunau Varilla, while Colon and Panama City belong to the Republic of Panama. There it was that I dropped anchor, near an immense steel superstructure, which seemed as though it had originated in one of H. G. Wells's dreams, and worked day and night with a rumble like thunder, caused by electric trolleys and cranes capable of coaling the largest ships in a few hours.

The new town of Colon, built on the site of the old one

which was burned down, is laid out symmetrically like all American cities, and is remarkable only for the diversity of its inhabitants and the great number of its cabarets. The entire business of the place seems to be in the hands of the Chinese, except the barbers' shops, which are run by Japs. In the great square are preserved two huge sixteenth-century anchors nearly nine feet high.

During her brief stay at Colon the officers of the French steamers *Alcantara* and *Porto-Rico* came to visit the *Firecrest* and invited me to dine with them. I likewise had the pleasure of making an excursion in a motor-launch up the old stretch of the French canal, which is not used for traffic.

On the morning of April 11th the pilot came on board and I weighed anchor, being taken in by the *Coco Solo*, a motor-launch of 4 h.p. belonging to the agent of the French line at Colon. The French consul was also on board the *Firecrest.* The few miles that separate Cristobal from Gatun were soon traversed and the gates of the great triple dock swung open to receive me. It was not without some apprehension that I entered the canal. Four years previously I had traversed the Garonne and the Midi canals from Bordeaux to Sète, passing through more than a hundred locks in three weeks. In those little locks, made for barges sixty feet long or so, the *Firecrest* had suffered severe damage. How was she going to fare in these immense locks over 12,000 feet long, made for steamers of 10,000 tons and more? I had prepared great fenders of plaited cordage to protect the sides of the boat, but when the gigantic gates closed and shut in my little sailing craft together with the Japanese steamer *Tatsuko Maru* I did not feel too confident. But to my great surprise the water began to flow in from below in a steady stream, and the *Firecrest* was floated up without a jerk, as though in a lift, against the steel wall of the dock. All I had to do was to take in the slack of two hawsers which held me moored to the quay on top of the lock. In the middle of the basin enormous fish were being shot clear out of the water by the force of the inrush. Astern of the *Tatsuko Maru* yellow heads were peering over the sides, betraying vast amusement at the unusual sight of so tiny a sailing boat in the Panama Canal.

Very soon the lock was full, the gates swung open, and, towed by hand, the *Firecrest* followed through the second and third locks in the wake of the Japanese boat, which was drawn by six powerful electric tractors. The Atlantic was now behind me, and I had only to cross Gatun Lake to reach Pedro Miguel lock, which would open to me the gates of the Pacific.

Gatun Lake is an artificial expanse of water some nineteen miles long, which has submerged a forest. It is a curious and unique sight; the channel passes between numerous islands and tree-tops almost entirely covered, upon which were perched pelicans and egrets. The small power of our tug prevented us making more than four miles an hour, and we were continually being passed by steamers going at ten or twelve knots. Every nationality seemed represented. English, American, Japanese, German and Norwegian vessels seemed in the majority; there were even some boats flying the flag of the Irish Free State. The pilot seemed ashamed of our slowness and exchanged various jokes with his friends on the boats that overtook us. Having passed the wireless station of Darien we arrived at the famous Culebra Cut, where gigantic dredges were ceaselessly at work clearing the canal of the rocks that had fallen in during frequent subsidences.

Towards the close of the afternoon we were in sight of Pedro Miguel (known locally by the name of Peter Mike) and Miraflores locks, and at last the *Firecrest* passed from the Atlantic into the Pacific, thus marking the end of an important stage in my long journey. At dusk I entered the artificial harbour of Balboa and dropped anchor near the American cruisers *Rochester* and *Cleveland.* A certain impression of sadness remained with me after my passage of the Panama Canal, for I thought that only faulty organization had hindered the genius of our own engineers from realizing a work that was entirely French in conception.

Perhaps my readers will have been astonished at finding in these pages none of the conventional exclamations of admiration and amazement with which travellers are accustomed to celebrate their passage through the canal. The canal is certainly an undertaking of daring audacity which required careful organization and long years of titanic labour, but to my mind, amongst other things, the delicate and intricate mechanism of a submarine is a far greater creation of the genius of man. My impression is that the Canal works are good, but that it is impossible to do better with the latest discoveries of science. What particularly struck me was the organization. Everything seemed to run perfectly smoothly, without the least waste of time, and in the greatest silence. Perfect order reigned everywhere. The labourers were housed in clean, well-regulated villages, and at either end of the canal were complete arrangements for revictualling ships that passed through. In a word, what impressed me more than the actual engineering work was the efficiency of the service ensured by the U.S.A. I must say that the *Firecrest* received special attention. Orders had been given that the sluices letting in the water should be opened gently. At each lock a special crew of men was on the look-out to make me fast; and thanks to this care the *Firecrest* was able to traverse the whole canal without so much as getting her paint scratched.

The harbour of Balboa has been created artificially and is nothing but a widening of the canal. Panama itself has no harbour big enough to shelter large vessels. On one side of Balboa are nineteen jetties with workshops, a dry dock and warehouses; on the other is the bush that stretches the whole length of the canal. Numbered stakes are uncovered at low tide, and on every available place a vulture is invariably perched. At the end of the harbour is a constant line of steamers, passing up and down the canal. Motor-launches carry to each vessel a pilot and the medical and customs officials. Powerful American cruisers are constantly passing to and fro, creating a tremendous back-wash as they go.

The town of Balboa has been built for the Americans employed on the canal. It is a fine, clean place with great avenues of royal palms. The Americans keep to themselves very strictly there, with their club-houses, automatic restaurants, ice-cream soda fountains, co-operative stores, and innumerable churches which have no resemblance to churches, not forgetting the no less numerous masonic lodges.

The day after my arrival the launch from the *Rochester*, the cruiser flying the American Admiral's flag, ran alongside the *Firecrest*. An officer came aboard and handed me an invitation to lunch with Commander McNair. He also offered me the assistance of his men to carry out any repairs I wanted done on the boat.

On the following day I went to the *Rochester*, where some forty officers, seated round an immense table, gave me a warm welcome. The *Rochester* was exactly the same age as the *Firecrest*, and had carried the American flag to every quarter of the globe; she was a veritable floating city, having some eight hundred souls on board. I was taken to see the admiral's quarters, and inspected all the most modern installations on the ship—douches, apparatus to distil fresh water from salt, electric dish-washers, etc. On deck, in tropic clothing, were the American sailors, all abundantly tattooed. Tattooing, indeed, is an institution in the American Navy, and scheduled time is allotted to the practice of this artistic diversion.

During my stay I enjoyed the most friendly relations with the officers of the *Rochester*, and especially with Commander McNair, a fine, all-round sportsman, with whom I had several good games of tennis. He lent me some American sailors to repaint and scrape the hull of the *Firecrest*. The utmost cordiality was maintained between us, and on one occasion the one-man crew of the *Firecrest* went to dinner with the crew of the *Rochester*.

The *Firecrest* had not received any damage in her passage from Bermuda to Colon, yet there was plenty to be done. I had to get ready for a long run down the Pacific and to provide for at least a year's absence from victualling and refitting yards. My space on board was very limited, and I had to weigh most carefully all the provisions and stores, as well as find room for new cordage, sail canvas and spares of all sorts.

I also ordered by cable from New York a very light mainsail of balloon-silk cloth, which could be hoisted without a boom and would enable me to take advantage of the slightest puffs of wind while crossing the doldrums.

Often enough, when my hard day's work was done, I would spurn the comfort and good order of Balboa and go on foot to the city of Panama, nearly two miles distant. The road passed by a cemetery where lay the remains of the first French workmen on the Canal, who died by scores from yellow fever.

Everything at Panama is picturesque and unexpected, and the old Spanish traditions have survived the contact with American modernity. In the street are bronze-coloured inhabitants of pure Spanish descent, Jamaican negroes, picturesque Mexicans with immense sombreros of many coloured straws, and U.S. soldiers and sailors glad to escape from dry Balboa. I also saw Indians from San Blas, barefooted, short and thick-set fellows, remnants of one of the most interesting races of Central America. In the streets innumerable barefooted, happy children exercised the profession of boot-shine, or sold lottery tickets. Above all else were the cabarets, from which emerged the sounds of negro music—places where soldiers and sailors were continually going in and out. The women had all the Spanish grace coupled with Creole nonchalance. Like Montmartre, Panama had its "Chat Noir"—El Gato Negro.

Boxing was very popular in Panama. I saw some excellent fighting, and some of the black pugilists were as good as could be found anywhere. A few of the combatants bore childishly pretentious names, and I remember watching a fight between two enormous negroes, one of whom was called Knock-Out George Washington, and the other King Solomon. The fights took place in the midst of perfect pandemonium raised by the shouts of the backers, reminding me of the "pelote basque" in Madrid.

Scorning to use a taxi, I usually made my way back to the boat on foot, running most of the distance to keep myself fit. I even won at tennis against the champion of Panama, despite my being out of training; but after a day's work the best sport I found was to go swimming in the cool, invigorating water of the harbour.

Balboa possesses an excellent swimming-bath, where a special display was given in my honour by the famous troop of the Red, White and Blue. The American instructor, Mr. Griser, has obtained really remarkable results, demonstrating conclusively the ease with which one can teach the American crawl to beginners who have never tried the out-of-date breast-stroke and trudgeon. I was very sorry that I had learned to swim at a time when the new strokes were unknown in France.

The U.S. steamship *Arcturus* put in at Balboa on her return from exploring the Galapagos Islands, and I had the pleasure of renewing my acquaintance with the leader of the expedition, Dr. Beebe, whom I had met a year previously at the Explorers' Club of New York. Interesting water-colours were shown me of deep-sea fish, with the colours they had when brought to the surface before dying. The expedition had been well organized with the latest scientific appliances, the entire cost being met by one of the great natural history museums of New York. The *Arcturus* carried several cinematograph operators, and the results of the cruise were to be projected on all the American screens. These practical methods differ from our own, for in the Old World it is not considered good taste to mix publicity with science, yet it is the only way, nowadays, to get the financial assistance necessary to carry out a great enterprise.

I also made an excursion to old Panama, completely destroyed and sacked by the buccaneer Harry Morgan, in 1673. At the entrance to a creek, some six miles from the present town, a few pieces of wall and ruined towers could be seen, all that remained of what was once the most opulent city on the Pacific coast.

. . . . .

After two months' stay I was ready to sail. I received some invaluable gear from France, including a new cinematograph camera, presented by my friend Pierre Albarran, and a gramophone sent by Jean Borotra, the tennis champion. From New

York I got the light mainsail I had ordered. In contrast with the Atlantic authorities, the customs officials of Panama treated me with the utmost courtesy and sent an *alguazil* along with me to see that my mainsail was safely put aboard the *Firecrest*. When I wanted to fill my water-tanks the motor-launch of the American admiral came and towed me alongside the jetty. The price of water had been fixed with regard to large steamers, and I well remember that the minimum tariff was a dollar for the first five hundred gallons! An enormous hose was put through the *Firecrest's* fore hatchway. I had asked particularly that the tap should be opened very lightly, as I only wanted about fifty gallons. I suppose they turned the tap full on, for the water rushed out with terrific violence, filling the tanks in an instant and overflowing into the hold. I dragged the hose out in a hurry, soaking myself as I did so, thus giving the usual crowd of loafers on the quay an unexpected diversion, but the water in the hold was already at the level of the floor and it took me some hours to pump it dry. Before my departure the officers of the *Rochester* gave me a farewell luncheon, when I was presented with a new French flag and a burgee of the Yacht Club of France.

I weighed anchor on the morning of May 31st, and was towed out of the channel by the launch of the *Rochester*. I anchored off Taboga Island, where, in peace and tranquillity, I wrote down these notes of my voyage.

CHAPTER V

FROM PANAMA TO THE GALAPAGOS

Yacht Firecrest *at sea, South Pacific Ocean*

ON June 11th I sailed from Taboga Island. The Galapagos Islands, for which I was making, were only eight hundred miles distant as the crow flies, but it meant a long passage, none the less, for it was extremely difficult to get out of the bay of Panama under sail alone, and gain the second degree of north latitude, where the trade-winds were to be found. According to the Americans sailing directions :

> "The passage under sail towards the West in the rainy season (which it was at the time I am writing about) is an extremely difficult and arduous undertaking; calms, squalls, sudden gusts of wind and contrary currents, heavy rolling, extreme heat and an atmosphere charged with dampness and rain are daily occurrences. It often happens that less than twenty miles are made in a westerly direction in the course of a week, and it is only by making industrious use of every puff of wind that the passage can be made at all."

It would mean inflicting unnecessary hardships on the reader to quote my log which, during this part of the voyage, was merely a succession of references to squalls, thunder, lightning, dead calms, deluges of rains, and trimming of sails. Early on the second morning I sighted Cape Mala, and that evening the blueness of the water, indicating a great depth, showed that I was getting out of the Gulf of Panama. During the first week the breeze was very light and exceedingly variable, constantly shifting from north to south-west, by way of east. Nearly the whole time on deck, trimming the sheets to get the most from the wind, I managed to keep up an average speed of one knot. But at noon on June 18th, when I felt confident that I was well south of the fifth degree of North latitude, my observations gave my position 5° 17′—that is, twelve miles more north than I had been the evening before. I had met a current running at more than thirty miles in twenty-four hours.

For some time following, the breeze, light and variable, was generally from the south, broken now and again by slight squalls from the north and north-west. My daily run varied from 7 to 40 miles a day, and constantly driven as I was by the currents, my course on the chart was a series of inextricable zig-zags. Thus, on June 20th, I had succeeded in regaining the south of latitude 5°, but on the 25th I was once more in 5° 24′. A light breeze bore me on the 26th to 4° 48′, and on the 27th I was once more sixteen miles north of 5°.

My observations on July 1st were particularly discouraging. On the whole the breeze had been more favourable and I reckoned on having made ninety-seven miles on a southerly course in the last forty-eight hours. I could already picture myself in the zone of trade-winds; yet when I took observations it was only to find myself in 4° 58′ N. I had been sailing against a current of more than eighty miles in two days.

Between June 17th and July 2nd the *Firecrest* sailed 450 miles. On July 2nd her position on the chart was only five miles south of her position on June 16th. I was getting desperate, for I could see no means of ever getting out of this calm zone. Was I to meet the fate of Pizzaro, who, the first to try to get out of the Gulf of Panama, in 1525, after seventy days' sailing was obliged to put back to the river Chiman? Even in recent days a three-masted French barque, after ninety-two days of vain attempts to get through, had put back to Costa Rica, with her crew dying of scurvy, to be there condemned and broken up, as her hull had become a mere skin, the work of that dangerous tropic worm the teredo.

The calm, however, gave me plenty of leisure, and I profited by it to read once again my favourite authors, correct my journal, and study the natural history of Polynesia and its languages. When the night was clear I shot with my sextant the southern stars, which were new to me. During the day I was never wearied of studying the abundant life around me.

In the Gulf of Panama I was surrounded by numbers of whales (probably *baleopteris Musculus*) and was able to film their movements. Far from the *Firecrest* the bonitos and dolphins chased vast shoals of flying-fish. In my wake a dozen dolphins were constantly rolling and jumping. From time to time a shark appeared on the surface with his attendant train of pilot-fish and other parasites. In front of all there was always, on either side, a little fish which invariably filled me with admiration. Silvery grey in colour, it bore on its back a dazzling red chevron; it was of extraordinary vivacity and I have never seen a dolphin succeed in catching one.

The sea birds were numerous and of many different sorts; some of them white as snow, others red, others half white and half black, or entirely black. Some dived after flying-fish, whilst others, furnished with long beaks, were of a less sporting spirit, and preferred to catch them in the air rather than wet their feathers.

At dusk I used to watch the extraordinary leaps and acrobatics of the dolphin fish, and of my own observation I was able to confirm the remarks of the old naturalists. I have seen dolphins jump as far as six feet in the air and to a distance of nearly thirty feet, which argues a prodigious muscular strength. I have also seen an enormous shark leap vertically, almost entirely clear of the water, and make a half-turn on his own axis before diving again. I often spent some time at fishing. The damp had taken a lot of spring out of my bow and I preferred to harpoon the dolphins when they passed near enough. I was never able then to get a shark, and my experience taught me that they are not always frightfully voracious, for I used a dolphin as bait, fastened on a hook bent to a chain; after the pilot-fish had looked around, the sharks nibbled the bait in little mouthfuls without even attempting to gulp it down whole. I was able to kill one of them, however, with my Springfield rifle, whereupon a ferocious battle of cannibals set in.

It was during this calm spell that I discovered that innumerable red flies had turned my stock of potatoes into one vast gelatinous mass. Something unexpected, indeed, was always happening. For example, June 24th was a day of captures. At 6 p.m. I harpooned an enormous dolphin and during the night, hearing a strange noise, I found in one of the lockers a winged cockroach nearly two inches long. This capture was, in my eyes, much more important than the former. I did not know then that it would be impossible for me to keep in check these redoubtable cockroaches, which were to establish themselves on the *Firecrest*, where they would cause serious damage to my books and charts.

However, at noon on July 3rd, my tribulations came to an end. My latitude was 4° 43′ N. In the afternoon and during the night a fresh south-westerly breeze gave me a speed of 4 knots. The swell was strong and the *Firecrest* scarcely had any way on her and pitched violently. The whole of that night I had to keep a sharp look-out, for my observations placed me near Malpelo, a small isolated island three hundred miles from Cape St. Francisco, the nearest point on the South American mainland. My reckoning with the currents was only approximate and I had to keep my eyes open. At daybreak Malpelo hove out of the mist and a solar observation showed that my chronometers had a different rate at sea from the one that they had been showing in Balboa at the Hydrographic Office.

Near this islet fish and birds were even more numerous. The breeze turned fresh and I had to go out to the end of the bowsprit to take in my flying jib. The swell was strong, the bowsprit buried itself in the water and I had hardly carried out this delicate operation when I realized that a great number of sharks were patiently waiting for me! I got back to the deck and dispersed them with a few shots from my rifle. Among the fifty-odd black brutes nosing around me, I saw an enormous one of a dirty white colour and over thirty feet in length.

. . . . .

South of Malpelo choppy water told me that currents were meeting there. I knew then that I was soon to leave the northerly drift which had prevented my progress so long. On July 7th the rain and damp ceased; the weather became drier and the breeze steady. At last, in latitude 2° 50′ N. and longitude 80°, I met with the trade-winds which, however, were not yet settled in the east, but blew from south-south-west, forcing me to keep continually tacking. With the trade-winds had come the flying-fish which constantly fell on the deck at night, bringing me a supply of fresh food.

During my stay in the calm zone numerous strands of sea-weed had become attached to the hull of the *Firecrest.* I even observed the same black and white flowers that had so retarded my passage across the Atlantic. Now I knew that they were crustaceans and if asked about them might have answered in the off-hand tone affected by scientists—"Oh, only *lepas anatiferas*, family of *lepatides*, sub-order of *thoracis cirripedes*, division of *entomostraceans*."

At 7 a.m., July 15th, I crossed the Line without the traditional baptism, in 85° 55′ W. longitude. The previous evening I had seen the Pole Star for the last time, and I bade farewell, perhaps for some years, to the northern hemisphere.

On the evening of July 17th, by observations of Centaur and Jupiter, I made out that San Cristobal, or Chatham, the only inhabited island of the Galapagos, was no more than forty miles distant. The *Firecrest* steered herself during the night, but I often came out on deck trying to discover land through the darkness. A slight current, combined with an error in my chronometer, might easily have made a difference of 30 miles in my longitude, and if I had slept confidently I might well have had a brutal awakening with the crash of the *Firecrest* on a reef. At dawn I was on deck and land was close by, stretching in a circle in front of me. I was less than four miles from the coast, in the bay of Rosa Blanca. My landfall had been very accurate, but my margin of error was really too small. A greater accuracy would have been even more dangerous. It was the thirty-seventh day since my departure from Panama; it had taken me four days more than the run from Bermuda to Colon, and this to cover a distance three times less as the crow flies!

CHAPTER VI

AT THE GALAPAGOS ISLANDS

At one time the Galapagos Islands were uninhabited and only visited by casual whalers who put in for water. They were formerly known as the Enchanted Isles, for a goddess was supposed to dwell there. Covered with volcanoes, some of which are still active, they are very interesting from a geological point of view. Charles Darwin visited them and described the flora and fauna in *The Cruise of the "Beagle"*, one of the volumes in my library on board. In our own days Dr. Beebe has explored them thoroughly.

Day was breaking. The green slopes of Mount St. Giachino, on the south of the island, contrasted strangely with the northern shores, which were jagged with little volcanic cones and almost entirely destitute of vegetation.

I doubled the northern headland and its dangerous reefs. The abundance of animal life about me was prodigious. Frigate birds and condors were planing at great heights, often swooping down with a giddy speed to snatch in the air their prey from the diving birds. A school of sharks followed in my wake. Bonitos and dolphins chased the countless flying-fish, which belonged to a different species in these waters. They had two pairs of wings, and their heads were prolonged into a sort of sword longer than their bodies, similar to the snout of the sword-fish. When they flew their body was curved into a sort of U. They had absolutely no chance of escaping their various enemies, and I was admiring the frigate and tropic birds, which never missed them and always seized them by this long sword. Attacked by other birds, who disputed their prey with screams and piercing cries, the raiders were often obliged to drop the victim; but such was the agility of these sea birds that the fish never reached the water.

Everything around me was new and strange. The barren

surface of the island, with its many extinct craters, showed its recent geological formation, and I was strangely attracted by the wild nature of the coast. I could now contemplate one of the greatest natural curiosities that had ever come in my way, for the Kicker Rock reared itself from the sea on my starboard beam. This is a basalt rock over two hundred feet high, of regular geometrical shape, with absolutely vertical sides. The summit, almost flat, is covered with a sort of grass whose greenness is in marked contrast with the bare rock. There flew and cried myriads of sea birds of all sorts.

The mountain peaks sheltered the bay from the strong trade-wind that only reached me in squalls and soon died down completely. I was getting a meal ready when I suddenly perceived that the island was rapidly receding away from me! A four-knot current was taking me westward. I knew by my nautical books that in these islands sailing ships in sight of port had sometimes been caught up in the powerful Humboldt current and been fifteen days and more before they could reach the anchorage. Was I to undergo a like fate?

Happily the calm lasted for barely an hour, and I was soon able to move on my course again. I now sighted Dalrymple Rock, which indicates the entrance to the only harbour in the island. It is a curious yellowish rock, called after a famous British naturalist; but as amongst our fishermen and mariners at home, the local name given by the inhabitants is infinitely more vulgar and realistic. I was soon able to sight Lido Point; then the little harbour Puerto Chico opened out before me, showing a beach of glistening white coral, a few huts, a lighthouse, and a little wooden jetty.

Before dropping anchor I had to exercise all the skill and art of the professional navigator. I knew from the charts that a narrow and winding channel, about 160 yards wide, gave access to the harbour, and that no beacon or buoy whatever was on the surface to show its capricious bends. To starboard, the sea was breaking like thunder on the Schiavoni reef, and the masts of the wrecked Australian steamer *Carawa*, which had been cast there four years previously, stood out of the water.

To port, Lido Point was hidden in spray. I entered the *passe* and began to beat up against the tide and a strong head wind. I had to be careful, for treacherous spikes of coral were waiting for me beneath the surface. It is not easy to tack single-handed under three headsails, and with four sheets to attend to. In this narrow channel I was not able to keep on the same tack more than thirty seconds, and during this half-minute I had to take bearings and run forward to look out ahead of my boat. The different colours of the water warned me many times of a reef, and no time had to be lost with the helm to avoid danger. Tacking more than thirty times without once missing stays, which would have been fatal with the adverse tide, at last I reached the inner harbour. Having assured myself as to the nature and depth of the bottom by sounding, I eventually anchored in six fathoms on a sandy bottom, some 200 yards north of the jetty. It was Saturday, July 18th, and 4 p.m.

As I furled my sails I noticed that the lighthouse was nothing more than a lantern on the top of a great pole, surrounded by two thatched huts. Farther off, and near the only wooden house, were hoisted the colours of the friendly republic of Ecuador. I returned the salute and was finishing to make everything shipshape when I perceived three persons waving to me from the end of the jetty. Understanding that I was wanted on shore, I proceeded to unfold and launch my Berthon collapsible dinghy. I was greeted by a great number of questions in Spanish, which I understand a little, though I cannot speak it. I gathered that one of the men was the harbour master and governor of the archipelago, so to him I showed my papers. When he knew that I was French he waived all further inspection and invited me to dinner. Just at that moment a little old man came forward and asked me in bad English if I was the only one on board. Dubious shakings of the head greeted my affirmative reply, and he said: "You were two and you have drowned the other!" He told me then that he had come to the archipelago more than fifty years ago, that he had done a bit of everything, had in turn been sailor, carpenter, trader, even skipper of a schooner, and at the actual time was in charge of the lighthouse. He had married a woman from Ecuador, had forgotten his native English and had never properly learned Spanish. My boat, he told me, had the look of an English craft, and when I said that he was right he translated my reply with pride to the others, though without producing the slightest impression on them. He told me that he was born in London in 1848, asked me if I knew Tower Hill, and seemed delighted when I said that I had often stayed in his native city.

We went to the governor's house, where, by lantern light, and surrounded by particularly voracious mosquitoes, I consumed not less voraciously some beef steaks and numerous roasted bananas. The old Englishman acted as interpreter, and I had to answer endless questions about my cruise. I was told that if I wished to cover the five miles distance to the "*pueblo*," the owner of the island, el Señor Don Manuel Cobos, would be pleased to send me a horse and receive me as his guest of honour at the Progreso *hacienda*.

The following day, at the appointed hour, I sighted a *peon* holding a horse by the bridle; so I went on shore. Sailors are known to be fond of exchanging the heaving deck of their ship for an equally unsteady seat on horseback. During my voyage I had obeyed my mania and found charm in heaving things overboard. I had left in my wake shirts, clothes and shoes scorched by the humid heat of the tropics, so that I only possessed a few sailors' clothes of white duck. With bare feet, wide-bottomed trousers and a sailor shirt, I certainly cut a picturesque figure of a horseman when I started on the five-mile trail to Progreso *hacienda*. The path lay over lumps of lava which rolled beneath my horse's hoofs, and through a yellow-flowered bush which formed the only vegetation.

The path continued to ascend until, having climbed three steep hills, the landscape changed completely, and I suddenly found myself in the midst of luxuriant vegetation, among which I recognized trees bearing lemons and oranges, bananas, pineapples and wild guavas. Above everything hovered great quantities of birds with golden plumage. I passed a detachment of

Ecuadorian soldiers, then two young boys carrying birds which they had knocked down with stones. To my great surprise, I discovered that the birds, not frightened of human beings, allowed them to approach quite near without flying away. Farther on, a youth on horseback, wearing a brilliantly coloured *poncho* and carrying the traditional lassoo from his saddle-bow, greeted me with a "buenos dias." At last, having climbed a sharp hill and skirted various ramshackle buildings, a sugar refinery and a sawmill, I reached the *hacienda.* El Señor Don Manuel Cobos himself, a young man of about twenty-five, came to meet me and wished me welcome, with a good Parisian accent. He at once informed me, with all the courtesy of a true *hidalgo,* that his island, his *hacienda,* his *peons,* were entirely at my service. He told me that he had spent four years in Paris, at the school of Sainte Marie de Monceau.

In front of his house was the *peon* village, formed of a semi-circle of thatched huts. It was, indeed, nearly a vision of South America, with *gauchos,* horses roaming about at large, lassoos and many-coloured *ponchos,* and dirty, ragged but picturesque *peons.*

We went up an exterior staircase to the first floor of the house, where I was introduced to a lieutenant in uniform, commandant of the Ecuadorian troops quartered in the island to guard the convicts, to the Commissary, the Major-domo and to several very charming young *señoritas.* I heard that a detachment of soldiers had been sent down to the beach to keep guard over the *Firecrest* in my absence.

The first and only storey of the house consisted of a large room with bare and rather cracked walls, out of which opened a number of smaller rooms, kitchens and store-rooms. Seeing over the various apartments of the house, I was struck by the almost total absence of books or illustrated magazines. On the other hand, the quantity of firearms was amazing. There were automatic Mauser pistols everywhere—on pillows, beds, dressing-tables. The bedroom of the proprietor himself was a veritable arsenal.

A bell was rung and we seated ourselves before an excellent meal consisting entirely of the products of the island, which astonished me by their variety. There was bread made with manioc flour, roasted bananas, grilled steaks, oranges and pineapples. While eating I noticed that the staircase by which we had ascended to the first floor was closed by a door, before which stood a servant fully armed. In the embrasure of each window was likewise a *peon* on guard.

My host explained to me that he anticipated an attack, that his father had been murdered by the *peons*, that he and his assistants never went out without being fully armed, and that it would be most imprudent for me to venture ashore without a revolver. I thought to myself that the multiplicity of firearms was the chief danger of the place. It seemed that some months earlier, while Don Manuel was inspecting his sawmill, the *peons* had seized the armoury and had opened fire on him from the windows. He had had to get away as best he could on horseback and had spent four days in the country before he was able to return.

He told me a lot about the fertility of the island, of which only a tenth part was under cultivation. The difficulty of procuring labour and the total lack of any means of communication retard the development of this colony which had a great future before it, and upon which the Americans have cast covetous eyes on account of its position on the Panama route.

I had to reply to a number of toasts drunk to the health of France, of Ecuador, of our respective governments and of the colony of San Cristobal. It was decided to give a ball in my honour, and the couples glided on the floor in the latest dances, while a half-breed sang, as he accompanied himself on a mandolin, a strange and crude sort of song in which words meaning love and death occurred at frequent intervals. Inflamed to the height of courage by the drinks that had circulated freely, several of the gentlemen actually offered to accompany me, but naturally this was not to be taken very seriously.

In the front of the house the *pueblo* stretched in a semicircle of little thatched houses and huts. Numerous groups stood at the doorways playing at cards or throwing dice on blankets. Some of the youths were amusing themselves at a ball game with enormous rackets covered with cowhide and weighing several pounds. Dirty, ragged children were running about everywhere. I was quite taken by the novelty of the sight, the Latin grace of movement, the gay colours of the *ponchos*.

Dancing went on until late in the afternoon, while my host and I talked about France and, above all, Paris, which he hoped to see again one day. We also spoke of my friend Ralph Stock, who, five years previously, had stayed at San Cristobal with his sister, while sailing on the *Dreamship*. When I tried to take my leave, my host insisted with such courtesy that I was obliged to remain and partake of his evening meal with him.

Towards the middle of dinner the conversation took a rather alarming turn. Once more I was told how dangerous it was for me to go about unarmed, and was warned to keep a special look-out on my boat. Some months previously five convicts had taken possession of a thirty-foot cutter; a month later a steamer had picked up three of its survivors near the coast of Panama, dying of hunger and probably sole keepers of an atrocious secret. The convicts would certainly not hesitate to get hold of the *Firecrest* if they got a chance. So I was advised to keep a good look-out and overhaul my arms.

The night was pitch dark and it was raining heavily. From the window I could not make out my boat, and I grew uneasy. Recollections of a favourite book of my childhood—"Children of Captain Grant"—came to my mind, and I had visions of the *Firecrest* in the hands of convicts. My mind was soon made up, and I announced my intention of returning on board at once. I was deaf to all remonstrances that the rain was too heavy and the road too bad to return in the dark. I took leave of my hosts and mounted the horse that had brought me here. The night was, indeed, pitch dark. My horse, which had seemed to know the road well enough in daylight, was absolutely at a loss in the blackness. He kept on stopping, stumbled against stones and appeared to take a malicious pleasure in wandering off the path and plunging into the prickly brushwood at its side. I was always having to dismount and set out on a voyage of exploration to regain the track. My clothes were sticking to my body with wet, and disquieting shadows constantly flitted across the path. On one occasion I felt something damp and hot touching one of my legs; a grunt reassured me, it was a wild pig. After one particularly bad stumble, my saddle-girth broke, and I clutched my horse's mane just in time to save myself from a nasty fall. Yet I was glad to have difficulties to overcome, and I really enjoyed the humours of a situation that a writer like Mark Twain would have known so well how to describe.

After a long time I sighted at last the light of the lantern at Puerto Chico, and reached the governor's house, where I found, fast asleep, the soldiers sent down to guard my boat, which was riding at anchor and had not been run away with after all. Two days later the proprietor, accompanied by the governor and some young *señoritas*, came to visit me on board. I showed them some pictures of my cruise and my tennis trophies, and played for their benefit some records on my gramophone, but a slight swell kept the *Firecrest* on the move, and my visitors were only too glad to get back to land as soon as they could. A *muchacho*, about ten years old, with dirty and unkempt hair, tried to point out to me the inconvenience of sailing single-handed, and the incalculable benefits of having a companion, especially himself. At my stern refusal he became glum, and exhibited all the desperate looks of one determined to put an end to his miserable and wretched existence.

My stay at the Galapagos was very brief. I took on water and provisions, and my deck disappeared beneath the heaps of bananas and oranges given me by my host. I raised anchor on the morning of July 30th, bound for a distant goal—the mysterious coral islands three thousand miles away.

CHAPTER VII

FROM THE GALAPAGOS ISLANDS TO THE GAMBIER ARCHIPELAGO

ON July 30th I sailed from Puerto Chico, the little harbour where I had laid at anchor for ten days. A fresh fair southerly wind enabled me to clear Schiavoni reef easily, as well as the breakers off Lido Point. On leaving the harbour I set a westerly course in order to pass to the north of the dangerous MacGowen reef, between the islands of Santa Fé and Santa Maria. During the afternoon the breeze increased again, and the sea became choppy; strange to say, almost on the Line as I was, it was positively cold. It rained hard, San Cristobal soon disappeared from sight, and I could hardly make out Santa Fé on the starboard bow.

The *Firecrest* steered herself that night, but with so many islands about I had to keep a good look-out and was constantly on deck trying to peer through the darkness of the night. Humboldt current bore me to the west, and if the *Firecrest* had altered her course it would have taken me straight on the reefs. All went well, however; at dawn Floreana was already astern of me, away to the east was Isabella, and far to the north-west lay Turtle Island.

I was now clear of all dangers, and changing my course to south-south-west, I steered for the Gambier Archipelago, three thousand miles away. To my great regret, I found I should have to abandon my projected visit to Easter Island, with its gigantic and mysterious statues. There were various reasons for this, the chief being that the island having no sheltered anchorage, it would be probably foolhardy to land and leave the *Firecrest* alone at anchor.

The Marquesas Islands, nine degrees south of the Equator, were three thousand miles away. With the trade-winds and an equatorial current running at a speed of from ten to seventy miles a day, that would have been the shortest and easiest course to take. On the other hand, to reach the Gambier Islands, or Mangareva, situated in 23° S. latitude, I knew it would be necessary to get out of the zone of trade-winds and into the region of calms, heavy weather and contrary currents. I had read Stevenson's and Herman Melville's enthusiastic descriptions of the Marquesas, yet it was for the Gambier that I set my course, for that archipelago was to me the great unknown.

My passage began well. The breeze blew freshly and the *Firecrest* made good headway. The day after my departure from Galapagos a bonito (*thynnus Pelamys*) made an extraordinary leap out of the water and, striking the mainsail about twelve feet up, fell with a thud on the deck. The creature weighed nearly thirty-five pounds, and I cooked it all, thinking that it was lucky for me that sharks and whales did not indulge in the same antics.

The wind was abeam, which was the best quarter for sailing without my having to stay at the helm, and the *Firecrest* beat all her previous records. Until that time my best run with no one at the tiller had been 105 miles in twenty-fours hours. During the first four days of this passage the distances covered were 113, 144, 122 and 122 miles respectively, and I only went on deck to change or splice ropes and gear worn through by friction. The winds became less strong and more following, and this obliged me to lower the mainsail, thus reducing my speed to eighty miles a day; but even then I had plenty of leisure to employ in making two new sails. By this time I had succeeded in simplifying my meals to the last degree. Apart from a few flying-fish that I picked up on the deck and an occasional dolphin that fell to my harpoon, I lived entirely on rice, porridge, biscuits and potatoes. Considerable experience had shown me that a vegetarian diet suited me best and gave me the greatest amount of physical resistance. On it I kept in perfect health the whole time and was always in excellent form.

I also used my spare time to determine my exact position.

It is well known that latitude, or distance from the equator, can be easily obtained by measuring the height of the sun at the meridian, or true noon. Longitude is the distance of the meridian from that of Greenwich; it is obtained by calculating the difference between the local time, ascertained by sun or star observation, and Greenwich Mean Time given by chronometers. When one knows that an error of four minutes on the watch makes a difference of sixty miles in longitude, it can be realized how important it is to know exactly the chronometer's rate. No chronometer is ever perfectly accurate and the time it keeps depends more than anything else on the temperature and on the motion of the boat. On big liners the exact time is obtained every day by wireless and the exact time can be reckoned to the fifth of a second. My great difficulty on the *Firecrest* was to know the error of my chronometer in the constantly varying conditions of my voyage. I had two strong chronometers of the type known as deck watches. At Bermuda I tested their accuracy, and passing St. John, in the Antilles, found that they went slow on their previous rate. At Panama, again, I left them at the hydrographic office where they were rated every day by wireless. Their error was about two seconds slow in the twenty-fours hours. Passing near the rock of Malpelo I found they had lost nearly four seconds a day, which was confirmed by a series of observations taken at the Galapagos. At sea I was able to work out a series of temperature curves that enabled me to know approximately how my instruments were going. I sometimes amused myself by calculating the longitude by the distances from the moon to stars, a method no longer used at sea, but one which would have helped me to ascertain my position in the event of the chronometers stopping.

In this way the days passed quickly enough and I was reckoning on a short passage when, on August 26th, in 17° S. latitude, I lost the trade-winds and on the 31st ran into a dead calm that lasted a whole week. The wind returned on September 6th and blew up freshly with a choppy sea. About 11 a.m. it had the strength of a real gale. My rigging had been worn by friction and charred by the sun; and so it was that almost simultaneously the port preventer backstay snapped and wound itself round the forestay, getting inextricably twisted and tangled in the hanks of the trysail, while the two topping lifts that kept the boom up also gave, as well as six of the hoops on which the mainsail runs up and down the mast.

Without the topping lifts it was very difficult to get in my mainsail. I managed it, however, and then laid to under the staysail alone. As the evening wore on the sea grew rougher. At 9 p.m. the oak tiller broke, but luckily I had a spare one of iron ready for use. Towards midnight I got under way again under the trysail and staysail. At break of day I inspected the damage I had suffered and set to work to repair it; I had to go aloft several times to change topping lifts blocks. I also had to ride down the forestay to unwind the shroud that had twisted into the hanks. I could only hang on with my legs; every instant the wind bellied the sail out and threatened to throw me into the sea. When I got down my knees were covered with blood, but I had put everything in order and having renewed the lacings of the mainsail to the boom, I got on my course again, all sails set. I was pleased to find that my comparatively long inaction had not impaired my strength, and that I was in as good form as ever.

The wind held very unevenly. During the night of September 13th a violent shock shook the *Firecrest*. By daylight I found that the copper sheathing had been torn from the stem just below the waterline. Apparently I must have struck a piece of half-sunk wreckage. There was yet another danger to be encountered on my route, which was the Minerva or Ebrill Reef, marked P.D. on my chart—P.D. meaning "Position doubtful." Reported by various captains with slightly different bearings, it was sought for in vain by the *Abet* in 1880. It is supposed that the *Sir George Grey* was lost on it in 1865. These reefs marked P.D. on the charts constitute a grave danger for mariners, for their position is not known with any degree of accuracy. Almost the only thing certain about them is that they are never to be found on the place indicated on the charts. And so, taking no steps to avoid them, I confined my endeavours to keeping a sharp look-out, and saw nothing save a slight patch of broken water, when I was going too quickly to take soundings.

On Wednesday, September 16th, my observations made me forty miles from Mangareva, the peaks of which ought to be visible in fine weather at that distance, but low clouds and rain made visibility very poor.

My course lay near the low-lying atoll of Timoe—a mere ring of coral with coco-nut trees on it, which was only visible at a distance of a few miles; so from noon on I kept on climbing aloft trying to see through the haze of rain. I was afraid that an error in my chronometers might have led me wrong and was beginning to get almost apprehensive when, at 1.30 p.m., I saw palms apparently rising right out of the sea, away on the port bow; their trunks were bent by the wind and there was not a vestige of land visible. Here was Timoe Atoll, and when it was abeam I saw the coral reef on which the surf was breaking.

I could congratulate myself on a perfect landfall. After forty-eight days at sea I was less than two miles out in my longitude. As I passed the atoll I was filled with amazement and admiration of the extraordinary labour of the madrepore, just as Quiros, Cook, and Bougainville had been when they discovered the Tuamotus.

At 3 p.m. I sighted land—the archipelago of Mangareva some twenty miles away. When night fell I laid to under shortened sail so that my drift took me nearer my goal; then I turned in with an easy mind, glad to have reached yet another stage in my cruise, and looking forward to Polynesia and its Kanakas, who had so often figured in my boyish dreams. I knew I was a century too late, and that Polynesia had been civilized long since and I was somewhat apprehensive. What was I going to find—joy or disillusion?

At dawn the following morning I was only seven miles from the island of Akamaru, nearly in line with the south-eastern channel by which I had resolved to enter. I hoisted all my canvas; the breeze was fresh, the *Firecrest* made seven knots and I stood at the tiller, drenched in spray. There was no need to look at my charts. Every detail on them was engraved on my memory, for I had pored over them many a long hour, taking delight in repeating to myself the sweet-sounding names of the various islands.

I left on my port the islands of Kamaka and Makaroa, the latter looking like a ship, and threaded my way through the girdle of reefs until I was so near the cliffs of Makapa that spray was dashed on to the *Firecrest*. When I had doubled the point, Akamaru Island was abreast, quite close, and I could not help exclaiming aloud in admiration. There it was, Polynesia! All the descriptions of my favourite authors faded beside the more beautiful reality!

A dazzling white coral beach was bordered by great plantations of coco-nut trees, whose branches were swaying in the wind. As a background rose the slopes of the mountain-side, covered with the fine and picturesque foliage of ironwood trees. I felt that I should never find words to describe the contrast between the green of the trees and the wonderful varied colours imparted by the coral bottom to the water of the lagoon. I could not perceive the houses that must have been hidden among the trees; and from the whole island emanated an atmosphere of calm and tranquillity beyond all description.

In the course of my travels those impressions engraved most deeply and vividly on my memory are of Nature when it has not been altered by the hand of man. Nothing could ever efface the memory of the wild ruggedness of Pointe du Raz and Baie des Trepasses, or the fascination and horror of the sea moaning into Plogoff's Hell. Now it was Nature in a calm and peaceable mood, and I felt that I had reached my goal. Here was the land where I would by choice settle and die had I not chosen the life of a sailor.

For the moment I had to give all my attention to steering the boat. To pass through the coral reefs I had to take continual compass bearings and plot them out on the chart. I had to be careful, too, of a westerly current that constantly drove me off my course, and necessitated continual corrections for drift.

Within the lagoon the breeze only blew in gusts. I steered at first for the highest peak of Mangareva, then, when I saw right ahead the dangerous reef on which the sea was breaking, I looked for the two steering marks on the mountain-side; but the fine rain prevented my sighting them and it was only by dead reckoning and working with the compass that I was able to enter the narrow channel that pierces the circle of reefs between the isles of Mangareva and Akena. I had to be constantly running forward to watch the colour of the water and discover the dangerous edges of the coral.

When I reached the outside harbour of Rikitea, seat of the government of the island, I saw a jetty, at the end of which was a mast on which the Tricolour was flying. For the first time since my departure from France the *Firecrest* was floating in French waters; and it was a great joy to me to see my country's flag so far from any continent.

I had no charts of the inner harbour, but it was well buoyed, and I dropped anchor off the government jetty, just as a sailing cutter came towards me. Everything seemed unreal, but no, I was not dreaming. A gendarme in uniform with well-waxed boots and moustache, just as one sees in cartoons, came aboard, followed by some natives. He proceeded to examine my papers very closely, far more closely than any examination I had undergone since leaving France; then seeing some firearms below he declared, rolling his r's : "There is not game here, but if you wish to go shooting you must obtain a shooting licence."

Oh, blessed gendarme! There could be no shadow of doubt that the French laws were firmly established here in the heart of Polynesia!

CHAPTER VIII

MANGAREVA

AFTER forty-nine days at sea the *Firecrest* dropped anchor within the coral reefs, in the inner harbour of Rikitea. As I furled my sails and made everything shipshape on deck I gazed round at the beautiful sight before me. Mangareva lay around me in a semicircle. Mounts Duff and Mokoto reared their barren heights some twelve hundred feet; on the lower levels of the island coco-nut trees waved their heads. The vegetation was luxuriant and almost entirely concealed the houses. All that could be seen were a few roofs and the two blue towers of a church.

Near my boat the water was a limpid green; farther away the coral beds below were indicated on the surface by a reddish tinge. To the south-east lay the islands of Aukena and Akamaru, and on the eastern horizon were the islets, covered with coco-nut trees, that encircled the lagoon.

When I had finished what I had to do, after a hurried meal I launched my Berthon boat and rowed ashore. Naturally my arrival had aroused the keenest curiosity, and a crowd of inhabitants were waiting on the jetty. My first impression of the natives was very deceptive. The Mangarevians wore the conventional uniform imposed by the missionaries and pastors all through Polynesia. The women wore a one-piece cotton garment, with long sleeves and a high neck; the men linen trousers and a white cotton vest. All had bare feet and wore straw hats.

The words "tamari harani," which means "Child of France," were the first that met my ears. However, if the appearance of the natives shocked my æsthetic feelings, my own appearance made a great impression on them. They thought that splendour in dressing was proportional to the importance and standing of the individual; owner and captain of a ship as I was, what was their amazement to see me come ashore in nothing but a sailor shirt and football shorts, barefooted and hatless. The sun had burned me brown, and I did not correspond in any way to their notions of a Frenchman from France.

The Residence was a wooden house, surrounded by a large veranda covered with corrugated iron, and not unlike the country houses in the neighbourhood of New York. There was only one street in the village, with houses on each side and some half-mile in length. Here again I was astonished at the total lack of local colour; imported deal boards and corrugated iron were the predominant materials in house construction.

The warrant officer of gendarmerie who had come out to the *Firecrest* turned out to be the sole representative of government in the island, and bore the high-sounding official title of Special Agent of French Establishments in Oceania. He received me very courteously, led me to the Residence where he lived with his wife and two daughters, and invited me to accompany him on the morrow upon a tour of inspection to the island of Akamaru. Overcoming my repugnance to official visits I embarked with him at dawn on the following day. In addition to the owner of the cutter and two sailors we carried an old native, who answered to the picturesque name of "He Who Throws Stones." The gendarme was in full uniform.

There was a dead calm and we had to row the five miles that separated us from Akamaru, where we ran alongside a jetty upon which the chieftain and a number of inhabitants were waiting for us. As in France, a lot of handshaking had to be done before we went to the chieftain's house. It was exactly like an official reception in a small French village. All the schoolchildren were marshalled out for our benefit; at our arrival they raised their hats, crossed their arms and cried : "Bonjour, monsieur !"; then they sang the Marseillaise. Finally a child of eight came forward and recited in a dull manner, without understanding a single word of what he was saying—just as a French child of the same age would have done—a fable which must have been "The Grasshopper and the Ant," if it was not "The Bee and the Fly."

The chieftain's dwelling was a wooden shanty consisting of

two rooms. An immense European bed, a table and a chest constituted the entire furniture. A meal was awaiting us—cooked, alas, in the French style—and was served by our host who, following an ancient Polynesian custom, ceremoniously refused to sit with us.

After the repast I was given several presents, chiefly of mother-of-pearl, shells and some beautiful plaited pandanus hats. The natives could not understand my habit of going about bareheaded. When I went out for a walk, even to cross the village street, one of them would run up and try to put a hat on my head, explaining that the sun would do me harm. I compromised by carrying a hat in one hand.

More woody than Mangareva, Akamaru seemed very picturesque to me, as I walked about, and I was sorry not to be able to settle in one of its little huts beneath the trees and get to know the inhabitants and their ways of life better by staying among them for a few weeks. At a bend of the road I found just the sort of home I should have liked, made of reeds with a roof formed of inter-thatched palm leaves. It was half hidden in a clump of trees among which I recognized coco-nuts, bread-fruit and the miro or rosewood trees. In thought I peopled this hut with the savages who originally inhabited it, wearing nothing but their simple loin-cloths of *tapa* bark, and leading a life more in harmony with Nature. Before going away we visited the school where a dozen or so pupils, taught by a native woman, were examined by the gendarme. I observed that they knew the history of France, and all about its sub-prefectures, but were totally ignorant of where Polynesia lay in the world, and of its marvellous history. It led my thoughts back to my school-days and to the useless things I had been taught.

Some days after my arrival I was awakened at dawn by shouts and hails from the shore. Going on deck I saw a schooner coming in at the passage. The whole population of the island was collected on the sea front and showed by its excitement how important was the arrival of the boat which brought the post twice a year from Tahiti. Yet the schooner, which ran in under auxiliary motor, with sails furled, was nothing much to look at. Her hull was dirty, and the deck was in an inconceivable disorder, cluttered with passengers and bales. Enormous clusters of bananas hung from the rigging, and two superstructures, forward and after, seemed to defy at the same time the strength of the waves and the laws of stability. As she ran past the *Firecrest* I could read her name painted on the stern : *Vahine Tahiti,* or Tahitian Girl. This name on such a huge, square stern seemed an insult to the women whose beauty had charmed Louise Antoine, Comte de Bougainville.

The arrival of this ship caused a great commotion at Rikitea. All day long dug-outs carried across to her natives who wanted to buy stuffs or clothes. Towards evening some dances were arranged, to which my gramophone and I were cordially invited. In a house quite close to the jetty some thirty people were assembled. The women had put on their best muslin clothes, with silken Chinese shawls that made a very fine effect against their brown skins. Everyone had bare feet and wore wild flowers woven into their hair. A place of honour had been reserved for me and a very charming Mangarevian girl crowned me with flowers.

I watched the natives dancing to the music of an accordion, but I was sadly disappointed, for they danced the latest European steps, which had come hither straight from Tahiti.

The young girls were nearly all pretty and graceful. At the age of fifteen they were already women, but they seemed to have an unfortunate tendency to grow very fat before they had even reached their twentieth year.

Late in the evening the dancers began to get lively. There were one or two attempts at a *upa-upa,* which is a suggestive and voluptuous dance of Tahitian origin. In that respect it had nothing to learn from the dances of the Turkish odalisques. Neither the youngest nor the prettiest girls took part in it, and before long everyone else had yielded the floor to a few women who had acquired some reputation as good dancers. A thin Mangarevian with hair in long plaits shook her haunches in unison with another woman, large and fat. The spectators accompanied their motions by clapping hands in time and singing Tahitian airs rather more melodious than the harsh Mangarevian tongue. When some more than usually suggestive figure was cut it was greeted with a roar of good-humoured laughter, in which the dancers themselves joined most heartily.

The Mangarevians, who sing very harmoniously, do not get much out of the mandolin and accordion, and their favourite accompaniments for dancing in the old days were wooden drums. One of the passengers on the schooner, an English mining prospector, made a great success by exhibiting his skill on the accordion. There was also a mysterious American who had landed on the island a year previously, no one knew why, and was living there with a young native girl.

I left when the dancing came to an end and passed before the open door of a room in which I saw the entire family of my host, some twenty persons in all, half of which were children, all lying fast asleep, huddled together on mats woven of *pandanus* leaves.

. . . . .

I spent about two months at the Gambier Islands, during which time I acquired a rough knowledge of the Mangarevian dialect and made some study of Polynesian customs. At the beginning of my stay the inhabitants had exhibited a certain coldness towards me; their distrust was explained by the fact that this people, belonging to the most generous race in the world, had been shamefully exploited by the whites whom they had welcomed so warmly. But when they found I wanted nothing, and that I had not come to their island from any selfish motives, their shyness and distrust soon vanished. As for me, I grew extremely fond of this delightful race, especially of the children, who were fascinating as are the children of all primitive races. Full many a merry game did we have together.

The opening of the pearl-diving season was fixed at Mangareva for November 10th. Diving is by no means free in the Tuamotu Archipelago, and is strictly regulated and controlled in order to preserve the oysters and prevent them being exterminated.

The whole of the week preceding the opening of the fishing the lagoon presented a spectacle of unwonted animation. The natives were all occupied in painting and repairing their craft. New dug-outs, in course of construction, were blessed by the missionary in the presence of a great congregation. My talents as a painter—every sailor has to master this art—were even brought into requisition, and one afternoon I inscribed the name of "Maputeoa"—the last king of Mangareva—on the stern of a little sailing cutter.

Tuesday, November 10th, the opening of the diving season, was almost a dead calm. Leaving the *Firecrest* at anchor in the bay of Rikitea, I took my little collapsible Berthon boat to go to the coral islet which lay in the centre of the pearling ground, some six miles away. I had with me a Winchester rifle and some photographic and cinematographic apparatus.

My boat being heavily laden I made but slow progress. When I got to the middle of the lagoon, where the depth was more than thirty fathoms, numerous sharks made their appearance in my wake, some of them more than eighteen feet long. When an enormous bluish-looking fellow, who seemed particularly ravenous, came so near that he actually grazed my boat, I could no longer resist the temptation of giving him a bullet from my gun. It was a very risky thing to do, for, hit in a vital spot, the enormous brute gave a terrific leap from the water and fell back thrashing his tail madly. My little cockleboat would have been smashed to atoms if he had struck it. The creature continued to struggle, leaving a train of blood in the transparent water of the lagoon, but it was not long before his voracious companions had settled on him. I could now continue my trip in perfect peace; looking astern, a seething, whirling flurry of fins and tails was the only trace of what was going on.

I rowed hard for a long time and was still a long way from the diving ground when I saw, emerging from the water, the heads of three natives wearing spectacles, alone in the middle of the lagoon, two miles from land and in fifteen fathoms of water infested with sharks, and those three heads were laughing merrily enough and seemed perfectly at their ease. I approached them, full of curiosity, to find that each diver kept himself afloat with a bundle of hibiscus wood, to which was attached a net into which the oysters would be put. They told me that a sailing cutter had dropped them there during the morning and would be back to fetch them during the afternoon! They then disappeared below the surface.

Much farther on some outrigger canoes from Akamaru made a compact group. Each contained a couple of natives. They greeted my appearance with cries of delight and offered me oranges and manioc. One of them told me that he would dive for me and open a shell in my honour. He went down in a depth of some ten fathoms and soon afterwards reappeared with an oyster in his hand. When it was opened it did not reveal the hoped-for pearl, which was not very surprising when it is remembered that the proportion of oysters containing *poe*, or pearls, is only one in several thousand. The mother-of-pearl, however, was given me as a souvenir, whilst I swallowed the oyster flavoured with a squeeze of lime juice.

I went on and looked at the diving flotilla; everywhere I was hailed with cheers and laughter and offered mother-of-pearl. At last I reached a little fleet of dug-outs where I found several of my friends from Rikitea, with whom I decided to spend the afternoon watching the diving and taking some films. The natives, who worked in couples, were a jolly party and their shrieks of laughter could be heard from afar. They continually moved their positions in search of places richer in shells, which they spotted by means of square boxes with glass bottoms, looking through which showed the ocean bed with absolute clearness.

Suddenly one of the divers gave a loud shout of delight as he spotted a particularly rich bed, and prepared to dive. He took off his hat and clothes, and stark naked he seemed a veritable young bronze god. Lowering himself slowly in the water, keeping one hand on the outrigger, he got ready for the dive. First of all he took several deep breaths, exhaling with a curious sort of whistle that could be heard from afar. I believe this whistle is peculiar to the divers of the Tuamotu, and I cannot imagine that it serves any other purpose than to regulate the respiration.

Like all pearl divers he wore home-made wooden spectacles, the glasses fixed in with glue, to preserve the eyes from ophthalmic dangers often to be met with under water. At last, after some minutes of deep respiration, he disappeared beneath the surface and soon afterwards came up with a shell in his hand. While he was down below his comrade followed every movement anxiously, ready to go to his help if he were attacked by a shark, or to assist him in case of accident.

As they plunge into the water divers grip their noses with one hand, and assert that at a depth of more than five fathoms air is expelled through the ears; but the possibility of this has been finally disapproved by scientists, and the idea probably originates from an illusion caused by the pressure of water on the tympanum. Good divers remain, as a rule, from one to two minutes under water, and are more anxious to make a number of descents than to break the record for long submersions.

The shells are not opened at once, each diver waiting to examine his luck in privacy. Good divers get over 200 lbs. of shells in the day's work, and some exceptional men obtain twice that amount. Mother-of-pearl shell fetches about a franc a pound in Mangareva.

Pearls are rare, and the total value of those exported is only equal to that of the mother-of-pearl. The previous year had been a particularly good harvest, and a large black pearl, brought up before the arrival of the Jewish merchants from Paris, had been snapped up by a Chinese merchant of the neighbourhood, who paid the lucky diver 110,000 francs.

I passed the whole afternoon with the pearl divers. As was my usual custom, I had only got on my shorts and was bareheaded, while the natives wore hats and clothes to preserve them from the sun's rays. Towards evening the dug-outs began to come in, and I expected the invitation of some natives to pass the night on the little islet where they had built huts of scraps of corrugated iron. There we made a meal in the open air, of which the memory will always remain vivid. There were bananas boiled in water, oysters that had been grilled, one after the other, on wooden skewers, and *popoi* at least five years old. *Popoi* is the fermented paste of the breadfruit tree wrapped in leaves and kept in the ground. It has a smell like some of our strongest cheese, and few Europeans get to like it. It constitutes the principal food of the natives.

The meal was, as is always the case in Polynesia, a very serious matter and everyone ate in silence. If I turned my head for a moment to glance at the sky, the country or the waters of the lagoon, one of my hosts would call me to order, saying "Kakai," which means "Eat," and more food would be passed me. Such were the rules of Mangarevian society.

I passed that evening, the night, and part of the following morning on the island. The utmost cordiality reigned, and the hours I spent in the natives' company were very delightful. When I wanted to go away the following morning they all besought me to stay and to fetch the *Firecrest* there and partake of their life on the little island. It would certainly have been a very agreeable existence for me, to live that healthy open-air life I love so much, but the sea was calling me again and I could not resist her. So, promising to return and visit them in a few years' time at the diving season, I launched my Berthon and made for Rikitea and the anchorage of the *Firecrest.*

The next day I was ready to sail, and with a fresh wind of more than seven knots I left the harbour of Rikitea, while the children crowded on the jetty to wave me farewell as long as I was in sight.

CHAPTER IX

THE MARQUESAS

THE evening of my departure from Mangareva the wind blew up fresh and I had to roll one turn of my mainsail. Rain fell in torrents and the sunset was very threatening. A north-westerly blow soon obliged me to lie to close-reefed. While the waves dashed against my valiant little craft and their blows resounded on her hull, which quivered and moaned at each shock, I lay in my bunk reflecting on the discomforts of my present position. What demon was it continually urging me to go to sea? I had found a land that delighted me, far from the constraints and restrictions of civilization; I might have laid the *Firecrest* up for an indefinite stay, have accepted the engaging offers of the pretty young Mangarevian girls, and had a family of bronze children who would grow up free and happy beneath the warm Polynesian sun. With Mangareva as headquarters I might have explored Rapa, Easter Island, the Austral and the most isolated of the Tuamotu Islands.

But the sea was calling and I could not resist her appeal. So once more I took up with the rough hermit life of a sailor, with the Marquesas Islands as my next port of call, a thousand miles away to the north.

The second day after my departure the bad weather left me and I had every hope of making a good passage and falling in with the south-easterly trade-winds. But it all turned out quite differently. It was the southern summer. On Thursday, November 19th, I passed exactly under the midday sun at the zenith in a cloudless sky above an ocean with scarce a ripple upon its surface. Dead calms, slight breezes succeeded other calms, and I was slowly progressing to the north, but the trades were not always to be found there. The calm zone of Capricorn seemed unending, like the monotonous music of the sails that flapped ceaselessly, with never a breath of wind to fill them, the blocks hanging against the deck. Instead of my heavy mainsail I hoisted the light sail that had proved so useful when getting out of the Gulf of Panama.

At last, December 6th, at 10° 40′ S. latitude, I struck the trade-winds, twenty-four days after leaving Gambier Islands. In the evening the peculiar appearance of the clouds in the north indicated the vicinity of land. It lay hidden there beyond the horizon, the island of Fatu-Hiva, the most southern of the Marquesas. When night fell, observations of Canopus, Sirius and Achernar enabled me to ascertain my position. By next morning the island was already astern, thirty miles to the south-west, so hoisting all my canvas I passed the uninhabited island of San Pedro and sighted Hiva-Oa, where I hoped to anchor for the night. But the wind dropped and, reducing my sail, I let myself drift with the current. The following morning I was still fifteen miles from Atuana.

The coast presented a wild and strange aspect, very high mountains falling almost sheer from their summits to the water level. I could see no plateaux, and only a few valleys running into the mountains. The coco-nut trees that bordered the water's edge were hardly discernible, and the tops of the mountains seemed greener than the bases. It was a wild and savage-looking island, strangely unattractive, yet so different from what I had hitherto seen.

I was still lying becalmed in Traitors' Bay, two miles from Taha-Uku, when a whaling boat came out and a Breton hailed me with lusty welcome. Even here, alas, my fame had preceded me! At last I dropped anchor in the narrow bay of Taha-Uku, between two high cliffs. I had been twenty-six days coming from Mangareva.

The peak of Temetiu reared its head above the clouds some four thousand feet, the slopes descending from an immense semicircular crater. The erosion caused by cascades of lava had left great scars on the mountain-side. The clouds, driven up by the trade-winds, collected against the mountain-tops; on one side it rained, on the other it blew.

Between the mountains lay the valley of Taha-Uku, planted

with magnificent coco-nut trees. The wild beauty of the scenery passed all description. There was no trace of habitation save a matchboard cabin with a corrugated iron roof which, perched on the western cliff, was an insult to Nature.

After three weeks at sea I could not make up my mind to go ashore at once, and I was thinking of all the mariners of olden times, of the Spanish flotilla sent by Don Garcia Hurtado de Mendoza, viceroy of Peru, who, with Mendada and Quiros, discovered the southern group in 1595 and gave them the name of Marquesas, in honour of the Marquesa de Mendoza. A hundred and eighty years later Cook landed, while on his second voyage. Then Marchand discovered the northern islands and gave them the name of Revolution Islands. The descriptions left by Cook, Radiguet, Melville and Stevenson had always enthralled me, but I knew that only a few rare specimens remained of the magnificent race that had once been the finest and fiercest in the Pacific, notorious for its terrible warriors and its cannibals; yet at the same time the most civilized, to judge by the incomparable art manifested in its tattooing and sculptures.

I launched my Berthon boat and made for a point below the cliff where there seemed to be a sort of landing-place. When I got there it was to find only a few steps cut out in the rock some few feet above sea-level. The difficulty of landing in the swell was so great that I moored a few yards out and swam ashore.

The road from Taha-Uku lay along the side of the cliff to the west of the anchorage. When I had rounded the Kaledo point the bay and valley of Atuana lay stretched before me. Breakers were crashing in thunder on a beach of black volcanic sand. Immense coco-nut trees, dominated by two wireless aerial masts, hid the houses from sight. There were just a few wooden houses, belonging to the French, English or Chinese traders, and the dwellings of the French officials.

The vegetation far surpassed that of any island I had yet called at—gigantic mangroves, coco-nut trees, orange trees and breadfruit trees. Concealed by the foliage and scattered down the valley along the banks of a tiny stream, were the native dwellings, close to their plantations. Here in a small hut now disappearing under the quickly growing bush had lived and died the famous painter Gauguin.

As I passed the warehouses of the steamship company some Frenchmen wanted to drink my health in champagne. They were nearly all Bretons and they argued vociferously about my birthplace with an old Southern Frenchman, an ex-schoolmaster, who kept on launching into interminable patriotic tirades. To keep the peace I said that I had renounced the land, that for seven years the *Firecrest* had been my only home, and the open sea my only country. They gave me a delightful welcome, however, which enabled me once more to observe the really extraordinary way white men pass their existence in the tropics. Why drink wine and champagne when there is exquisite coco-nut water? Why erect uncomfortable dwellings of pine planks and corrugated iron when the leaves of the coco-nut trees are there to furnish an ever-fresh cover? Why wear hats and clothes when pigmentation of the skin is the best defence against the tropical sun, whose beneficent rays give you strength and health? For my own part, I had long ago made up my mind to care nothing for public opinion, and I usually wore nothing but a loin-cloth.

Some way along the road lived Dr. G——, who had temporarily filled the function of administrator and whose friendship was one of the greatest pleasures of my stay at Atuana. At his home I passed the first evening in turning over the illustrated magazines and reading French newspapers, for it was more than a year since I had had any news from France. But I must confess that after so long an interval general news interested me but little and what I wanted most to see was what my friends had done in the tennis championships in England and America.

In this way began my stay in the island which was to last for nearly three months, three months filled with too many incidents ever to be recorded in these pages. From the first I realized that a sort of melancholy apathy reigned throughout the valley. The old Marquesan dances and games had been suppressed, and the money paid to the inhabitants for their harvests of copra and the cultivation of vanilla was unable to procure them any real pleasures.

Happily the children had kept intact the best qualities of their race, and it was amongst them that I passed my happiest moments, riding the surf and going long excursions up the valleys. Sometimes Dr. G—— and I went riding on horseback, and when we passed native huts the inhabitants would come out and salute the Doctor with "Kaoha," which is the usual Marquesan salutation. It was a great delight to me—almost unique in the whole of my voyage—to find an official who had won the love of the natives.

For nearly three weeks the *Firecrest* lay alone at anchor in the bay of Taha-Uku, but on Christmas Eve, late at night, I was awakened by the rattle of a chain through hawse-pipes. It was the schooner *Hinano* dropping anchor. She had come from Tahiti with the new administrator of the Marquesas Islands. During the next few days three more schooners put in to the narrow harbour, which became rather crowded. All these sailing vessels belonged to different trading houses, and the competition among them was very keen. They were like floating department stores, and sold cloth, rice and canned food; but their principal business was to obtain dried copra from the natives. Each captain had his agents and spies on shore who let him know when any copra had been gathered in one of the valleys; whereupon he would repair thither at once with his schooner. They employed all sorts of ruses to get the better of one another, and were always bluffing and shrouding their movements in the most profound secrecy and mystery. So it was with Captain C—— who commanded the *Gisborne*. I made his acquaintance the day after his arrival when I was swimming back to my boat—a short distance of three or four hundred yards—as had been my custom for several days, as the Berthon boat was being repaired. He was kind enough to send his whaleboat to take me on board and told me that several weeks earlier a little pig of his had fallen overboard and had been snapped up by a shark before anyone had been able to save it. In contrast with the other captains the skipper of the *Gisborne* seemed very fond of his boat and seldom went ashore. We were very near neighbours in the harbour, within hail in fact, and having noticed my liking for Tahitian dishes he often invited me to share his meals, which usually consisted of fish served with a sauce made of coco-nut milk or *mitiari*. Yet even with me Captain C—— was very mysterious when it became a question of business, and if he told me he was sailing westward I was pretty certain to see him sail the following morning on an easterly course.

This competition between the traders in quest of copra was in some respects very inconvenient. The Marquesan cares little for money, and to obtain copra certain of the captains exploited his love for spirits, which are strictly prohibited in the island, though it is next to impossible to keep them out. One of the captains, who enjoyed a great reputation as a skilful navigator in the archipelago, walked about with a Bible under his arm and worked on the natives' love of the marvellous and their tendency to discuss biblical miracles—which in some certain respects resemble their own ancient myths—always ending by proving conclusively by Saint Paul that he was the only one to whom they ought to sell their copra.

On December 30th I tore myself away from the charms of Atuana and set sail for the island of Nuku-Hiva, some hundred miles away to the north-west. The breeze was of the lightest, but the current carried me rapidly from Traitors' Bay into the Bordelais Channel, between the islands of Tahu-Ata and Hiva-Oa.

I was very anxious to visit this northern island. I had read and reread the charming descriptions of it in *Typee*, the most delightful of all Herman Melville's books—to my eyes much better than *Robinson Crusoe*—and one which deserves to be translated into French. Very often as I did a spell at the helm, book in hand, I had dreamed of the idyllic life led in those deep valleys before the white man carried thither his destructive civilization.

At daybreak the following morning the island of Ua-Uka lay ten miles to the north-east. Right ahead of me, wrapped in mist, Nuku-Hiva seemed even wilder than the island of Hiva-Oa. Cliffs fell sheer to the sea, their bases beaten by the waves that broke against them with a roar of thunder. On the starboard bow was Controller's Bay, into which opened the deep valley of Taipi. The whole length of the coast the cliffs were broken by little coves of delightful green, into which opened charming valleys, and between them rose the mountain heights covered with short grass, and looking savage and grim, huge and desolate. The coco-nut trees rose out of the water and I was soon able to distinguish the narrow entrance to the Bay of Taioae, on either side of which two great rocks, aptly called sentinels, seemed to have been placed on purpose to stand guard over it. The wind failed me between these two rocks, only coming in little puffs, and the *Firecrest* tacked slowly into the bay, which opened out into a semicircle, forming probably the finest harbour for warships that we French possess in the Pacific Ocean.

I dropped anchor at the bottom of the bay, off a little hill upon which were still the ruins of a fort. I now had the impression of being enclosed in a sort of circular basin, for the entrance to the bay seemed very small at a distance. The ruined buildings, last vestiges of the occupation of the island by our navy, betokened that the island had once enjoyed great prosperity. The mountains, rising to majestic heights, formed a kind of immense natural amphitheatre round the bay, whose shore was edged with stretches of white sand that glistened in the sun or was broken by little streams dashing down from the valleys, vast fissures of a dazzling green between the mountain heights, and all radiating from the bay. Thus must the place have appeared to the frigates of the French admiral, Du Petit Thouars, in 1842, and to Herman Melville, when in company with Toby, he escaped from the whaler *Dolly* and climbed the mountains to reach the valley of Taipi. But, alas, where were those picturesque native huts, with their leaf roofs and walls of bamboo, so artistically woven?

A single road ran along the bay, studded with large, hideous wooden habitations, which were used for the traders' offices and storehouses. The almost total absence of natives was more apparent here than anywhere else in the Marquesas, and in itself gave conclusive evidence of the desolation that follows in the train of what is conventionally called white civilization. Less than a century of occupation sufficed to empty the islands. The whole population of Nuku-Hiva, estimated by the Russian Kreusenstern at 16,000, had already diminished to half when Du Petit Thouars called in there, and at the time of my visit scarcely amounted to 600. All these considerations filled me with melancholy and made me curtail my visit to Taioae. I did not even want to visit the famous valley of Taipi, where a dozen or so natives were dragging out a miserable end to their days—last survivors of thousands who led an idyllic and happy life when Herman Melville was there, less than a hundred years ago.

At Taioae there were, it is true, some of my own countrymen, who gave me a hearty welcome, but I like to study humanity during my voyages; and to probe into the various concepts of Good and Evil of many races, and the native way of thinking, which is so different from that of the white men. That is why I used to repair, of an evening, to the veranda of Bob the trader, where the youth of the country used to assemble. Bob was an old sailor from Liverpool who had been long settled in the Marquesas as a trader. He attracted me from the first simply because he was loved by the natives. He was a born story-teller and his conversation was very instructive.

The *Firecrest* lay at anchor more than half a mile from the shore, and it was my custom to swim to the beach and pass part of each afternoon sporting in the surf or stretched on the sand, basking in the burning rays of the tropical sun. Late one evening, as I went into the water to swim out to my boat, an enormous shark passed close to me. I splashed and made some noise. It was the shark which got frightened and swam away; all the same, to avoid surprise attacks, I did not again venture far out into the water at night. Before long the schooners I had met at Taha-Uku joined me in the harbour.

On the morning of January 11th I weighed anchor and, sailing out of Taioae Bay, steered eastward, passing under cliffs that rose sheer from the water's edge, and soon arrived off the narrow channel leading into the Bay of Taioa. The scenery was impressive and even surpassed the harbour of Taioae in its strange beauty. A narrow cleft in the clifts gave on to a very green valley, bordered on the west by an absolutely vertical wall of basalt more than 1,500 feet in height. Four or five cable lengths in the cleft expanded to the right, terminating in the circular basin of Hakatea, in whose calm and tranquil waters, surrounded by green-clad mountains, I dropped my anchor, sheltered from winds and waves. At the end of the bay was a shining white stretch of sand and wild brushwood, a marvellous solitude disturbed only by the bleating of the wild goats that frisked on the mountain-sides. Launching my Berthon boat, I made for the beach of Akaui, at the end of the neighbouring bay.

Several natives collected round me as soon as I reached the shore, to help carry the boat up, and one of them taking me by the hand, led me to his hut situated near the beach, at the end of a spit of sand, between two streams that came down the valley. The hut was no more than a shelter of leaves, and there I was invited to partake of a meal with his family, consisting of his wife and two charming young girls. It is my almost invariable custom to obey the maxim of doing at Rome as the Romans do, so I tasted all the strange dishes of which the meal was composed. There was raw octopus pickled in wild lemon juice, octopus roasted on red-hot stones, *kaku*—a delicious dish made from breadfruit paste cooked in coco-nut milk, goats' flesh or *mene-mene*, and finally the inevitable *popoi*. For drinking there was the fresh water of young coco-nuts. It was a real pleasure to me to find myself among these bronze creatures who even yet practised the generous and spontaneous hospitality primitive men always show towards wayfarers.

While I was being thus entertained a crowd of natives

stared at me from afar with curiosity, waiting to invite me in their turn; for it would have been the height of indelicacy for them to invade the house of my host while I was his guest. They all disputed for the privilege of entertaining me, and at last Stanislas Taupotini, great grandson of Queen Waekehu, famous for her tattooed leg, and, with his brothers, owner of the valley, bid me welcome and invited me to picnic at the head of the valley for the following day. Stanislas, or rather Piutete, to give him his native name, had a splendid head, with an almost classic Roman profile, and was, like most of the descendants of the chiefs, taller, sturdier and of a lighter colour than the common people. Although he was the owner of the valley, the inhabitants of which were employed by him to gather copra, his house was one of the smallest in the village, and there seemed nothing to show that he enjoyed more comfort or wealth than the other natives. This was so formerly in the Marquesas, where only a few specially fine mats in his house, and the profound respect borne him by his people, differentiated the chief from the rest. The Polynesian government was exceedingly democratic; the chief was responsible for arranging the planting so as to avert famines, and had to lead his warriors to war.

Stanislas' house was a tiny erection of wood and corrugated iron, and the inside was hotter than a green-house. It was a type of dwelling imposed on the natives by French law, and in which the modern Marquesans are dying of consumption.

During my stay at Akaui I had numerous visitors, discreet and naïve folk who were surprised at all they saw on board, and whose exclamations of surprise, uttered in long drawn out murmurs, "e mea Ka-na-ha-aa-aa-ou," still echo in my memory.

On Monday, January 18th, I weighed anchor at 7.30 a.m. and left the narrow passage of Akaui, a very difficult undertaking for a sailing boat, against a current of two knots and a head wind. In fact, it is thought almost impossible locally for a boat without a motor to get out, and trading schooners never attempt it under canvas alone. But my narrow cutter sailed nearer the wind than a schooner, and after much tacking, during which missing stays would have been fatal, I managed to clear the narrow pass. As I left it I cast a final glance at the marvellous valley, and saw the inhabitants collected on the beach to wave me farewell.

Once clear of the island the current carried me rapidly towards the west. Hiva-Oa, my next port of call, lay to the south-east, and as I made a long tack to avoid the island of Uapou, I saw an eastward schooner tacking. The *Firecrest* was pounding heavily in a very choppy head sea, burying her nose in the waves.

Next day I sighted Hiva-Oa, and during the night passed to the south of Tahu-Ata in order to avoid the current running out of the Bordelais Channel. The following day the wind dropped to a slight breeze, veering towards the north-east, which obliged me to beat up against it all night. At last I arrived within some miles of my anchorage at Tahauku, but I was becalmed until early dawn, when a slight air enabled me to glide gently into the harbour. I had taken seventy hours to sail what I had covered in twenty-five hours in the other direction; and astern of me was the schooner *G——*, of 120 tons, who had left Taioae twelve hours before me and proceeded constantly under sail and motor, consuming twelve barrels of petrol. This did not surprise me greatly, for most of these schooners were built in a somewhat haphazard manner; if their owners had only taken the trouble to build them according to the plans of some competent architect they would have made an enormous saving, both in time and cost of running.

If my first sojourn had left me with agreeable memories, I have yet pleasanter ones of my second visit, and I certainly intend to return to these islands one day, for I feel myself bound to them by many ties. Once again I had some delightful rides on horseback, with the doctor and his friend Tea, a young and charming Marquesan girl. Together we went to the fertile valley of Taaoa, right at the end of Traitors' Bay, where we called on Madame M——, who was half Marquesan. There were always delightful parties in the native style, and instructive talks on olden times in the island. We made excursions up the valleys where, after bathing in the fresh and limpid waters of the mountain torrents, I learned to enjoy the exquisite freshwater shrimps wrapped in hibiscus leaves and roasted on red-hot stones, a food fit for the gods. I also met my young friends again and renewed our sports on the beach of Atuana. After playing almost naked in the sun I became as brown as a Marquesan, and my skin began to regain its natural colour, that is to say, what it would have been, had I always lived in the open air and the sunshine without any clothes.

But I had to be off once more. An important mail was awaiting me at Tahiti, the first for a whole year, and I had to renew certain portions of the *Firecrest*'s rigging and get new sails made. The Marquesas Islands were one of the rare stopping places on my cruise that I left with real regret, for I felt that I might have lived there in the greatest happiness.

On the morning of February 9th I weighed anchor and, under a full spread of canvas, passed the beach of Atuana, where a number of the young people of the country were collected. As a signal of farewell I fired three rounds from my rifle, then steered for the isle of Fatu-Hiva, sixty miles to the south-east. But this time my thoughts were not for my destination; they centred round the pleasant memories of my stay at Hiva-Oa. By dawn next day I was becalmed in sight of Fatu-Hiva. Not until noon did a light breeze get up and enable me to make the land.

This island surpassed in wildness the other Marquesas. Black mountains of basalt rose vertically from the sea, and when I drew near the shore the wind came in gusts that heeled the *Firecrest* right over, and I could only approach the shore very slowly by steering the boat, which carried all her sail, with the utmost care. I knew the dangers of the violent squalls in Virgin Bay, and that the schooners of the place always took in their canvas and entered under power alone.

Virgin Bay, the native name of which is even more melodious —Hanavave—provides a perfectly fantastic spectacle that only

Poe could have described. Towers of basalt taking the strangest shapes of minarets, towers, steeples, pointed rocks pierced like a needle's eye, form the background of the bay, and a narrow cleft in the mountains opens on to a valley. The breakers roared like thunder on a beach of black shingle. A line of coco-nut trees showed minute against the mountain-sides. Smaller yet were two tiny native huts, and smaller still a few dots on the shore, which were men. Never had I felt such a sensation of the insignificance of man beside the grandeur of Nature.

Running in so close that my bowsprit almost touched the headland, for the mountain-sides fell sheer into the water, I dropped anchor in twenty fathoms on a treacherous sloping bottom. A canoe, manned by a young native, came out to the *Firecrest*, but I had no wish to go on shore; I did not want to be disillusioned that evening by meeting actors less beautiful than the stage. So I turned in, rocked by the swell, and soothed by the roar of the breakers and the plaintive cries of goats on the face of the cliffs.

The following morning I tried in vain to land with my Berthon boat. The surf broke too heavily on the shingle and would soon have smashed my little canvas canoe to bits. So I had to anchor it a few yards from the shore and swim to land. Some of the population were waiting for me there, but what sad specimens of humanity they were. In very truth I do not believe there was a single individual in sound health in the whole valley. Elephantiasis, tuberculosis and lymphangitis had made unbelievable ravages among them. When I stepped ashore they thronged round me, wanted to know the reason of my visit, and displayed the utmost astonishment when I said that I had come simply because it interested me, not because I had something to sell them.

The greater part of the old natives were tattooed; this did not surprise me, for Fatu-Hiva had always been celebrated for its tattooers and sculptors. The women, as was the case in the old days, were only slightly tattooed on the face—a few curls round the lips and the lobes of the ears. The foot, up to the ankle, and the right hand, as far as the wrist, were covered with a delicate pattern like lace. No one was allowed to put a hand not tattooed into the domestic dish of *popoi*.

Naturally I had to submit to the inevitable rites of Marquesan courtesy, and a splendid old native, suffering, alas, from elephantiasis in both legs, led me to his hut, where I partook of an excellent meal of breadfruit paste cooked in coconut milk. The hut was atrocious, built of deal and corrugated iron. It was a perfect example of the bad influence and of the execrable artistic taste of the white race. The shady pathway, which led to the chief's hut, continued along the valley. On the right was a charming little old church surrounded with rose laurels and half hidden in the foliage; farther on there was a native house with its grove of palm trees and walls of reeds interlaced in chequer-board pattern, which allowed the air to circulate freely. On the terrace in front of the house were seated the inhabitants with whom I had to partake of a meal, for it would be a grave insult to a Marquesan to refuse his hospitality. Yet even there it was very sad, for everyone seemed ill, and one young girl, exceedingly pretty, was suffering from the hideous complaint of the country.

I followed the valley which meandered far into the mountains with a stream running along it. The vegetation was luxurious, and this was undoubtedly the most fertile vale I had seen in the Marquesas. Very soon the dwellings ceased, and there was nothing but brush and abandoned *paepaes*, or terraces, to show what a large population had lived there before they had been desolated by the white race. In spite of its surpassing beauty, the countryside had an abandoned air, sad and melancholy. I nearly put my foot on an enormous centipede, the bite of which would have meant death—there was nothing but death and desolation everywhere.

I rarely went for a walk in the valley, for it was not wise to let the *Firecrest* out of my sight. The bay, indeed, had a very bad bottom, and I was always afraid that one of the violent squalls would make her drag the anchor and drive out into the open sea.

I spent the afternoons seated on the shore before the boathouse, an open shed in which were kept dug-outs. There the young people would gather around me, sickly fellows for the most part, very few of pure blood and most of them showing traces of the white race who had sailed hither from distant lands. The old American whalers had left their mark unmistakably.

I had realized from the first that I should have to stay near the shore so as to keep a watch on the *Firecrest,* for the unsatisfactory bottom filled me with apprehension; so I refused all invitations from the natives to pass a night away from my ship. Towards one o'clock one dark morning the squalls blew more violently than ever, and I was awakened by the anchor dragging along the bottom. In a very short time I was out of the bay and the current carrying me free. By daylight I had nearly a hundred fathoms of chain with my anchor at the end of it to haul on board—a colossal task to perform single-handed, and it took me nearly four and a half hours to do it. It was not until evening that I got back to my moorings. Under these conditions, despite a very keen desire to stay longer in the island and to learn from the surviving tattooers and sculptors what remained of Marquesan art, I weighed the anchor, after a week's stay, and steered for the Tuamotu Islands.

CHAPTER X

AN ARCHIPELAGO

BETWEEN the Marquesas and Tahiti lies an archipelago dreaded by all navigators. Everyone knows that an atoll is a coral ring lying at almost water level, and enclosing a lagoon. At its most elevated spot an atoll rarely attains a greater height than ten feet, and the tops of the coco-nut trees that grow on the ring cannot be seen more than a few miles away, which makes navigation in those waters most dangerous. In no other part of the ocean is there such an agglomeration of atolls as in the Tuamotu; the currents are dangerous and uncertain, and the charts often quite wrong.

This being so, the archipelago is carefully avoided by mariners. In spite of using a local pilot, Stevenson lost his yacht there; Jack London could not get to the Ragiroa atoll, and in his cruise from London to the Toga Islands Ralph Stock was no more successful. An excellent English navigator, Lieutenant Muhlauser, who recently sailed round the world on his yacht the *Amaryllis*, would not risk sailing in those waters.

As a general rule atolls can only be entered by a very narrow channel through which the tide rushes in or out with a great speed, and this makes the entrance very arduous for sailing craft. The thought of surmounting all these difficulties thrilled me, so I made up my mind to pass right through the middle of this dangerous group and visit successfully the atolls of Raroia and Makemo, famous for the strength of current to be met at their entrance channels.

After seven days of light breezes my observations, at daybreak on Wednesday the 24th, showed that I was ten miles or so from my first calling place. I knew this, besides, by the peculiar tinge of the western sky, which indicated unmistakably the existence of an atoll somewhere near. At 7.30 a.m., I saw coco-nut trees apparently rising out of the water, and on the starboard bow sighted the atoll of Takume; on the port bow lay Raroia. I immediately made for the wide strait, several miles across, that separates them.

I had already seen several coral reefs at Mangareva, but this was the first time I had been near an atoll. It was like fairy-land! For about a cable's length I followed the submarine reef that surrounded the atoll, and was only perceptible by the emerald green colour of the water. Every now and then enormous blocks of dazzlingly white coral stood out of the sea as though tossed up by some gigantic eruption. What struck me most of all was the transparent blueness of the air, the marvellously delicate hue of the sky above the lagoon, and the violent contrast of green tree-tops and vivid blue sky.

The sea was breaking heavily on the coral. The coastline of the atoll was far from presenting the regular appearance shown in the charts; it was a succession of bays and little points, not continuous, but broken into little islands separated from each other by miniature channels. Towards noon I was opposite the Ngarue channel. Now was the time to verify some of my theories. Every skipper I had talked to had advised me to enter at slack water of low tide when there was practically no current, but I resolved to make my way in at the full strength of the flood, thus profiting by its assistance. As a matter of fact, I never take much notice of advice tendered to me, but invariably follow my own inspirations.

The tide was rising when I got there, and the sea sweeping in with an enormous swell. There was no sign of a buoy to mark the channel, and I had to trust entirely to the compass to get my bearings. The breeze was light, but when I actually reached the entrance the current raced me onwards at a speed of eight knots.

This was really most impressive. The reefs seemed very close on either side. The water boiled and swirled and the *Firecrest* did not answer to the helm. Ahead were several large lumps of sunk coral. In the middle of the channel my boat spun round twice on her own axis, and I thought myself in great danger, but by this time I had been swept into the lagoon, where the water was marvellously calm and so transparent that I could perceive many dangerous reefs just below the surface. Navigation was now increasingly difficult, and I had constantly to leave the tiller to go forward and make out the various coral boulders which the chart indicated under particularly melodious names—Mapiropiro, Otikaia, Temarii, Temahine, Nekatautau. Before long I cast anchor off the little village of Ngarumaova, happy to have surmounted such difficulties and to have undergone an unforgettable experience. I felt something like pity for those who, by fitting a motor to their boats, lose the entire art of navigation and miss the thrill of entering a narrow strait under sail.

. . . .

On the white sandy shore, facing my anchorage, a few inhabitants had collected, and they seemed to be following my movements with keen curiosity. I was beginning to furl my sails when a dug-out left the shore, and its occupant, an old native, came alongside. His language was rough and different from that of the other islands I had visited; however, I managed to make out that he wanted me to go on shore and eat with him. So when I had got all in order on the *Firecrest* I followed him ashore. A score of natives were gathered round his hut, and they stared at me with frank curiosity. One woman spoke a little French and told me that the inhabitants were afraid of me. It seems that five years previously a schooner had run aground in the Tuamotus with only two men on board—one of whom was the cook—who had mutinied, seized the vessel and murdered the captain, and those two were the only survivors of the crew. They had been taken and sent to Australia to be tried. Seeing me alone, the inhabitants naturally imagined I had eaten the rest of my crew and took me for an armed desperado, ready to defend myself to the last. They were now somewhat reassured, but were greatly intrigued as to the reason for my visit, and wondered why I wore a loin-cloth instead of trousers.

The old native, the only one who dared come out to meet

me, was very proud of his pluck, and he and his wife laid themselves out to provide a feast suitable for the occasion. When all was ready, the rest of the folk effaced themselves with true Polynesian tact, and left me alone with my host. His hut was tiny, probably because he was extremely poor, consisting simply of a few stakes driven into the ground and roofed with palm leaves woven together and the walls made of the same material plaited in the form of rough curtains. Small as it was, this was the most comfortable hut in the whole island, for I noticed that not only the roofs but also the walls of the others were made of corrugated iron, which engendered a perfectly infernal heat under the tropical sun.

Poor as my hosts certainly were, for their cabin contained nothing but a few bits of fishing tackle, they did their best in my honour, and on a little table served up an enormous fish cooked in coco-nut milk. Beside the dish were placed their gifts, shells of most marvellous colours and five little pearls. To take their seats by my side was out of the question; they were there to wait on me. Such was the traditional Polynesian hospitality in honour of the passing visitor.

Thus began my stay in this island, where I met such a hearty welcome and where all the inhabitants exhibited a hospitality unequalled among the greatest nations that call themselves civilized.

The following morning, having work to do on board, I did not go on shore. I was surprised to see my host of the evening before bringing me out a cooked fish which he had caught during the night, thinking, as he said, that having so much to do I should have no time to get any food. It was quite impossible to get him to accept any present in exchange. Every time I went on shore I had to accept the hospitality of the inhabitants, who entertained me in turn and loaded me with gifts. Perhaps the present that pleased me most was that of my friend Tiari—a fishing hook of mother-of-pearl and bone, that flashed through the water like a flying-fish, and was useful for catching bonitos.

. . . . .

The atoll had a circumference of some fifty miles and was about ten miles across. The widest strip of land was no more than three hundred feet from side to side; on this narrow strip lived nearly sixty people. The village was divided into little properties, but the coco-nut trees that surrounded the lagoon belonged to the whole community. The copra they obtained, which formed the sole wealth of the island, was evenly distributed among the various families.

The village of Ngarumaova consisted of a single street, around which were clustered the huts I have already mentioned, most of them made of corrugated iron. On one side was the sea, which broke on great boulders of coral and organic refuse whitened by the salt of the ocean. They were the work of countless thousands of years—shells of all sorts and whale teeth cast up no one knows when. As a contrast, the side facing the lagoon was strangely calm, a sheet of water of surpassing tranquillity, scarcely ruffled by the trade-winds, where great fish of dazzling colours could be seen. I do not think the greatest height of the atoll was more than six feet above the water level. None of the trees was old, for a cyclone had passed across the island ten years before, levelling most of the palms and carrying away all the huts. The inhabitants had only managed to save themselves by clinging to the strongest tree trunks, which were the only refuge from the surf and spray that accompanied the cyclone.

Coco-nuts, fish from the lagoon, and a few turtles furnished the principal food of these islands. When green the coco-nut yields a most refreshing milk and the kernel of the ripe nut is a complete food in itself. From the grated kernel a creamy milk is obtained by pressure, which is used in cooking; a limpid oil is also extracted from copra. When the nuts are very ripe they contain a sort of sponge which is considered a great delicacy. There are coco-nut trees of all sorts, the nuts of some of them having such soft shells that they can be eaten as well as the inside. Monotonous as this diet seems, I preferred it infinitely to the canned food which the inhabitants felt themselves obliged to offer me. The coco-nut tree, indeed, is able to supply every need of the inhabitants; the trunks are used to build houses; the leaves furnish the roof or can be woven into comfortable mats; the fibre round the nut is worked into stout imperishable cordage; the oil is used for lighting; and it was by rubbing together the dried sticks of the branches that fire was formerly obtained.

The girls of Raroia all seemed to me very pretty; strong and well shaped, they had a very slightly darkened skin and their features were nearly European in cast. Two little girls, in particular, were of a type almost exactly the same as that of the street beauties one meets in Seville.

When the time came for me to go I entered the only shop in the village, which was kept by the chieftain, to procure some provisions, and began by ordering 5 lb. of rice. I was amazed to see the native who served me weigh out 10 lb. When I was going to stop him he informed me with a smile that it would cost me nothing. Another inhabitant coming in at the same moment, and hearing what the chieftain had done, ordered 20 lb. of rice which he put in my hand. It was impossible to refuse—to have done so would have been a mortal offence. Other natives came in and pressed on me the whole contents of the shop. I had the utmost difficulty in persuading them not to do so, and getting back on board I set sail immediately, and soon I left the dangerous channel leading from this hospitable atoll, helped by the ebbing tide.

. . . . .

Makemo Island lay nearly eighty miles from Raroia. My course thither took me between the atolls of Nihiru and Taenga, twenty miles distant and only the approximate position of which was marked on the chart. I had to keep a sharp look-out all night long. I passed between the two atolls without seeing them, determining my position every second hour by stellar observation; the conditions for this were exceptionally favourable, and I used a telescope of small magnifying power, but great luminosity. I was constantly on deck, straining my ears for the sound of breakers, which, in the darkness, was all that denoted the proximity of atolls. With her helm lashed down the *Firecrest* must have followed as steady a course as a steamer, for at daybreak the eastern extremity of the long island of Makemo was only five miles away.

After running along the reef for some hours I arrived opposite the channel of Pueheva, a very narrow passage with an entrance even more difficult than that of Raroia. I could see the huts of the village and a native dug-out coming out to the *Firecrest*. The breeze was light and I was already halfway through the passage, letting myself drift in on the tide, when the unexpected happened. The dug-out drew alongside and before I could protest two natives jumped aboard. This was going to rob me of the pleasure of tackling the dangerous channel by myself; to their great amazement I flatly refused to let them take the least part in managing the boat, and concentrated my attention on threading my way through the maze of coral rocks which I had studied so carefully on the chart, and whose poetic names I had off by heart. As we passed I called these names aloud to my unwelcome passengers, who were astounded that a stranger should know their Rikiriki, Uparari, Tutaekiore and finally Matarangameha, near which I dropped anchor at the spot I chose for myself. At some cable's length from my anchorage there was a little wharf, and the picturesque huts of Pueheva were visible among the trees on the spit of land at the right of the entrance. It was a charming sight—the green waters of the lagoon, so clear and transparent, the white coral shore, and the vivid green of the palm trees.

There appeared to be considerable commotion near the wharf; when I got ashore the whole population were waiting for me, and the chief had put on European costume for the occasion. In front of a new building, which bore the high-sounding appellation of Town Hall, a great pyramid of coconuts had been collected, and this was formally presented to me by the chief, while the natives were chasing fowls for me. Not liking the presence of these creatures on board the *Firecrest*, I refused them, but seeing the disappointment of the donors I compromised by accepting one. After this, numbers of men came one after the other with presents of multi-coloured shells and little pearls. Here, once more, I had a taste of the welcome accorded to strangers by primitive people who have not yet been spoiled by contact with civilization.

Standing near by were two Europeans, one of whom was an old man with a white beard, whilst the other, gaunt and ascetic-looking, wore clothes of a clerical cut. The old man was a Danish skipper who had acted as pilot to Robert Louis Stevenson in his voyage from the Marquesan Islands to the atoll of Fakarava on the *Casco*. His long residence in the islands had certainly not improved his temper, for the very first words he uttered were full of envy and hatred. "I call that," said he, looking at my presents, "offering an egg in the hopes of getting a fowl"; a statement which was utterly false, for during the whole of my stay in the island I found it quite impossible to get the natives to accept the smallest present. The other European was a Seventh Day Adventist missionary, and with him I had many interesting conversations.

Short as it was, my stay at Makemo proved to be one of the most agreeable in the whole cruise. For the first time, I saw a Polynesian population absolutely fit and in good health, leading a natural, open-air existence. If they were apt to put on European clothes too often, yet they were still frequently to be seen in the lagoon, wearing an elegant *pareu* in red and white flowers.

The day after my arrival, crowds of children were fishing from tiny little outrigger dug-outs not far from the *Firecrest*. They often disappeared into the water to have a look to see whether the bait was still on the hook. Noticing the presence under my boat of great sombre shapes passing over the coral bed I warned them that sharks were about, but my words were greeted with laughter, and they went on diving and gambolling as merrily as ever. As for myself, I soon got to bathe in the waters of the lagoon without heeding the monsters which passed a dozen fathoms or so below me.

I was very happy among these amphibious people, fishing in the depths of the lagoon or having diving competitions with the youngsters. The perfect ease of their motions under water was truly extraordinary. Where I could dive with the utmost difficulty to five fathoms, it was mere child's play to them to get down to ten. Yet the best divers were absent. They had gone over to the Island of Hikueru, where the best mother-of-pearl in the whole archipelago was found, for the pearl fishing had opened. Among a race of divers those of Makemo were noted for their excellence. I was told that certain of them could go to thirty fathoms and that even a woman had dived to twenty-five fathoms.

The fowl which had been given me by the inhabitants proved a nuisance from the very first day. It took away my sense of being alone on board, and the intolerable creature would not let me sleep in peace. Surmounting my extreme repugnance, for it was the first time I had done such a thing, I decided to slaughter it, and this I did with a rifle; then, assisted by a young native and armed with a cookery book I plucked and cleaned it according to all the rules of the art, and ended by boiling it in the native fashion.

I only spent seven days in this delightful island, for I felt I would have to leave it before I got too attached, and yet I can still retain an unfading memory of the extraordinary beauty of that narrow strip of coral crowned with verdure, with the sea eternally near—calm within the interior of the lagoon but thundering in terrific breakers on the blocks of coral outside.

Several young natives besought me to take them with me. Never was I so tempted to take a crew as among these descendants of the famous Tuamotu navigators, whose exploits now belong to the world of legend; but I wanted to end my voyage by myself. Seeing these happy youngsters in their sunny island and contrasting their own youth with my sad childhood, far from fresh air and sunshine, the idea which had been conceived at the Marquesas began to develop in my thoughts and set me dreaming of a far distant atoll, the future haven for my ship, where I should make a home and thither return between my cruises to distant shores.

When I came to weigh anchor I found that the chain had become completely twisted round some coral boulders at the bottom, but several fishermen saw my difficulties and immediately came to my help, some on the deck hauling the chain while others, perfectly at their ease at the bottom of the lagoon with ten fathoms of water above their heads, unwinding the chain and setting it free. The current was very fast in the narrow channel, the swell enormous and the seas which swept on the deck of the *Firecrest* would have made me think I was in grave peril had this been my first experience of such things. The eddies made the sea boil and foam for more than a mile outside the passage, but this was only to be expected, for the lagoon at Makemo—an immense basin 50 miles long and 10 wide—has only two narrow channels by which to empty itself when the tide goes out.

CHAPTER XI

TAHITI

ON the afternoon of the day after my departure from Makemo I sighted the atoll of Katiu. At sunset I was off the entrance to the passage through the reef and within view of the village of Toini. A crowd of natives stood on the beach and waved as I sailed by. During the night I passed between the atolls of Raraka and Katiu, and the following day slipped through the dangerous reefs that surround Faaite and Taanea. With something of melancholy I saw the tops of the trees sink below the horizon, for I had a foreboding that nowhere else in my cruise should I find any islands dearer to me than the Marquesas and Tuamotus.

A little later I perceived, far away to the southward, a wonderful green reflection in the sky. It was caused by the shallow lagoon of Anaa atoll, the most populated island of the group. It was now the southern summer and the trade-wind was light. On March 14th the mountainous island of Mehetia was in sight to the north-west, and the following evening I saw at last the topmast peaks of the island of Tahiti. The wind continued very light, with every now and then a dead calm. By the morrow I was off the peninsula of Tairarapu, the headland of Tautira and the reef on which Captain Cook had so nearly lost his ship on the second voyage.

I expected much of Tahiti, but its beauty in no wise disappointed me. With the summit of Orofenua lost in the clouds, the curious and amazing Diadem Peak, the deep valleys that wandered down to the sea, the belt of coral that encircles it, upon which the ocean ceaselessly thunders—it seemed to me more majestic than any other island I had seen and in very truth the Queen of the Southern Seas. The weather was calm, but light breezes enabled me to leave astern a schooner that had borne me company all the morning, and so doubled Venus Point and Matavai Bay, whose names evoked memories of Wallis, Cook and Bougainville. Night was coming on and there was a dead calm by the time I was off the passage giving entrance to Papeete. A motor-boat came and offered to tow me in. Contrary to my custom I accepted, and at 6 p.m. on March 18th I dropped anchor in the waters of the lagoon, happy to have reached at last the island I had dreamed of so long.

By daylight I found that the town stretched along the shore among the trees by the water's edge. Even the corrugated iron roofs, the jetties and the warehouses were unable absolutely to destroy the beauty of the landscape which must have been wonderful before the arrival of white civilization. Before long I heard the noise of motors and began to regret the less civilized isles of the Marquesas and Tuamotus.

After the unforgettable welcome I had received from the natives of those islands I dreaded to have my solitude troubled. Tahiti was, in fact, the first island with a French colony that I had put in at, and I was afraid of receiving a too enthusiastic reception. I need not have worried, my arrival in Tahiti was absolutely ignored officially and no one disturbed me during the whole of my stay there. However, I had the satisfaction of receiving a letter of congratulation from M. Georges Leygues, Minister of Marine. This gave me great pleasure, for it was the first time I had ever had any recognition or the least interest in my cruise had been shown by the Government.

Papeete in no wise disappointed me, for I had expected nothing. It was a town inhabited chiefly by half-breed whites and Chinese. The white population consisted of business men and officials, the first had brought thither their love of money, the others all the prejudices of European civilization; they liked exactly what I hated, they and I had scarcely a thing in common, and I lived on board the *Firecrest* at Papeete almost as solitary as if I had been in the open sea. The Papeete of Loti was certainly dead long since, but I did not regret it, for that was not the town I wished to know but the old Papeete of the early European navigators, of Wallis, Cook and Bougainville—the Papeete that flourished when Tahitian civilization was at its zenith with its feudal constitution, its wonderful lyric poems, and its surpassingly beautiful dances.

It would be quite alien to the object of this book if I were to set forth my reflections on the decadence of Tahiti. I was particularly struck by the invasion of the Chinese and by the total absence of any of the native arts; they have quite disappeared never to be replaced. There is nothing picturesque to be found there now, not even the native costumes, for the French law forbids the wearing of the *pareu,* or loin-cloth, in the streets of Papeete; as the old dances and songs by the waterside are likewise prohibited, Papeete is indeed nowadays a very quiet small town.

Yet, notwithstanding all this, there are still a few pure Tahitians there, though they are not to be met with in broad daylight, for they are out and about all night fishing on the reef, whence they carry their catches, at very early morning, to the market-place. This market is one of the rare picturesque spots yet to be found in modern Tahiti, with its brilliantly coloured fish, its tropical fruits that smell so sweetly, and its enormous bunches of bananas. Sometimes, too, wonderful specimens of native beauty are to be seen there.

I often amused myself by strolling along the quays, where the numerous and inevitable little Chinese are always to be seen fishing, and where the schooners coming in from Tuamotu discharge cargoes of mother-of-pearl, that for so many people represent the spice of romance and poetic adventure, while for me they signify only exploitation and the spirit of trade.

One day I noticed a stout ketch with the name *Curieuse* painted on her stern. A single glance at her rounded lines told me what she was. It was the valiant little boat on which Rallier du Baty made a long expedition to the Kerguelen Islands and which he sold in Australia after war broke out. Family ties kept him in France afterwards, and thus prevented him from realizing his dreams and making a voyage round the world after having visited Tahiti and Polynesia, yet the *Curieuse* was lying there, where her owner would so dearly have liked to bring her.

My life on board was not entirely solitary, however, at Papeete. There were a few young Tahitians who found grace in my eyes, for they were fond of play and in them were still to be found some of the ancient qualities of their race. They alone were allowed on board the *Firecrest*, and they enlivened the boat with their songs and laughter. We were always having interminable matches at diving and water-polo.

Every Sunday I used to charter a taxi and we all set out, a joyous band, for the lovely beach at Arne, not far from the tombs of the Pomare kings. There we had some splendid surf-riding, and when the sun sank behind Morea I returned to my boat worn out with fatigue, to fall asleep on deck beneath the stars, wrapped in that deep, satisfying slumber that comes with extreme physical weariness.

I found it very difficult at Tahiti to satisfy all my longing for some form of active sport; there was only a feeble imitation of a tennis court and a poor football field traversed by a road, where there was not so much as the sign of a match during my whole stay in the island. Sport, indeed, seemed to meet with little encouragement from the Government.

In front of the governor's palace stood a house, buried in foliage—it was the home of Marau Taaroa a Tati, the widow of King Pomare V. I often went to see her and my conversations with her who was queen of Tahiti made an indelible impression on my mind and inspired in me a profound gratitude towards this lady who told me so much about the ancient legends of old Tahiti, its epic history and marvellous literature. Often, during long solitary spells at the tiller, have I recalled my old friend, as she narrated the prodigious history of her race and clan with her own peculiar eloquence and the extreme dignity of her bearing; a queen if ever there was one, born to rule and command.

I recall, too, a visit to the valley of Papenoo, to see Terii a Terioteraì, a direct descendant of one of the greatest Tahitian families. Of his extreme courtesy and his amiable reception I have the most vivid memory, as well as of two other guests, foreign traders, who had no interest save for their own business. The market price of copra was constantly being intruded into our discussion of things of the past!

The valley of Papenoo, alas, which was once the most populous in the whole archipelago, is now almost deserted, and the mixed population of half-breeds and Chinese were of no interest to me, compared with the marvellous race that is so fast disappearing.

I made my way to Point Venus and the monument erected near the tamarind tree which Captain Cook planted, where the Royal Geographical Society of London has placed a stone bearing what is said to be a mark of the meridian inscribed by the famous navigator to observe the transit of Venus. But the story is probably merely a legend, and the stone in question is almost certainly nothing but a sighting mark placed by the astronomer Wilkes, a hundred years after Cook, to gauge the growth of the coral.

At Tahiti the *Firecrest* was furnished with new storm-sail and flying-jib. On May 21st, 1926, I set sail before a light breeze, but it was a false start, for the wind dropped to a calm before I was clear of the lagoon and I found myself driven on to one of the coral slabs near the island of Motu-Atu. Jumping out on the reef I shoved the boat off and then, clambering on board, regained my moorings without the hull having been so much as scratched. My departure was thus postponed until the following day. At sea one day follows another with seeming monotony, yet no two days are alike. On the morrow there was almost too much wind! Clearing the lagoon easily before a brisk south-easterly breeze I was caught at the end of the channel by a sudden gust that heeled the *Firecrest* over and ripped the mainsail from top to bottom before I could lower it. At the same moment the whole island disappeared from sight in a squall of deluging rain. Hauling in the sail, I ran before the gale under three headsails, passing on the next day in sight of Huahine and Raiatea, where I was unfortunately unable to put in. By daylight on the following morning the island of Porapora was only thirty miles distant, showing me her sad and dreary east side, the only one that Loti had observed. But this was only an illusion, for when I entered the strait that separated it from Tahaa, Porapora appeared before me radiant, green and fertile. The breeze dropped and it was almost dark before the entrance of Teava-nui, "the great bay," opened before me. Then began some interesting navigation. I had to beat up against wind and current, guided only by the noise of the breakers on the reef that flanked the channel. But these perils were soon left behind and I was aided by the light of the moon which rose early over the scarcely ruffled lagoon between the isles of Tupua and Porapora. As I drew nearer the shore clouds and a torrential rain hid everything from sight; but I had time to take two compass bearings of the mountain-top of Pahia and the island of Tupua. I dropped anchor in fifteen fathoms of water and when the squall had passed and the moon appeared once more through the clouds, I saw the wooden jetty and wharf of Vaitape less than a cable's length off. Had it been broad daylight I could not have moored in a better place.

Songs and laughter were wafted across from the jetty, for my arrival had been signalled before darkness fell, but no one came aboard that night and I had no desire to go ashore. The following morning I received the French resident, an old planter who had been fifteen years in the country. He combined his functions with that of a schoolmaster, was married to a Frenchwoman, and had two daughters.

Some days after my arrival the chieftain of the island gave a feast in my honour. An open hut had been specially built for the occasion and decorated with sweet-smelling *hinano* and *tiare* flowers. An enormous pile of fruit, coco-nuts and bunches of bananas flanked the entrance. We took up our seats on the ground around a mat on which were placed the various dishes; there we sat cross-legged, and wore garlands of flowers in our hair, in true Polynesian style. As for the menu, it was the very best Tahitian cuisine. For *hors d'œuvre* there was raw fish soaked in wild citron juice and served with wonderful sauces;

sucking-pigs baked under ground in the Kanaka oven, with taros and sweet potatoes; fish cooked, also under ground, in coco-nut milk; then finely chopped-up chicken, boiled with saffron in bamboo tubes; finally, *taro poi*, which is the favourite Hawaiian dish, and was made of taro and bananas. As for drinks, we had the delicious water of the young coco-nuts. We ate without forks, and between each course calabashes of water were passed round to wash our hands in. But the speeches will always stay in my memory. At the end of the meal the chief arose and made a speech in Tahitian. Unfortunately I could not understand all he said, nor can I render justice to the fire of his oratory, the dignity of his demeanour, the perfect rhythm and harmony of his periods. When the interpreter translated the substance of his speech I was struck with admiration. The chieftain began by excusing himself for not being in a position to give me a worthier reception, but the cyclone that had devastated the island in January had destroyed his home. He offered me the pyramid of fruit and other food that lay heaped outside, and wished me welcome to his island of Porapora. Then he adopted me in true Polynesian fashion, and declared that the entire island would in future know me by my Tahitian name, which, alas, I can no longer remember, though I know it meant "The Song of Sugar Canes." To explain this, he related the wonderful story of a Porapora warrior, of incomparable courage and strength, who, surrounded on the summit of a hill between Mount Faitape and Faanui, and sorely wounded by the spears of his enemies, put his back against a clump of sugar-canes to meet his death. The wild war song that he uttered until his last breath left him became legendary and by it he was known to all future generations. "And so," concluded the chieftain, addressing me, "because he was the bravest of all our warriors and because we admire thy bravery sailing along over the mighty seas, we give thee his name, and it is the best we have to offer thee!"

Considering that the island of Porapora was famous throughout the whole archipelago for the indomitable courage of its warriors, I felt bashful and confused at this speech, for never had such an honour been paid me, and I could only answer that I appreciated such an honour and express to them my gratitude and love. I was grieved not to be able to understand Tahitian perfectly, but I promised myself to return there one day to gather together and study all the legends and stories of the Porapora heroes.

I have remarked that a cyclone had recently devastated the island. It had stripped all the trees of their leaves and fruit and demolished the houses. One witness assured me that corrugated iron roofs were flying about everywhere and were very dangerous. Only a few of the larger native huts remained intact; these were the places where the natives were accustomed to assemble of an evening and sing the wonderful songs for which Porapora was famed throughout the neighbouring islands. Rebuilding was started at once, always, alas, in that dreadful white deal that seems part and parcel of our civilization. I deeply regretted the disappearance of all the picturesque native huts built on piles along the edge of the lagoon, which must have been infinitely more in harmony with the landscape than these modern abortions.

At Porapora there was no European except the French resident who received me on my arrival. I formed a fast friendship with the young folk of the island, thus getting to know even better than at Papeete this interesting branch of the Polynesian race. In the daytime I walked with these jolly youngsters all over the gay and smiling island that gleamed so green and pleasant beneath the forbidding heights of Mount Pahia. In the evening the inhabitants of the village used to gather by the water's edge round a flamboyant and dance, crowned with garlands, hibiscus flowers in their hair and their bodies anointed with sweet, scented oils. Hand in hand we wandered among the dancing groups, my young friends and myself; and sometimes I, who never danced in France, let myself be drawn into the simple native dances.

The population of Porapora has maintained a rather greater purity of blood than that of Tahiti, despite an apparent mixture of white and Chinese; the young people wear their hair long; the greater part of them have large and languorous eyes and that seductive beauty peculiar to the Polynesians.

One day an English sloop-of-war put in to Teavanui, the great harbour of Porapora. I made the acquaintance of the commander and his officers, dined on board their vessel, and Commander Brooke returned my visit and came on the *Fire-crest*. They only took a small walk on shore, and put to sea on the morrow.

Eight days later an almost identically similar vessel, but flying the French flag, appeared at the entrance to the channel. It was the sloop-of-war *Cassiopée* coming from Samoa. She soon dropped anchor, not far from the *Firecrest*, and a steam launch came alongside. In it was one of her officers with a message from his commander, proffering any help I should need. I went on board the *Cassiopée* at once to thank Commander Jean Decoux for his courtesy, and he kept me to dine with him.

For the first time in my cruise I met a warship of my own country, and I was immensely struck by the smartness of her appearance and of the crew. It was exceedingly pleasant to meet French sailors, men who felt an interest in all the things that thrilled me so much.

By a singular coincidence one of the young sailors on the *Cassiopée* had written to me after my crossing the Atlantic, to ask me to take him with me. Upon my refusal he enlisted in the navy, and now we met in mid-Pacific. During the afternoon I showed him all over the *Firecrest* and explained the minutest details of my equipment.

Commander Decoux also paid me a visit on board and stayed a long time. He showed great interest in my instruments and methods of navigation; poring over my charts we discussed at length all I had done and what I meant to do in the future.

That evening a grand fête was held on the greensward in honour of the warship. The *Cassiopée* lit up the field with its searchlight. First of all the natives, seated on the grass, sang a weird sort of chorus in eight parts, with a strange and curious harmony and final notes drawn out very long. After this the best dancers in the island executed a *Hupahupa* of exceptional skill, accompanied by almost acrobatic contortions. The executants must be trained from their earliest years to do this dance properly, and Porapora is noted throughout the archipelago for its dancers and for its singers.

The commander, his officers and a number of the crew sat watching this fête. I wandered among the various groups, delighted to see the pleasure it all gave my native friends, who were overcome with gratification at entertaining Frenchmen who were interested in them and liked them. Then I seated myself by the commandant, with my young friend Tepera at my feet.

When the songs and exhibition dances were finished, the usual round dances began. Very soon the sailors were taking part, as well as the black Kanakas from the Loyalty Islands, who formed part of the crew. There was a surprising contrast between the dusky natives and the white-faced French sailors who, from continually wearing sun helmets, had not been burned by the tropical sun. Everyone joined hands and was gay and happy, for the affectionate smiles of the Poraporans needed no interpreters to translate the welcome they offered.

Next day the *Cassiopée* sailed for Tahiti, but during the two days that elapsed before my own departure for Samoa I was able to realize what an excellent impression the visit of the warship had made, and how necessary it was that, to make them love France, French people should from time to time come among the natives without any ulterior motive, not to exploit them or get money from them.

I weighed anchor during the afternoon of Saturday, June 12th, 1926, and sailed out of the marvellous harbour of Porapora. In the Teavanui channel an outrigger dug-out passed close to me; on board were two natives dressed in their simple *pareus*, their bronze bodies glistening in the sun. They were my friends Mana and Terai coming in from fishing. They shouted a sad farewell "Apae!"—and besought me to put about and return with them, but Porapora already belonged to the past, and all my thoughts were for the future, for Samoa and the Navigators' Islands of La Pérouse, which lay twelve hundred miles away to the east.

CHAPTER XII

THE NAVIGATORS' ISLANDS

In leaving Porapora lagoon I passed near a small sailing cutter coming in from the Maupiti Island and tacking against the south-east breeze. Happening to look a-weather I noticed some big black clouds scudding quickly across the sky. The squall was upon me in an instant, and the *Firecrest*, heeling over on the side, shot over the waves at her greatest speed, whilst the native cutter disappeared from my sight. The sea was breaking and I was continually shipping green seas.

My trysail was soon too much canvas to carry, and I was forced to take it in; but having lashed the helm, I left the *Firecrest* to run before the storm under the jib alone, and went down below, where the utmost disorder reigned. All my books were scattered on the floor and whatever was loose in the galley had got mixed up with the food and fruit that I had not had time to lash down.

The following day I passed quite near the low-lying dangerous atoll of Fenua Ura. Throughout the whole of my passage the trade-winds blew hard and the sea was high and covered with white horses; as the waves were continually breaking over the deck, I was obliged to keep the skylights closed tight.

The *Firecrest* was steering herself under three headsails, leaving behind her a fine straight wake as she made a regular eighty to one hundred miles every twenty-four hours. As the deck was practically always awash I remained below, only going above to take an observation when the sun showed itself through the clouds, or to keep an eye on chafed gear.

I could neither sit nor stand in the saloon below, and I had to lie down on the settee, half reclining on the side, for the *Firecrest*, like all other narrow cutters, sailed in a gale at a big list, with her rail in the water. So I whiled away the time reading some books I had received at Papeete from France, or playing over again, on a little folding chess-board, the games of a recent New York chess tournament. The hours passed very quickly in this manner, and as the fifteenth day was dawning I sighted Fau and Olesinga Islands, which belonged to American Samoa; but unfortunately it was impossible for me to put in there owing to the absence of any safe anchorage.

A little later I sighted the island of Tutuila, and after steering for nine hours on end at last arrived off Pangopangi harbour, just as the British sloop *Laburnum,* which had left Porapora ten days before me, steamed out. The officers on her bridge waved to me as I entered the harbour between Points Breaker and Distress.

The harbour consisted of a deep bay between high mountains, extending from north to south for over a mile. The heights were covered with trees and vegetation, from their topmost ridges down to tiny beaches of white coral, where little naked children were playing in the sun. Amongst the coco-nut trees, by the seashore, I was delighted to see picturesque Samoan dwellings, instead of the appalling hovels made of planks and corrugated iron which are the disgrace of Southern Polynesia.

The sea was breaking on the reefs, which ran the length of the shore, but the surface gave no sign of the presence of the dangerous Whale and Grampus Rocks. The bay bent inwards towards the west and soon I was able to see the steel aerial masts of the wireless station, and the buildings and piers of the U.S. naval base.

Alongside a wharf was the U.S. sloop-of-war *Ontario,* and close by were numerous officers and men, who beckoned me to come nearer; but I was afraid of the crowd. What I wanted was quietness and seclusion, and as usual I dropped anchor a long way off, at the other end of the harbour, near the village of Fanga Tonga.

Soon a motor-launch put off from the wharf and came alongside the *Firecrest.* Two naval officers stepped aboard and placed the resources of the naval base at my service in case I had any need of repairs.

Just as twilight was deepening an outrigger canoe shot out from the shore and made for the *Firecrest*. A boy was paddling, and two young native girls were singing. They had flowers in their hair and garlands about their waists, and their fresh clear voices carried far over the sea. I was delighted to hear the Samoan language, with its intonations which were new to me, as it possesses the "s" and "l" sounds unknown in Eastern Polynesia. Several words, however, were familiar, as well as the "ng" sound that I had learnt on the Mangareva Islands.

"Why have you come here?" they asked me.

"To see you."

"To see us? ah! *Talofa li!*"

It thrilled me with pleasure to recognize the salutation of the Marquesas Islands: the *Kaoha*, which is but the *Aloha* of the Hawaiian Islands, modified by the interchange of consonants that is so frequent in Polynesia. I knew at once that I was going to have a pleasant sojourn in the island of Tutuila, for a people who use the word "love" in their daily salutations could not fail to be agreeable and well worth staying among.

The day after my arrival I went ashore and was welcomed by the naval officers; they introduced me to Admiral Ryan, who asked me to dine with his family. In this manner I spent a very pleasant evening, ending up at the cinema, where we were entertained by some very lively Far West films.

The American Admiral told me that the officers of the *Laburnum* had complained from bad weather, and that, worn out by their rough passage, the crew had been unable to take part in the games and sports that the American Navy wanted to arrange in their honour, but had preferred to remain aboard to rest and sleep.

As for me, I had but little time to rest, as was usually the case when I put into port. The passage had been a very rough one and everything below had become damp and drenched with sea-water. I had to get everything dry; clean up and wash down, so that, with all the work upon deck, and the care of the rigging, I was continually occupied.

The *Firecrest* was moored to a big buoy at the far end of

Pangopango Bay, about one mile from the shore. The bay was on all sides surrounded by mountains, and was dominated by the Rain-Maker, whose summit was practically always enveloped in cloud. When I did leave my boat it was to play tennis, the first I had had since leaving Panama, or else to swim or take long walks. There were some very fine hard tennis courts at Pangopango, and a beautifully kept stretch of grass where baseball was played. The cleanliness and order everywhere bore witness to the able administration of the United States Navy.

The dwelling-houses of the Base were comfortable and well built, and the road running by the shore was cleared of all useless vegetation. Through the luxuriant undergrowth, and quite cut off from the white men's settlement, picturesque native villages were visible, with the curious Samoan huts that are at once so clean, hygienic and artistic. Stakes placed round a circular space covered with small pebbles held up a conically shaped roof of thatched palm leaves. There were no walls, only movable screens made of the branches of the same trees, which are placed in whichever direction the wind or rain may be coming from. This ensures a healthy and well-ventilated abode, and one admirably suited to the tropics.

The Tutuila natives wear either loin-cloths or *lavas-lavas*; they are a fine healthy race and the island is thickly populated. As a direct contrast to our French administration in Oceania, which does its best to educate the native according to European culture, the naval régime maintains a rigid barrier between whites and natives, obliges the latter to retain a large number of their old customs, which is certainly better for them. While upon my walks, I often stopped at these huts, where I was always offered "kava," the traditional native drink, made of ground-up *Piper Methisticum* root mixed in water.

American Independence Day, falling as it does on the Fourth of July, was celebrated a few days after my arrival, and I was glad to be able to watch the sport and dances organized for this occasion; the only two boats then in harbour, *Ontario* and *Firecrest*, had all their bunting flying. The morning began with whale-boat racing, and contests were run on the fine baseball field between *Fitas-fitas* and the United States sailors. *Fitas-fitas* are Samoans belonging to the native army and police force; they wear black loin-cloths with red edges and a red turban. Chosen as they are from amongst the biggest and strongest Samoans they are splendid, athletic fellows.

A very interesting item was a six-relay-race, over some 800 yards, which the natives just managed to carry off. The American sailors, stalwart fellows as they were, looked quite small beside the enormous *Fitas-fitas*, who, however, ran in a bad style, with their chests thrown backwards.

A swimming race over a two-hundred-yard course was won by a Hawaiian native. Indeed, the Samoans struck me as being much inferior to the natives of Honolulu in the crawl. During the afternoon, a baseball match was played between the Americans and a native team. The Samoans presented a very curious sight. They had adopted the peculiarities of their opponents, wore the same little caps and striped shirts, and amongst the onlookers one could hear "Attaboy" and "That's the guy!" shrieked in a naval nasal accent by some small native boys, just as though it was a match in New York.

At last the game came to an end, and the native dances, to which I had been looking forward with impatience, began. About sixty miles west of Tutuila is the island of Manua, where, far from the contact of white men, noble natives have carefully preserved the old traditions. The previous evening, therefore, the *Ontario* had brought across two hundred of these natives, and they now made their appearance. They were dressed with a mere loin-cloth of *siapo*, which is the bark of the paper mulberry, or of finely plaited matting. Under these we could catch glimpses of the curious Samoan tattooing, which is only done upon the middle of the body, and looks just like a pair of short knickers painted on the skin in a dark blue colour. Their bodies were anointed with coco-nut oil and glistened in the sunlight, whilst they had painted themselves with moustaches that made them appear very fierce.

Some of the dancers wore long blonde wigs of coco-nut

fibre, and in front of the whole procession two little old men performed all sorts of antics as they juggled with two long and heavy axes. The remainder, however, were fine fellows, tall and muscular, each carrying a wooden wand with which to beat time, while chanting in a strange and barbarous manner. In this way, the party crossed the entire field, and came before the grand stand, on one side of which stood the American Admiral, surrounded by his officers, while the dignitaries of the native government were on the other. Their whole bearing, martial air, and proudly poised heads were really admirable. They were truly worthy descendants of those grim warriors who had massacred some of La Pérouse's crew.

It was a primitive dance, with few gestures, and lasted a long time. During the entertainment, I wandered amongst the picturesque crowd of spectators, with their multi-coloured *lavas-lavas*. Their straight, short hair was very different from that of the inhabitants of Tahiti or the Marquesas Islands, and most of the men had it brushed straight back from the forehead. A great number had bleached their hair with a kind of lime, made of coral, which, if used continually, gives a particular shade of chestnut, so that in this manner at least half the natives had fair hair.

As soon as the fierce Manuans had left the field they were replaced by a troop of natives from the island of Olesinga, dressed in light coloured *lavas-lavas* and garlands of flowers. The new-comers took up their position on mats placed before the platform, and then commenced one of those extraordinary sitting dances, or *sivas-sivas*, peculiar to Samoa—not exactly a dance, indeed, but a kind of pantomime, accompanied with song. There was also a burlesque note when two young natives, whose bodies were whitened with flour, crawled round the field on all fours, continually capering and jumping in the air. They had long tails fixed behind, and their noses were flattened by a bandage, to make them represent monkeys. They jumped on the backs of two others, and remained there, making the most extraordinary grimaces, and cracking jokes which amused the crowd.

The whole, indeed, was yet another extraordinary spectacle to add to my memories; to my impressions of the perfect artistry of the old sacred dances of Mangareva, the voluptuousness of many of those performed in Tahiti, and the extraordinary acrobatic facility of the Poraporan dances, now came this strange sitting dance, which indicated, however, that Samoa had never known that high degree of artistic culture that Tahiti and Raiatea had attained in days of yore.

As I wished to fill my tanks before leaving, I left my anchorage at the far end of the harbour, and moored the *Firecrest* along the quay. As I had dreaded, a crowd of visitors immediately besieged me and from that moment I had no more peace. The Samoans acted as if the boat belonged to them, and jumped from the wharf on to the deck without even asking my permission; then they would inspect the *Firecrest* from bow to stern without taking the slightest notice of me.

I could not help comparing these people with the inhabitants of the Marquesas and Tahiti, who had never worried me in this manner. Here I had the impression of being amongst a totally different race, and in the end I was forced to forbid anyone to board the *Firecrest*, but the more inquisitive ones still continued to gather on the quay, however, watching my every movement, and I was obliged to shut my skylight to keep out prying eyes. It was not long before I regained my lonely mooring at the far end of the bay.

On July 23rd, after I had awaited the San Francisco boat, which brought me some charts and nautical instructions, I weighed anchor just as the trade-winds began to blow again after three days of absolute calm. As I was obliged to tack continually, I made but little headway against the contrary current. Lieutenant Hayes, of the U.S. Navy, came alongside in a motor-launch to wish me a pleasant journey, and take a few photographs, and he offered to tow me out of the harbour. I declined his offer, however, for entering and leaving ports, testing, as it does, one's seamanship to the full, forms one of the chief attractions of sailing. So, after having had to tack about for a long time, I managed to get out of the bay, and sail along the coast of Tutuila, which is formed of enormous blocks of basalt, falling perpendicularly into the sea.

I rounded Step Point, a very dangerous headland where far out from the shore the sea was breaking over some half-submerged basalt rocks. All at once a sharp gust of wind from the south-west blew my jib to shreds. While I was setting the second jib my position became more and more dangerous, for the drift and current were bringing me ever nearer to these dangerous breakers. I was therefore obliged to tack again in order to get back to windward, but soon the wind suddenly veered round and I was able to leave astern this dangerous cape, the westernmost point of Tutuila, which shelters the bay of Asau, ever memorable as the site of the massacre in which Count de Langle and Chevalier de Lemonon perished, together with several of La Pérouse's companions, in 1787.

Out of the shelter of land, the trade-winds were blowing hard, and throughout the night the *Firecrest* rolled in a very heavy sea. I was forced to sleep stretched out on the deck of the cabin, as it would have been quite impossible to stay in my bunk. It was then that an event occurred which showed me that the greatest perils at sea, and indeed elsewhere, often come from the most unexpected quarters. A particularly violent wave threw a heavy bronze lead-weighted lamp out of its gimbals; this crashed to the floor a few inches from my head. I should have probably been seriously wounded had it hit me.

Early the following day I was off Upolu Island, and was admiring its great fertility, and different appearance to the more easterly islands I had visited. The low mountains, sloping gradually to the sea, were green and well cultivated. This was the island which Dumont d'Urville, agreeing with La Pérouse, described as surpassing in beauty even Tahiti. While I sailed in the offing, I drew comparisons, but I had to disagree with Dumont d'Urville. Tahiti, with its deep valleys and high majestic mountains falling perpendicularly to the sea, appeared to me far more beautiful. I ranked my favourite islands in the following order. First and foremost, any atoll in the Tuamotu Group, such as Makemo, consisting of the minimum of land—sea all round—sea within—a veritable mariner's abode. Next Fatu-Hiva, the island of fantastic beauty; then the other Marquesas, Moorea, Porapora and Tutuila, with finally Tahiti, the most majestic of them all. But I must say I prefer the beauty of wild nature to that which is cultivated and artificial.

In the afternoon, having passed between the two projecting arms of the exterior reef, I dropped anchor in the roadstead of Apia, just off Matautu peninsula, famous in Samoan history. As soon as the Health and Port authorities had left the *Fire-crest*, numerous canoes came alongside. But the natives, alas, were far too inquisitive and anxious to know what they could get out of me during my stay. So I made up my mind to refuse all visitors.

Although I had never seen it before, the countryside here appeared very familiar, for I was able to recognize the places described by Robert Louis Stevenson in his "Letters from Vailima"—the peninsulas of Matautu and Mulinuu, the beach of Apia, and the wreck of the German Cruiser *Seeadler*, which was lost with four other battleships in the great cyclone of 1889. This place had been the scene of many legendary events in the war between King Malietoa and King Mataafa, when England, Germany and America were trying to gain control of the Samoan islands.

There, too, I saw Vailima, now the Government Residence, and Mount Vaea, which recalled the tomb of the illustrious author whose works had so often charmed away my long hours on watch. The town of Apia, which is inhabited entirely by whites and consists chiefly of shops and offices, possesses little interest to the traveller. By the seaside, however, there was a curious native market, where were sold cooked fish wrapped up in banana leaves, taro, crabs, and *palosami*, or young shoots of taro cooked in coco-nut milk, a dish very greatly esteemed at Samoa.

My stay was short and I was kept busy the whole time in mending the sails and trying to get in working order my photographic and cinematographic appliances, which I had not been able to keep from getting spoiled by the damp. The impossibility of making the skylights watertight and, above all, the bad ventilation below deck were the chief faults of the *Firecrest*. They are to be remedied on her successor, whose design I was continually improving in my mind from the experience gained on my cruise.

I was invited to lunch by the Bishop of Apia. His palace was on a hill about five miles from the town and I had a pleasant ride on horseback there, through fertile country, and past curious native villages, where the huts faced one another; the one used as a dwelling, the other to receive visitors. The mission station was a magnificent site overlooking the sea; unfortunately most of the palm trees had been destroyed by the rhinoceros beetle, which had ravaged large parts of the country.

During my stay I also watched a Rugby football match between two native teams from Samoa and Tonga. The ground was situated on a race-course, about a mile from the town, and was rather too narrow and short. The players were very picturesque, however; the Tongans had bare feet, but the local team, in which were several half-castes, wore either rubber shoes, or just socks and garters. The game was very quietly played, without any roughness, and ended in a sweeping victory for the visitors, who really had the making of good players. Under the New Zealand administration Rugby is gradually replacing a local game originally founded on cricket, and much in favour in the Islands. The matches between the village teams drew large crowds.

Those Samoans whom I met seemed to differ entirely from the Polynesians of the Eastern Pacific, who are less sophisticated and offer the passing stranger a large hospitality. I wanted to know if this was due to contact with the whites, and I should have enjoyed living for a while among the natives of some unfrequented village. That is why I decided to leave Upolu and sail for Savaii Island, which had few sheltered harbours and was little frequented by ships. In the village of Safune, on the northern coast of the island, the film "Moana of the South Seas" had been shot, and I was not keen to go there. One place tempted me much and that was Asau, with its long, shallow and narrow entrance which rendered access to the place very difficult. But once the channel had been cleared there was protection afforded from every wind, and in the lagoon I should have a wonderful opportunity for carrying out various urgent repairs in the *Firecrest's* rigging. Moreover, there were only two small villages, and I should not have been disturbed in my work.

CHAPTER XIII

A VERY UNLUCKY PASSAGE

As I sailed out of Apia harbour I passed a great cargo boat of the Clan Line, the crew of which cheered me loudly. I noticed then that it was Friday, August 13th, but this did not worry me at all, for I am not in the least superstitious by nature. Little, however, did I anticipate the trouble that lay before me. My voyage, indeed, seemed to start under the most favourable auspices. A smart breeze from the east took me by daylight the next morning to the offing of Savaii, a volcanic coast, inhospitable and forbidding to look at. The stern mountain heights, rising sheer from the water's edge, were scored by great streams of lava and strewn with enormous boulders of basalt, relics of the last eruption, in 1906.

The trade-wind freshened and blew in violent squalls, but I was close to the harbour which, as I thought, I could easily put in to. Breakers foamed on the coral reef that protects the harbour of Asau, and only the absence of surf showed the way in to smooth water. As I entered this passage the wind suddenly shifted, and the boom swept across so violently that the mainsheet broke.

The passage through the reef was little more than a hundred yards in width, and farther in, narrowed to considerably less than this. To attempt to go in was to court disaster, so without a second's hesitation I tacked and made my way out of the passage, nearly grazing the dangerous coral as I went.

The mainsail was flapping against the shrouds as I was drifting and the boom kept burying itself in the sea. Having half lowered the mainsail, I got out to the end of the boom to bend on a new sheet, which was a risky enough thing to do considering the conditions in which I had to work. At last I managed to haul in the boom above the deck, and then it was I discovered that the big block of the mainsheet was broken.

So I was forced to dive down into my narrow sail-locker and rake out a double block from among the mass of gear, sails and spares of all sorts. The violent tossing of the *Firecrest* made the work more difficult.

When I had bent on the new sheet I set up the mainsail again, but by this time the boat had drifted far under the lee of Asau, and I had to beat up again in order to make the harbour. Scarcely had I begun to get under way when the jib and fore-staysail sheets parted.

It was now too late to think of making the harbour before darkness fell; I should have had to spend the whole night tacking to weather Asau before the morning.

The Wallis Islands were only two hundred and fifty miles to leeward, which meant less than three days' sail before a good fair wind. As luck seemed against me, I decided it was better to change my plans rather than lose twelve hours of a favourable breeze. In the sheltered waters of the Wallis Islands I should find ample leisure to repair and refit as much as was necessary. So without further ado I changed my course, as darkness set in, and ran before it steering for the west. Strange to say, six hours later the wind dropped to a very slight breeze, but I had already gone too far to turn back. However, Asau harbour had enchanted me.

I had had time to notice natives fishing in a dug-out near the coral reef, and the bay, calm as a lake, surrounded by high basalt mountains, whose dreary blackness contrasted sharply with the vivid green of the coco-nut trees. Often was I to dream of this port I did not reach and picture to myself an enchanted stay which soon became as real to me as many uneventful spells ashore in the islands when I was living in a perpetual dream, ignoring reality.

After four days' sailing before a light breeze the Isle of Uvea, one of the Wallis Islands, hove in sight just before sunset, some dozen miles away to the north-west. According to the charts there should be a gentle current to the south-west; so lowering all sails I left the boat to drift throughout the night. However, as the wind was constantly blowing fresher I was continually up and down during the hours of darkness, though it was so pitchy black that I could see nothing.

In the first dim light of the dawn, what was my stupefaction to find that the outer reef of Uvea was only a few cable lengths distant! Contrary to all indications, the current had borne me steadily northwards during the night! I set the mainsail up as quickly as I could, but by that time I was less than a cable's length from the reef, and was being driven hard on to it, while the swell added to my difficulties. A narrow-built and deep cutter like the *Firecrest* behaves well in a rough sea, and with every tack I was making headway against wind and current, when glancing aloft, I noticed a great rent in the topmost corner of my mainsail—a rent that every moment grew larger and threatened to split the canvas in two before many minutes were passed. I could not lower the sail, for to do so meant being driven on to the reef. I had to go on trying to gain enough and be far enough to attend to the repairs. And so, for close on half an hour, I tacked out to sea, handling the helm with the most delicate touch to keep the wind from ripping up the canvas. When, at last, I saw that the catastrophe was imminent, I let go the sail with a run, and snatched up my needle and sail-twine to patch it up again.

The repair was made in record time, despite the pounding of the sea against my boat, and the mainsail was hoisted again. All the same, when I got under way again I found I had lost all the wind which I had gained with such labour and trouble and was close on the reef once more. Hard by the very edge of the reef I could see a little green islet, on the white shore of which were several natives watching my strange manœuvres with astonishment.

Having made innumerable tacks, in a sea that was every moment getting rougher, by two o'clock in the afternoon I was off the south-eastern entrance, or Honikolu passage, which is considered very difficult to negotiate on account of the strength of the current. A long time ago the French man-of-war *Lermite* had been wrecked there, and her funnels, still rising from the water, indicate the entrance of the passage and warn navigators of the danger they run. My pilot books advised entering at slack water of low tide; but I preferred to get in on the rising flood, and it was thus that I made the attempt. Visibility could hardly have been worse, for a fine rain had begun to fall, and I was quite unable to make out the high wall which serves as a landmark on one of the heights of Uvea. Aided by the current I sailed through the passage easily, but as I was tacking at two hundred yards from a beacon, I ran aground on a spur of coral not marked on the chart, which I had been unable to see owing to the driving rain. There I stuck. Hurriedly I carried out a small grapnel in my Berthon dinghy and tried to warp the *Firecrest* afloat, but just as she was beginning to shift the hawser broke. Luckily the rising tide floated her and a moment later I could drop my anchor in the roadstead opposite the village of Mua. A dug-out, manned by three natives, put off from the shore and ran alongside, one of the men making me understand by signs that he was the local pilot.

I did not like the anchorage at all; it was too far from the shore, the bottom was hard rock, and the constant pounding of the boat was putting a great strain on the cable. So I determined to get under way again and sail for Matautu, the capital of the island, which lay some six miles farther north up the lagoon. I hoisted the sails once more, raised the anchor until the stock was up to the bob-stay of the bowsprit and then hurried aft. I had been rather surprised at the ease with which the anchor had come up. I was at the tiller, steering clear of the numerous sunken reefs, with a native on the look-out forward, when a thought suddenly struck me and I hurried forward to get the anchor clear of the water. My worst fears were realized, it had snapped at the middle of the shank, and only the top half of it was dangling from the cable. It was unbelievable! I had used this anchor all the way from Panama, and at the point of breakage the metal was more than five centimetres thick. At Nice the *Firecrest* had been hoisted on dry land by a crane with a shackle of a smaller diameter. However, after such a series of misadventures as had befallen me I was not so stupefied with surprise as I might have been.

I soon found myself off the jetty at Matautu, but there was not, as I had hoped, any boat at anchor, nor moorings for me to tie up to. The situation was, indeed, very awkward. I was continually obliged to tack, in order to avoid the numerous reefs, but just as I had come to the decision to leave the lagoon, get out into the open sea and make for the Fiji Islands, a little motor-boat passed near me on its way back from fishing. As I tacked close to her I was able to shout across and explain, to the owner on board, my situation and he very kindly lent me an anchor. So at long last I was able to go ashore, though it was with an uneasy mind. The anchorage was hardly sheltered at all from the trade-wind which blew very freshly, the bottom was hard and my cable had too great a strain on it. I ought really to have been moored with two anchors but I had already lost the only two I had on board, and there was none other to be found in the whole island. At ten o'clock in the evening I came back on board again, after having dined with the doctor governor. The wind was still blowing half a gale; there was a heavy swell on the lagoon and the bowsprit of the *Firecrest* was continually plunging into the waves.

I was lying half asleep, ready to spring on deck and pay out a little more cable if the anchor dragged, when I was roused by the noise of the cable dragging against the bottom. The next moment, before I could lift a hand, the *Firecrest* had struck against the reef. I had only to haul in a few feet of chain to find that it was broken. The wind had veered to the south and was blowing a gale; the *Firecrest* was heeled over on the side and at every wave she rose and dropped on the coral with an ugly cracking noise. The situation was desperate. In the harbour not a boat; not an anchor I could carry out to kedge myself off. Besides, with such a wind blowing it would have taken a steamer to have towed the boat clear.

There was still a little flood but I could only think of how, when it ebbed, the *Firecrest* would be broken to pieces. Standing on the deck, drenched by the waves, there was nothing I could do but stand helplessly by and witness the dying agony of my faithful companion. I had been an hour on the reef when suddenly my boat heeled right over on to one side, the deck became almost vertical and the water began to pour in at the skylight. I had already started swimming towards the shore when, to my utter amazement, I perceived that the *Firecrest* was following me; in fact she reached the beach almost at the same time as I did myself and drove herself hard into the sand at the very limit of the highwater mark.

I discovered that very little water had entered her. The night was pitch black and it was half-past one in the morning. I made my way sadly up to the residence convinced that the *Firecrest* had ended both her career and my cruise.

By daybreak the sea had retired, leaving the boat high and dry. I then saw that her lead keel was missing and that the ten bronze bolts which had kept it in position had broken near the wooden keel. The constant beating against the reef had evidently torn off the metal and, freed from the enormous weight of four tons of lead, the weight of the rigging had heeled the *Firecrest* over on her side, and lightened, and drawing but very little water in this position, she had simply floated ashore.

Some superstitious people would not fail to attribute all the troubles which had overtaken me to the date of my departure, and one of my English friends, an author, and himself a sailor, will not hesitate to tell me that I tempted Providence by doing so. But if it had to be done again I would set out without the least apprehension. Even at the time of my departure, one o'clock—or thirteen o'clock—on Friday, the 13th, at Apia, at that same instant it was Saturday the 14th in Paris, as well as in the Wallis Islands and in Australia. When I turn over in my mind everything that happened I smile philosophically and tell myself that it might have been worse. The main-sheet might have broken farther in at the passage of Asau, in which case I should have been dashed on the reef; if the keel had not been torn off, in all probability the *Firecrest* would have been smashed to pieces on the coral. I know perfectly well that certain parts of the rigging might have been in a better state, but in the course of my long voyage there had been no chance of obtaining proper spares, and at Samoa I had not found the gear I had hoped for. Again, my cable was nearly new; it might, it is true, have been stouter. "Too strong never parted," is an adage of our French sailors, but I had constantly to drop anchor in depths of twenty fathoms and more, and a heavier chain would have been exceedingly difficult to veer single-handed without a windlass or a capstan.

CHAPTER XIV

THE *FIRECREST* AFLOAT AGAIN

SLIGHT as was the damage suffered by the *Firecrest* the difficulties I had to overcome before it would be possible to make her float again seemed wellnigh insurmountable. To search for the four-ton lead keel, drag it up to the beach near the *Firecrest,* repair the broken bolts, some of which were more than a yard in length, and, if necessary, make new ones, put the keel in place and then launch a vessel drawing nearly six feet of water over a coral floor of a little over four feet deep, all these seemed to me an accumulation of insoluble problems. In the island itself there was no help to be got. There was not even a blacksmith. Among a population of 5,000 natives, of whose language I knew very little, the only artisans were two Chinese, who did a little of every trade but were not good shipwrights. However, before worrying about the future the immediate need was to right the *Firecrest,* as lying on her side strained her very seriously.

First of all I cleared her of part of the rigging. After this I emptied most of the ballast and took away all my personal belongings, some of which were carried to the Residence, and the rest to the house of the French trader in Matautu.

The next day sixty natives were placed at my disposal by the King, at the request of the Resident. With the help of J. S. Brial, the trader, who served as interpreter and very kindly gave me every assistance he could, the *Firecrest* was righted by means of tackle seized to the mast and then firmly shored up. As for the lead keel, it was found high and dry on the reef at low tide. I had it lashed with crossbeams and steel cables to a lighter, normally used for loading copra, which at high tide lifted the heavy piece of lead and brought it up near the *Firecrest.*

Now I was able to live on board my boat again. She was

safe enough, but I was not in much better plight than before. The problem of getting her afloat seemed harder than ever, and before anything else could be done it was necessary to make new bolts.

I knew only too well that months might elapse before any ship put in. Had there been in the whole island the very flimsiest sailing canoe, seaworthy enough to put out in, I should not have hesitated to borrow it in order to make a trip to the Fiji Islands, where I could get new bolts forged. But in the whole lagoon there were nothing but flimsy dug-outs only suitable for navigation within the lagoon and alas, none of those wonderful canoes of old in which the ancestors of the natives sailed frequently to the Tonga Islands. The most famous of those craft had been the *Lomipeau*—in English "Rider of the waves"—which had been employed to carry the heavy building stones used for the tombs of the Kings of Tonga.

Nor could I hope to ballast the *Firecrest* with sand and cement in order to make the Fiji Islands. My boat was too narrow and had a too small stability of form and it was impossible to do what would have been easy and safe on a beamier and shallower craft. So there was nothing to be done but to wait and hope, consoling myself for my forced delay by enjoying the charms of an island whose isolation had made it highly interesting.

The Wallis Islands were discovered in 1767 by the English ship *Dolphin*, and consist of the Isle of Uvea, rising some 400 feet from the sea, and several other small islands in an immense lagoon enclosed by a coral reef. Uvea contains some 5,000 inhabitants, belonging to the Tonga branch of the Polynesian race. This group has never reached the high degree of civilization attained by the Tahitian and Hawaiian branches of the race, yet it possesses certain exceedingly interesting characteristics.

Wallis Island, since 1887, has been a French Protectorate. His Majesty Lavelua, King of the Wallis Islands, was an old man of sixty, whose appearance and bearing was not without dignity. In the shadow of the cathedral of Matautu stands the royal palace, a massive building of coloured bricks, which constitutes, in itself, a lasting memorial to the bad taste of the white men who built it. But the king preferred to live with his family in a native hut behind this house, and there I found him, some days after my arrival, when I went to pay him a visit, accompanied by the French Resident.

Built in an elliptic form with a roof of coco-palm leaves interlaced and enclosed on all sides, this hut had only two narrow entrances. Truth to tell, the native dwellings of Wallis are less clean and worse ventilated than those of Samoa, and less comfortable than the old Marquesans' huts, nevertheless they form an airy shelter, far superior to what is afforded by European houses in the tropics. There, seated on a pile of native mats, I tried to make the king understand the motives, or rather the absence of motives, for my voyage, at the same time showing him photographs of the different places I had put in at.

The king seemed to rule only in name, for all his acts were controlled by a council of ministers, chosen from the royal family by the Marist Mission, and he was continually held fast between this preponderating influence and that of the French Resident. However, he seemed to enjoy the entire respect of his subjects. This respect showed itself in certain traditional customs, one of the most curious of which was that of sitting on the ground when he was passing.

One fine morning, having been duly warned of the coming honour, I made my way to the royal palace, where I found the "Pules"—or chiefs of the different districts—assembled under the presidence of the king. In front of the veranda were heaps of kava roots, piles of yams and taros, a pig, and numbers of fowls, as well as an assortment of beautiful native mats. Kava, the traditional drink of Western Polynesia, which I had learned to enjoy at Samoa, was drunk with appropriate rites from handsome cups of coco-nut shells. The "Matapule"—or master of ceremonies—announced the guests in order of precedence. The first kava or kava of honour was offered to me, whereupon the first minister began a speech,

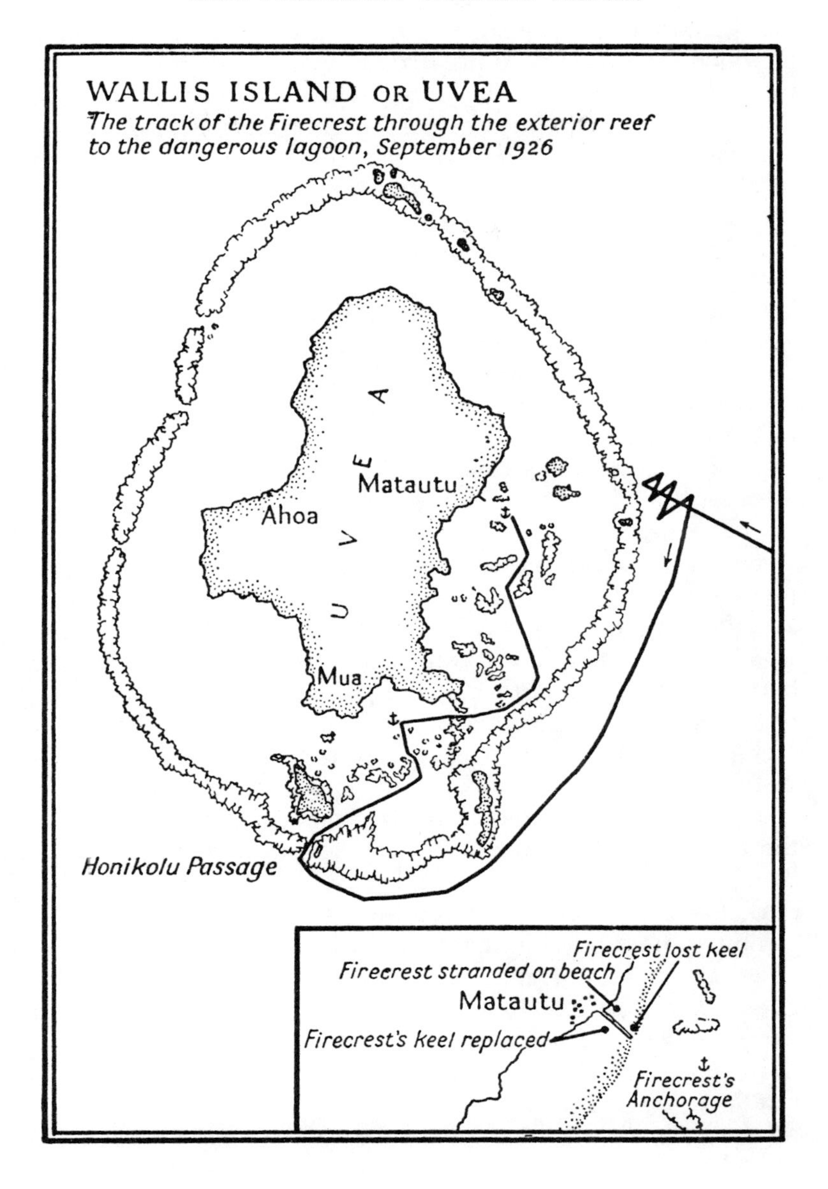
WALLIS ISLAND OR UVEA
The track of the Firecrest through the exterior reef to the dangerous lagoon, September 1926
UVEA
Mataútu
Ahoa
Mua
Honikolu Passage
Firecrest lost keel
Firecrest stranded on beach
Mataútu
Firecrest's keel replaced
Firecrest's Anchorage

and with much Polynesian eloquence delivered a long discourse of which the sense was translated to me by an Englishman who lived the country. "The young Chief had come," he said, "all alone, on a little boat across the seas. Far from his country and his plantations of yams, and coco-nut trees, he had come to the Wallis Islands alone, without servants to minister to his wants. The chiefs of the Islands of Uvea offered, in consequence, to their friend, the young chieftain of France, kava roots that he might entertain convivially, and all the provisions heaped up before the palace, in order that he might live worthily according to his rank while he stayed in the country." Such was the traditional display of Polynesian hospitality towards the passing stranger. All this he declaimed with emphasis in the harmonious Uvean language. I thanked him much for the presents, which, as a matter of fact, cumbered me up somewhat; so that I had to give the animals out to board with different natives.

The king, to whom I made the gift of a Winchester rifle, had already been to visit me on board. In the evening his wife and daughter came to pay a call, bringing with them the mats which the assembly had given me. The king's wife wore her hair short and fuzzy; that of the princess was long and hung down over her shoulders. All kinds of hair-dressing are to be met at Uvea, for little girls are shaven almost bare, young unmarried girls wear their hair very long, and married women keep it short and stiff. Following a usage almost universal in the Pacific, the hair was dyed with lime extracted from coral. The princess was very pretty and graceful, and although rather dark, had a type of face almost European. She and her mother exhibited their astonishment and admiration by all sorts of naïve exclamations, and seeing some Swedish matches lying about, thrust several of them into the pierced lobes of their ears, and wore them as ear ornaments.

By degrees I made the acquaintance of all the natives. On Sundays, gathering together the young people of the countryside on the "malae"—a large square that lies between the church and the shore—I tried to initiate them into the mysteries of football. But the ground was rough and littered with coral boulders. I was quite unable to stop my young friends from seizing the ball in their hands, and if I had had an oval one I would have taught them Rugby, for which they seemed to have a greater leaning. The favourite game of the island, as of Samoa, was a cross between cricket and baseball, and teams from neighbouring villages fought for honours with stern rivalry. The balls employed were wooden, and often caused really severe injuries to heads that chanced to get in their way.

Of an evening I often made my way to a large house situated behind the church, and known as the College, where a number of young men lived. As a matter of fact, it was nothing but a sort of bachelors' club, where the missionaries, who had separated the adolescent lads from their families, were keeping them together to make them work about the mission. In the same way the young unmarried girls of the village lived in a great house nearby under the wardenship of three French Sisters of Mercy, the only nuns in the island, and models of disinterestedness and devotion.

In this men's house or College, I used to lie on a pile of mats, sip kava, and watch the old-time dances my young friends loved to perform. Curious and savage they were, punctuated by raucous cries, yet more artistic and graceful than the dances of Eastern Polynesia. The movements were performed to wild music beaten on a drum made of rolled mats, which young children struck with sticks, accompanying the dull, heavy sound with weird songs.

I felt almost at home there, treated by all with care and affection. Fakate, chief of the district of Aoa, on the opposite side of the island, also took me under his protection. He was a magnificent old fellow, with a splendid torso and the profile of a Red Indian. In his company I paid a visit on horseback to the mysterious heart of the island, reached by way of narrow paths threading through a luxuriant and wild vegetation. A lake occupied the ancient crater of a volcano—an immense bowl, with steep sides to a depth of something like fifty yards, and the home of innumerable wild pigeons.

This expedition was followed by a great feast at the chieftain's hut, with pigs roasted in the ground, and various Polynesian dishes skillfully prepared. In the evening I made my way slowly back to my boat, followed by a string of porters laden with mats, native cloths and food—presents that I had been obliged to accept as marks of affection and good will on the part of a people whom I grew to like the more the better I knew them.

At last, one day a trail of smoke appeared above the reef of coral that stretched across the horizon, and soon afterwards a steamer appeared, threading her way along the winding channel that led across the lagoon. It was not the English boat that had been expected, but an old French tramp, the *Pervenche,* that for the first time had come over from Noumea, more than a thousand miles away, with the intention of linking up Wallis Island to our great possessions in Western Oceania.

Two Frenchmen, representing a syndicate of business houses in Noumea, informed me that they could be of very slight assistance. The wireless was scarcely in working order. But after some ineffectual endeavours we were at last able to get into touch with the station at Apia, and sent a radio to my friend Pierre Albarran, in Paris, informing him of my accident, and of the practical impossibility of my ever getting the *Firecrest* afloat unless the *Cassiopée,* our sloop-of-war in the Pacific, should call in at Wallis Island. As I was by no means sure that my radio message had been correctly transmitted, I gave a duplicate to the captain of the *Pervenche,* asking him to dispatch it from Noumea.

The *Pervenche* was a decrepit steamer, with plates fairly eaten through with rust. She had been knocked about badly during the passage from Noumea and leaked like a sieve. She carried lading for the trading station of Matautu, and had on board these two Frenchmen who had come to study the possibility of linking up Wallis to Noumea, and wresting the trade of the island, especially that in copra, from the English firm who periodically sent over from the Fiji Islands. They tried, too, though with very little success, to persuade some of the natives to go and work for them in New Caledonia.

The *Pervenche* had been gone eight days, and I had already spent six weeks on the island, when a bigger steamer made its appearance in the lagoon. She turned out to be one of the Burns, Philps and Company's boats, that run between the island and Suva. There was a forge on board, and several bars of iron, and Captain Donovan very kindly put his chief engineer at my disposal. The Resident let me have an old bronze propeller-shaft, and with two of my old keel bolts I managed to have made for me on board the steamer, four bronze and two iron bolts during the steamer's short stay. She had, moreover, brought an answer to my radio from the captain of the *Cassiopée*—an answer that left me with little hope of assistance.

So I made up my mind to try the impossible and float the *Firecrest* myself, unaided. Once the bolts had been made I was faced with the enormous difficulty of fastening on the keel. I had to have it carried by lighters, as before, to a part of the reef sheltered by the jetty; then I had to float the *Firecrest* on a high tide one calm day, bring her near the keel, accompanying her by swimming by her side. At low water she was laid on her side across the ends of some thick coco-nut trunks, along which we hoped to be able to slide the keel and thus get it into position. To carry out this task I had to employ some fifty natives, and I found myself obliged to engage the services of the two Chinese to act as interpreters. They responded with the best will in the world, but unhappily their truly Oriental pride forbade them to take any advice, and this prevented my directing the operations effectually.

It was exceedingly difficult to bring the holes in the lead keel opposite those in the wooden one to which it had to be attached. We could not hope to succeed in this save by means of heavy trunks, and we were only able to work at low tide, before the rising water floated the *Firecrest*. The first attempt failed, and ended in our having to shift the boat—and the keel as well—to another site. Eventually the third attempt proved successful and we were able to pass the bolts through the lead and the wooden keels. But I was not at the end of my woes. Some of the new bolts were thicker than the old ones, and the corresponding holes in the wooden keel had to be enlarged. Contrary to my orders, this was done with an extraordinary tool of Chinese device and make; and the result was that when the bolts were in place and the tide began to rise, the water oozed in through the enlarged holes in the wooden keel and the keelson and started to flood the hold. The pump had to be constantly going to keep the *Firecrest* afloat. Under such conditions it was useless to think of starting, so there was nothing to do but to shore the boat up again, which was a tough job with its increased weight now that the lead keel was attached, and some eighty men had to be employed to carry out the operation. Even the king himself came and lent a hand by heaving on the fall of a tackle attached to the mast.

By this time I was reduced to a state of utter indecision and embarrassment. The simplest solution of the difficulty would have been to remove the lead keel and plug the holes in the wooden one before inserting the bolts. But I could not make up my mind to set about this; to get the keel in place was a task of so great difficulty, and would take some days, necessitating the help of sixty hands or more, and I disliked intensely to have to ask for such help from the natives, who were already overburdened with all sorts of forced jobs they were obliged to do for the government, the chiefs and the mission. Nor was I able to reckon on the assistance of the Chinese, for the leaks were due to their own wilfulness in doing something I had disapproved, and they were a little disappointed at their failure.

I was, however, able to rely implicitly on the absolutely friendly and voluntary help of my young friends from the College of Matautu, and after a week of rest I determined to take out and refit, one by one, the bolts of the keel, stuffing the enlarged holes with tarred oakum, when one morning I had the pleasant surprise of sighting the black smoke of a French man-of-war approaching the harbour. At once I was filled with joy, for now I was certain of being able to continue my cruise. She was the *Cassiopée*, our sloop-of-war in the South Seas, whose arrival I had not dared to hope for. She steamed slowly across the lagoon and presently dropped her anchors before Matautu.

The anchor was scarcely in the water before her launch was lowered and came racing alongside the wharf. An officer landed and came up to me; he was the second in command, whom I had already met in Porapora. He informed me that the *Cassiopée* had been dispatched by order of the Minister of Marine, and was entirely at my disposal to carry out whatever had to be done, though no time must be lost about it, as she was already overdue at the New Hebrides; so the *Firecrest* would have to be refloated with the minimum of delay. I went on board at once to pay my respects to Commander Decoux, with whom I discussed what had to be done. He was vastly surprised to learn that the lead keel of the boat was already in place. The *Cassiopée* had brought some bronze bolts of a larger diameter which would have to be turned to the right size, a delicate job at the best of times. Luckily she had aboard her some excellent engineer artificers who performed this task in record time.

Once again the *Firecrest* was laid on her side, and one by one the bolts fashioned on the *Pervenche* were drawn out and replaced by new ones. When they came out it was found that the bronze nuts we had fitted to them had already corroded the iron bolts. If I had started in this condition, without having encountered the *Cassiopée*, it is more than likely that the keel would have dropped off in mid-ocean, in which case the *Firecrest* would almost certainly have capsized and my only hope of salvation would have lain in cutting free the mast and making some sort of raft to carry me to the Fiji Islands.

There was some difficulty in fitting in the new bolts, for the low water gave us but little time to get at the work. We had to drive in the bolts with a heavy hammer under water, and the slightest blow to one side would have snapped the bronze rods. However, the utmost good will on the part of the crew overcame all difficulties. The captain and his officers themselves worked at the job, sometimes up to their waists in water, often drenched by the heavy tropical seas, and always with an enthusiasm that I greatly appreciated.

I have already mentioned the fact that I was on the best of terms with the young men of Matautu. I had often spoken to them about France and about the real Frenchmen, who were very different from those who are usually met with in the colonies, whose ideal is to get rich at the expense of the natives. I still had much of the food that had been pressed upon me by the native chiefs, so I decided to give a native dinner to the officers of the man-of-war. My young friends hailed the idea with delight and were pleased to make the necessary arrangements for the feast. It turned out a very successful party. The commander and all his officers were present, and the natives had surpassed themselves in the preparation of the repast—sucking pigs deliciously baked underground on red-hot stones amongst taros and yams, and fish cooked in the milk of the coco-nut. There were plates of every kind of native dish, even to sweets and dessert, with all sorts of lovely names, such as "luloi," "peke-peke." There were young tops of taro, superior to the finest spinach, bananas cooked in coco-nut milk, and cakes made from breadfruit and banana paste.

Then some curious Uvean dances were performed. The dancers were the oldest of the young men, carefully anointed with red ochre, and adorned with collars of flowers and garlands of leaves. They gave us a splendid exhibition of their skill, performing all sorts of wild and savage movements full of gaiety and life. As I reclined on mats my eyes wandered from the officers in uniform to the natives, and I felt myself honoured indeed, in thus enjoying the confidence and friendship of the natives who were so pleased to entertain the young chiefs of the warship, my friends. It gave me inexpressible pleasure to be with countrymen of mine who were able, like myself, to appreciate the generosity and kindliness of the Uvean race.

When the dancing came to an end, I had yet another proof of the delicacy of mind of my friends. "Listen," said Amosio, who was one of the royal family and the chief of the young men : "We have not used the food the chiefs gave you for this feast, for we wanted you to keep it for yourself, and we wished to offer everything ourselves that was necessary to entertain your friends."

The repairs of the *Firecrest* advanced apace. The night of the third day, in pitchy darkness and amid a gale of wind, accompanied by drenching tropical rain, the last bolt was fastened in its place, and at earliest daylight the next morning we launched the *Firecrest*. I had already solved the problem of how to get her across the shallow coral to deeper water. Ten sailors at the masthead counterbalanced the weight of the keel and heeled the boat down on her side, the sea nearly entering through the skylights, so that she drew only a little over three feet of water. She thus floated easily over the reef and out into the deep sea, where we let her right herself.

The inside ballast was hurriedly shipped aboard, and soon afterwards the *Cassiopée* put out to sea, leaving me an unfading memory of the good will with which the French Navy had come to my help.

Before I could sail, however, I had to get all my rigging shipshape, and another three weeks passed before I was able to heave the anchor. During this time I became more than ever intimate with the natives. The arrival of the *Cassiopée* had again heightened my prestige, and numerous fêtes were organized in my honour in every village of the island. Unhappily, I have no space to describe them in this book, which is primarily dedicated to the story of my voyages, but my reception in the Wallis Island far surpassed any that I had ever received in any other port. It was there that the natives did me the supreme honour of begging me to become their chief and take up my residence amongst them. I would not accept, but this offer bound me to the island by spiritual ties, and determined me to use whatever influence the success of my voyage might give me to further the just cause of the natives and help them in their difficulties.

I will not attempt to describe the farewell scenes that accompanied my departure, nor my sadness at leaving a country to which I had become so truly attached. But I had to go, for the sea was calling me again, and I could not resist her appeal.

CHAPTER XV

HOMEWARD BOUND

On Thursday, December 9th, after a stay of four months at Wallis Island, I weighed anchor, and with a long beat against a southerly wind, sailed across the lagoon and cleared the narrow channel on the ebb tide. Outside the reef there was a heavy swell and the trade-wind was from the east. I was constantly shipping seas. Borne on a slow current and sailing herself under a trysail and three jibs, the *Firecrest* kept as steady a course as if she had been a steamer, though there was no one at the helm. By December 13th I had sailed more than 300 miles, and according to my observations I was somewhere in the vicinity of the numberless little islands that form the north-eastern barrier of the Fiji group. The chart was showing an inextricable medley of islands and dangerous coral reefs. To the north lay the Ringgold Islands, to the south the Exploring Islands; between these two groups was the North-Eastern or Nanuku passage, only fifteen miles across at its greatest width and simply marked by a small lighthouse on the atoll of Wailangilala. It was raining, and misty weather rendered visibility very poor. In spite of absolute confidence in my lines of position, I was feeling a little apprehensive. The slightest error would certainly put me on the dangerous reef of Nanuku. It was there that Jack London nearly lost the *Snark*, owing to a mistake on the part of his captain; there, too, the wealthy Lord Pembroke, who, like myself, was on a pleasure cruise, had piled up his sumptuous yacht *Albatross*.

At last, in a temporary clearing of the mist, I saw the flash of the lighthouse abaft the beam on the port side. I was on the right course and could now lash down the tiller. And thus, under her three jibs alone, heading south-south-east, and without helmsman, as the night wore on, the *Firecrest* left behind the isles of Naitamba and Yatata. The Sea of Koro, in which

I was next sailing, was calmer than the open ocean, for innumerable coral islands and reefs broke the heavy Pacific swell.

The day following Sunday the 12th was, so far as I was concerned, Tuesday the 14th, as at ten o'clock I crossed the Greenwich antimeridian and skipped a day in the calendar, in order to adjust myself to Fiji time, which goes on the Eastern dates.

The Koro Sea was dotted with pretty islands which I should have dearly liked to visit; but I was compelled to make Suva, the capital of the group, for after having been stranded so long in Wallis Island the *Firecrest* needed a thorough overhauling.

On December 15th Viti Levu hove into sight through the mist, and soon afterwards I was threading my way along the narrow channel of Suva, between two coral reefs upon which the sea was breaking with ominous thunder. I was tacking about within the lagoon in a feeble breeze and against the current when the harbour-master came out to meet me in his launch and towed me to a mooring berth, where I dropped my anchor as night was falling.

I was now lying in a profound calm in a wonderful harbour surrounded by high mountains. For five days the *Firecrest* had been battered by the sea, her decks awash with spray, but it had been the fastest passage in my whole voyage.

The day after my arrival I set to work and went to the Government yard to discuss the matter of hauling my ship ashore. It was absolutely necessary that the last bolt should be put in place which secured the leaden keel exactly under the heel of the mast; in addition to this, some of the copper sheathing needed replacing. But beyond everything else it was the inside of the boat that required attention. When the *Firecrest* had been lying on the reef a certain amount of salt water had got in between the outer walls and the inner bulkhead, and the whole boat was reeking with damp. This had to be dried and the woodwork scraped and painted. I began proceedings by emptying out all the ballast, consisting chiefly of rusty pieces of cast-iron, which was making the bilge foul and damp. This led to the discovery of a rat which had come on board at

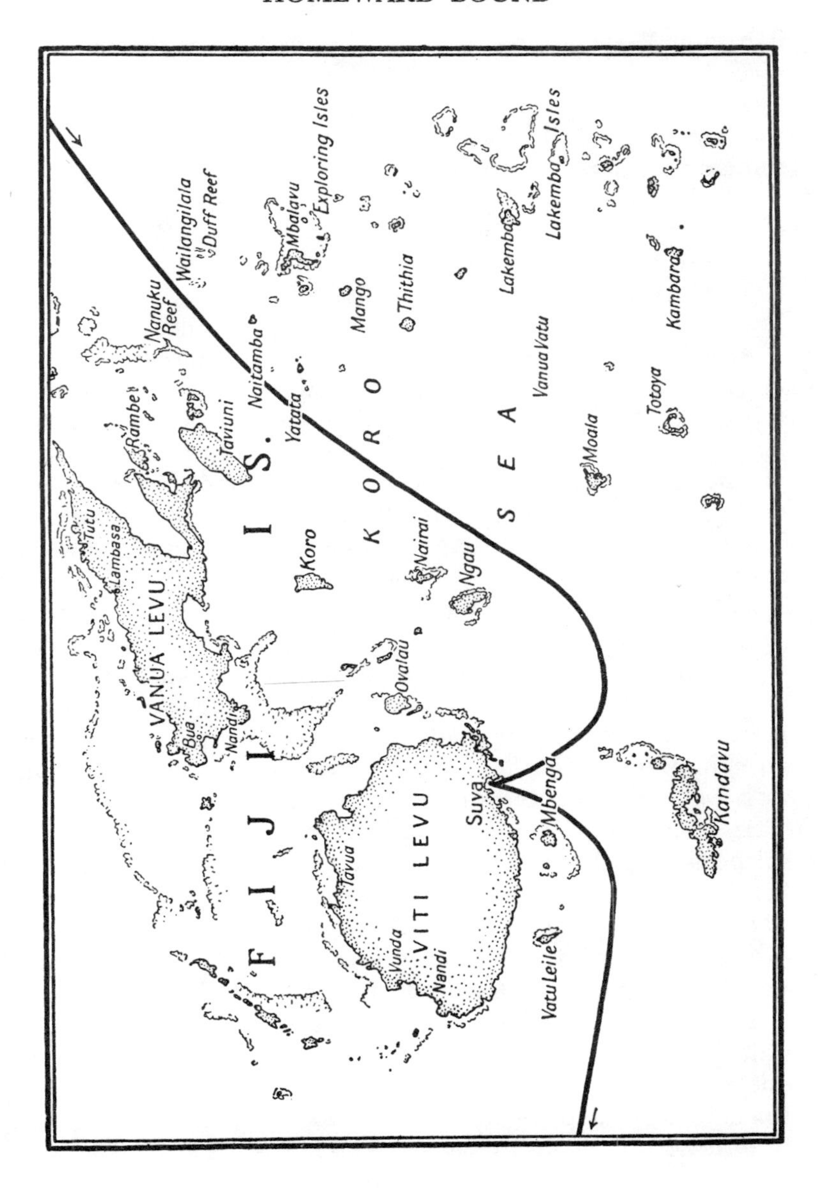
FIJI IS.
KORO SEA
VANUA LEVU
VITI LEVU
Tutu
Lambasa
Bua
Nandi
Rambe
Taviuni
Nanuku Reef
Wailangilala
Duff Reef
Mbalavu
Exploring Isles
Naitamba
Yatata
Koro
Nairai
Ngau
Ovalau
Mango
Thithia
Lakemba
Lakemba Isles
Vanua Vatu
Kambara
Totoya
Moala
Tavua
Vunda
Nandi
Suva
Mbenga
Vatu Leile
Kandavu

Samoa or Wallis Island, and had been crushed to death by the pieces of metal.

The English authorities gave their permission for me to have the *Firecrest* hauled up on their slipways, and even reduced the minimum charge from £25 to £20. And so, for the first time, the little *Firecrest* was pulled up on cars made for steamers of two thousand tons and more and a hundred yards in length!

The second bronze bolt was put in place and several of the copper plates renewed. The leaden ballast was retained, but it was sunk in cement, and this gave me a clean bilge.

According to the regulations of the port, I was obliged to get my repairs done by a private firm, but when I wanted anything, Mr. Sabben, the acting chief engineer of the Government dockyard, always treated me with unfailing courtesy and kindness. Assisted by a native Fijian, I scraped the *Firecrest* to the bare wood inside and out before painting and varnishing it anew. The mainsail's leech was also mended and a new jib made.

All these repairs kept me several months at Suva, where I made a very agreeable stay. There I met again Colonel Golding, with whom I had often played tennis in France, in 1913, at the Paris Tennis Club, just at the time of his marriage with the French covered-court lady champion. We played together an exhibition match before the Governor, Sir Eyre Hudson. At Suva there were splendid sports grounds, about ten excellent grass courts, a cricket and football field, and all of them in splendid turf. I could not help secretly drawing comparisons between this place and our own French capital of the Eastern Pacific, where the sporting spirit—or rather anti-sporting spirit—of our Government seemed precisely the same as that with which we were so familiar in France ten years before the war.

The Fijian race, which is a cross between the black Melanesian and the Polynesian, is, from the point of view of physique, one of the finest of the human species. Tall of stature, with a splendid torso and long, fuzzy hair somewhat resembling the bearskin of an English Guardsman, such is the typical Fijian. They are of a playful and peaceful disposition, make excellent sailors, and if ever I should want a crew for a future voyage it would be difficult to recruit a better one than I could get at the Fiji Islands.

There was already a glimpse of the East at Suva, with its numerous Hindu traders and tailors, its Chinese laundrymen and restaurant keepers. It would be nearly impossible to find a greater contrast than that presented by the Hindus and Fijians—between the little men, fond of covering their women-folk with jewellery and trinkets of all sorts, and the great strong fellows of the island, utterly indifferent to wealth and thoroughly enjoying life, careless of the morrow.

One day H.M.S. *Renown,* flying the colours of the Duke and Duchess of York, steamed into Suva roads, escorted by a fleet of native canoes whose sails were made of woven mats, in the real old style. The contrast was remarkable between this titanic monster, the very latest and most deadly creation of human genius, and my little *Firecrest,* which had brought me so gallantly to the Antipodes. I could not help reflecting on my own life which I would not have exchanged for that of any other human being. Was not I a freer man alone on the *Firecrest* than was the Royal passenger on the *Renown*?

The *Franconia,* another giant of 30,000 tons, was also at Suva. She was crowded with American tourists who, for the modest sum of some thousands of dollars, had the satisfaction of making a voyage round the world in less than four months. For my part I infinitely preferred the slowness of the *Firecrest* and the following of my own fancy, calling in at all sorts of curious little ports, to the monotony of a programme arranged long in advance, carried out along with unavoidable companions, and diverted with native dances all performed to order. All sorts of fantastic rumours circulated in Suva concerning the fabulous wealth of the passengers on the *Franconia,* but if anybody asked me I always replied: "I do not believe it; when millionaires travel round the world they sail, like myself, on their own private yachts."

Here, too, I saw the *Cassiopée* again, for she had come to coal at Suva. For the third time chance threw us together, and although the commander and some of the men were new, yet it always gave me the same pleasure to find myself amongst sailors of my own country.

I have a very clear remembrance of delightful automobile rides through the Fijian country with Tommy Horne, and of visits to his house away in the mountains, from which one overlooked the Rewa river. I should have liked to visit some of the islands farther removed from civilization, and would gladly have accepted the invitation of the great Fijian chieftain, Ratu Popi, to sail across to his island of Mbau. But the *Firecrest* was ready by this time for sea, and I had no time to lose if I meant to make the Cape before the end of the southern summer. Before my departure, however, I had to effect a capture of a very important nature. The rat which had been crushed in the ballast during my last voyage had not been alone, and every night I heard his mate gnawing the timbers and planking of the *Firecrest* for lack of better food. I much dreaded the ravages committed by rodents, who might well cause me a leak or make a hole in the water-tanks; and after many unsuccessful endeavours I succeeded in capturing my enemy, in a trap baited with a piece of sweet potato. It was a splendid beast, with a beautiful long rich fur coat and belonged to a species quite unknown in the Fiji Islands. Once it was caught I had no further trouble with rodents and had only to contend with cockroaches.

On the morning of Friday, March 11th, I left my anchorage near Government Wharf, amid the cheers of all the workmen in the dockyard, who had shown the greatest interest in my undertaking. For some time I was becalmed near the pass, and as I lay there a local motor schooner, on the way out to the sea, offered me a tow, which, according to my custom, I refused. A little later a slight breeze sprang up and I was able to make my way out of the lagoon. That evening and night were dead calm, and when morning dawned I saw the island of Mbenga five miles away. I was very sorry not to have time to put in there, for it was the home of "the Fire-Walkers," who are said to possess the secret of being able to walk with impunity over red-hot heated stones. On great occasions they give public exhibitions of their skill, and this power, known to Polynesians and Hindus alike, has greatly puzzled the scientists. For my part, I believed it was simply a cleverly worked illusion, and I should greatly have liked to verify on the spot the exactitude of my deductions.

The trade-winds had not yet definitely set in, for it was still the southern summer. There was a very feeble breeze, and I made but little way. On the morning of March 12th I was awakened by the hooting of a siren. It was the steamer *Suva* coming in from Australia and bearing down on the *Firecrest*, which was the cause of much curiosity on the part of her passengers.

For some time after this the weather remained very calm and I spent my leisure time in catching bonitos with the mother-of-pearl hook which Terio a Terio Terai, the Tahitian chief, had given me at Tahiti. On March 23rd one of the New Hebrides—the New Cyclades of Bougainville—the island of Erromango, hove in sight some seventy miles away to the south-west. On the morrow I sighted the Isle of Vate, and during the night the beam of Pango, beneath which I found myself when day broke. This was a lighthouse situated on the very extremity of a cape covered with virgin bush. I was no longer in the zone of the once civilized Polynesian, but had reached the first of the Melanesian Islands, with their primitive inhabitants. Doubling the cape, I made my way into Mele Bay, and thence into the channel of Port-Vila, where I had to beat up against a squally wind that heeled the *Firecrest* clean over on her beam. Soon I passed those wonderful islands, Iniriki and Vila. A motor-canoe, with Frenchmen aboard, sped out to meet me and followed me in all my tacks. At ten o'clock in the morning of March 25th I dropped anchor in sandy bottom one cable off Port-Vila jetty.

The town lies on the slopes of a hill—a town with dreadful roofs of corrugated iron jumbled together without any sort of order or artistic effect. I found there a number of my countrymen, for the islands are placed under the joint government of England and France, or *Condominium*, as it is called. Each nation looks after the affairs of its own nationals, and all difficulties are solved by a curious international tribunal presided over by a Spanish judge. This ingenious though singularly unpractical régime was known locally as "The Pandemonium."

I met several French officials at Port-Vila, and the day after my arrival I was taken for a ride on horseback, and was able to admire the extraordinary fertility of the island. I also received a cable from His Excellency M. Guyon, High Commissioner of the French Republic in the Pacific, bidding me welcome and inviting me to pay him a visit at Noumea. Unfortunately it was not possible to alter my plans to include this.

Near to the landing-place at Port-Vila, at the very water's edge, was a club where the French and English residents foregathered, men whose conversation was curious and interesting, for many of them remembered the "black-birding," in other words, the compulsory recruiting of native labour for the plantations. This system, which in former times lent itself to so much abuse, is now rigidly controlled and supervised.

Here, too, I met with yet another instance of the strange and foolish way in which white men fail to see the right way of living in the tropics, making abuse of alcoholic drinks, wearing European clothes and sun-helmets, which only afford a factitious and quite imaginary protection against the heat of the tropical sun. Very few were in good health or able to undertake anything like such physical exertion as came to me quite easily. As for myself, I had learned long before that only a natural existence and the adoption of age-old customs of the natives could ensure strength and good health.

Close by the entrance to the harbour was a charming island which I visited one day in my Berthon boat. Little naked Kanakas were playing on the beach, and they all ran away when I approached, though they trooped after me at a distance when I walked across the island, spying every movement I made. In front of the square-built huts, not at all picturesque and carefully hidden among the trees, the natives were cooking their meals in much the same manner as the Polynesians. They were amazed to find that I knew a few words of their language, which presented certain similarities to that spoken in the Tonga and Wallis Islands. Indeed, the small islands lying round the great island of Vate had formerly been peopled by a Polynesian migration from Wallis and Tonga, who had conquered the black Melanesians they found in possession. Intermarriage with the women of the conquered race resulted in the present inhabitants, some of whom were of a marked Polynesian type.

While adorable and graceful naked children were shooting birds with bows and blunt arrows, I made my way into a large hut where most of the male inhabitants of the island were gathered together. It was very high at the entrance, which was surmounted by two immense bulls' horns, but it narrowed as one entered. Within were some benches and a long drum made out of the hollowed trunk of a tree. It was probably used of yore to summon the inhabitants to their mysterious savage ceremonies. It re-echoed with a strangely dull yet sonorous rumble when I beat it.

Port-Vila was frequented by quite a number of trading craft from Noumea, whose crews, mostly from the Loyalty Islands, were of superb physique, with wonderful skins like burnished copper. They wore nothing but short loin-cloths, and were fond of painting their bodies and faces with red lines. I often went on board a cargo boat, whose Breton skipper before meeting me had always refused to believe that there was any truth in my voyage. When he met me, however, he gave me a very cordial reception.

After remaining a very few days at Port-Vila I sailed for the island of Mele, at the very far end of the bay, where I hoped to rest in peace and tranquillity. The island of Mele was on a coral reef of which the greatest breadth across was scarcely four hundred yards. Upon this tiny spot of land lived close on five hundred natives, descendants of men who had been driven there in olden times from the necessity of protection against attacks from the mainland. The vegetation at this end of the bay was astonishing, and there were several splendid groves of coco-nut trees. As I sailed near the island the slight breeze dropped to a dead calm, and numerous children paddling narrow, unsteady outrigger canoes shot out to pilot me to a mooring place between the island and the shore of the mainland. There I dropped my anchor in water of an amazing transparency and clearness.

The Isle of Mele was exceedingly interesting and, like Vila, inhabited by a race half Polynesian and half Melanesian. When I stepped on shore I found the children busy playing croquet, which seemed their favourite pastime. They spent a great part of their day in the water, however, fishing or racing on the surf which they were riding in their tiny little dug-outs. Never before did I see such a profusion of craft. I verily believe that every inhabitant of the island had his own canoe, made to fit him—long and narrow canoes hewn out of a single piece of tree-trunk, and needing the utmost skill in balancing to avoid capsizing.

Sometimes the natives went to work in the fields, whence they would return laden with yams and sweet potatoes, but I do not think they had to labour more than five or six hours a week in order to get all the food they wanted, such is the marvellous fertility of the soil in these islands. They were a happy people, as yet unacquainted with the needs created by white civilization.

On the shore, immediately opposite the *Firecrest*'s anchorage, dwelt a French planter whom I had met at Port-Vila; and he took me on horseback to see his plantation. I was amazed at the fertility of the land. Maize yielded two harvests a year and grew to a prodigious height. A few natives were employed on the plantations, but the greater part of the work was done by Indo-Chinese. There was a curious Annamite village where these people, so tiny and different from the Melanesians, lived in philosophical ease, chewing their betel and hashish.

The suppression of the forcible recruiting of black natives had, as a matter of fact, almost completely suppressed Melanesian labour. French planters had Indo-Chinese coolies imported by the Government; but the English, for lack of labour, had been obliged to abandon the greater part of their plantations, and had sold them to French syndicates.

On our return from this ride the planter showed me the hut of a New Hebridean worker, situated near the pathway. It was a typical native habitation, so cunningly hidden in the bush that from a few yards' distance it was quite invisible.

During my brief stay at Mele I rarely went ashore. Although the children came often enough alongside the *Firecrest,* the adult natives were very suspicious, and hurried into their huts whenever I approached. This was very different from the open hospitality extended to foreigners by the Polynesians, but the reason of it became apparent on the Sunday before I left. The chieftain of the island, who was at the same time the catechist appointed by the British missionaries, asked me to dinner, and I soon saw that the new religion was far too severe for these people and cast a shade over the spontaneous gaiety of native life. It was next to impossible to obtain any information about ancient customs, for the chief was inspired with all the fervour of the ardent neophyte and regarded with undiscerning horror anything appertaining to pagan days. He was entertaining me with hymns on a brand new gramophone when one came from the beach to say that the *Firecrest* had dragged her anchor and was drifting out to the end of the bay. In all haste I jumped into my dinghy, set out in pursuit, and reached her just in time to hoist the sail before she struck bottom. As it was Sunday, none of the natives had ventured to help me or my boat, for their version of the Christian religion forbids them making any use of their canoes on that day, even to help other people.

As I beat up against a light breeze I saw between the island and the main shore a graceful ketch making a wide tack to get into Port-Vila. It was the first time I had set eyes on her, but I recognized her at a glance. She was the *Snark*, Jack London's *Snark*, on board of which one of my favourite authors had made a wonderful cruise in 1907. A beautiful and gallant craft she was, for all that the critics had said in olden times. She sailed frequently between New Caledonia and the New Hebrides, and the sailors of those seas had nothing but praise to say of her.

A few days later I weighed anchor for New Guinea. It was noon, April 12th, and the letting off a few dynamite sticks was the rousing farewell that my friend the planter gave me.

CHAPTER XVI

THROUGH THE CORAL SEA

THE trade-winds were late to blow this season when I sailed from the Bay of Mele, and I was nearly becalmed for nine weary days. On April 16th, however, the *Firecrest* had a very narrow escape from disaster. I was doing something on the deck when I noticed speeding towards me on the surface of the water an enormous fin swimming in the direction of my boat very rapidly. When quite close it dived beneath the hull. This manœuvre was repeated twice over, but the third time a gigantic sword-fish shot out of the water clean over the stern of the *Firecrest*. If the brute had pierced my hull with its sword—and instances of this have been often reported by seamen—it would have undoubtedly caused my boat a very serious leak.

On April 22nd there was a swell, and various diving birds and sea-swallows flew around me and perched on the rigging. A fresh squally breeze blew up from the south-east, but—and this was a very exceptional thing for the month of April—the current streamed south-westerly. On the 26th the glass fell, the sea became very rough, the wind rose, and rain began to fall in torrents. Everything pointed to an approaching cyclone somewhere between where I was and the Australian coast. More scientific than the captain in Conrad's "Typhoon," I determined the probable trajectory and the location of the centre of the depression; then, running before it under my jibs sheeted flat, I shaped a course to get away from the track of the meteor. Less than twelve hours after I had changed my course the weather cleared and the trade began to blow again. Thanks to my handling of the situation, I had so escaped the terrific swell that I was almost doubtful of the reality of the depression, but on my arrival in New Guinea I heard that a cyclone had actually passed about two hundred miles from my position on that very day, and had done serious damage along the Australian coast.

Soon after this the breeze fell, and in the Coral Sea the current bore me steadily to the south-west, in contradiction to all information given on the charts. On April 29th a strong, choppy swell warned me of the probable existence of a shoal, and I regretted having no sounding gear at hand. On May 5th, about a hundred miles away, I sighted the mountain tops of New Guinea, and soon afterwards began to thread my way through the mass of debris of all sorts that the current had borne into the gulf. It was at this juncture that one of my chronometers began to go very irregularly and ended by stopping altogether.

After being becalmed some days, I sighted the lights from Port Moresby. At dawn, as I was still becalmed about five miles away I saw what appeared to be a steamer unnaturally motionless, but when the sea breeze started to blow I came nearer and saw that it was a wreck piled up on the great coral reef.

I made my way into the lagoon by the Basilisk channel, and there I noticed a strange craft following a course running obliquely to my own. Three long dug-outs were lashed alongside one another to support a large platform, on which were huddled more than forty natives, and the strange craft was propelled by two curious triangular sails, the upper points of which were cut out in a sort of crescent. What amazed me most, however, was to see how rapidly this queer raft—which the Papuans name a "*lakatoi*"—sped along the water. The *Firecrest* slid over the tranquil surface of the lagoon at a comfortable six knots, but she was hopelessly outdistanced.

Doubling the points of Bogirohobobi and Elakurukuru, I dropped anchor astern of a trading schooner, close to the jetty of Port Moresby. It was half-past four in the afternoon of May 10th, twenty-eight days after my departure from Port-Vila.

The European town stood on an arid and dreary bay, and consisted mostly of business houses. It was already growing late when an American yachtsman came aboard and asked me to go and dine with him. After four weeks of complete solitude it was not absolutely unpleasant to be in company and to get a chance of reading the latest news in the yachting magazines of my American sailor friends. But, alas, it was only relative civilization, and my whole evening was spoiled, for an instrument that stood behind me was emitting all sorts of abominable and indecent noises such as ought not to be tolerated in good company, but which radio fans do their best to excuse by naming them atmospheric interferences.

I met with a delightful welcome from the Australian society of Port Moresby, and got many a good game of tennis. There were some excellent hard courts situated in a most picturesque setting, with bougainvilleas all round, and nearby was a pleasant avenue of handsome villas by the seashore. The hard courts were up to the championship class, and once again I was forced to draw comparisons with our French Pacific colonies, where sporting grounds are unknown.

I often played bridge with Dr. Harse, a keen tennis follower, who had been an assiduous spectator at the Davis Cup matches in Australia, when Wilding and Brookes were the great tennis stars. We used to discuss the relative merits of the game in those days and in our own times, and were unanimous in thinking that the two great Australian champions had a genius equal to that shown by the best players of modern days.

Osborne Grimshaw, whose sister, Miss Beatrice Grimshaw, the well-known English novelist of the South Seas, was, unfortunately, over in Australia, asked me to dinner and gave me a superb warrior's spear with a tip made of human bone. I was also received by the Governor of British New Guinea, Sir J. H. P. Murray, who kept me to lunch with him. Sir Hubert was a man of most distinctive and interesting personality. He had been the amateur light heavyweight boxing champion of Australia at a time when the best amateurs were as good as the professionals, and it was now twenty years that he had been Governor of Papua. He had done a certain amount of exploring, and had studied profoundly the customs and dialects of the various native peoples under his control. His conversation was at all times most interesting, but it was when we came to speak about the various methods of administration for native races that I became entirely charmed. He was convinced of the dangers that beset the primitive peoples when they adopt our white civilization too precipitately, and he was trying to preserve as far as possible all that was good in their ancient customs, notably whatever concerned food and clothing. At the same time he did his utmost to protect them from being exploited by the traders, whose only thought was their own personal and temporary gain, but who cared not about the consequences to the future of the race. At last I had met an administrator to whom I could expound my own views, which he understood and did not dismiss as absurd Utopias. There will ever remain in my memory as one of the pleasantest episodes of my stay at Papua my conversation with this remarkable man who considered it one of the greatest duties of his administration to protect and defend the native races. My mind turned back, not without a certain melancholy, to my beloved islands in Eastern Polynesia, whose inhabitants had suffered so terribly from the effects of white civilization, and where a fast disappearing race of fine people might so easily be saved if the white race did really want it.

From the town to Government Residence a road ran along the hill-side, and from it there was a fine view of the wonderful harbour of Port Moresby. Below the Residence were the native villages of Hanuabada and Tanobada, and towards these I directed my steps. At the entrance of the first village numerous and small naked children were tobogganing down a steep path on the hill-side. These villages, which were densely populated, had been built out in the bay on piles by the Motu tribe, so that they might be defended the more easily against the raids of the redoubtable head-hunters from the jungle. At the entrance to each village were four great wooden posts, carved and coloured in brilliant hues; standing near by there was a raised platform, the whole reminding the visitor that he was in New Guinea, the land of witchcraft and totemism.

The village of Elevara was built on an island cut off from the mainland at high water.

The people were of good physique, with long, fuzzy hair that looked just like a sort of headdress. The men wore nothing but a loin-cloth, the women had a skirt made of strips of bark bound together round the waist. Such young girls as had not yet been deformed by hard, menial work, which is the lot of all Melanesian women, were very slender and graceful. They wore flowers draped round their arms and in their hair, and had their faces and backs tattooed in delicate and artistic designs, so finely executed that they could only be perceived at close quarters.

Notwithstanding this scantiness of clothing, the morality of these villages seemed better than it was in the East Pacific Islands, where the natives wear European clothing. That morality should exist in inverse ratio to the area of clothing worn seems to be a Law of Nature which my long voyage to many places enabled me to establish with finality.

The diversity of races in the island seemed to be great, and the streets of Port Moresby were thronged with natives of every shade of colour. There was one type, very black with a long, thin nose, that presented indisputably all the true Semitic characteristics, and very likely had for ancestors one of the lost tribes of Israel. There were yellow natives, others of a light coffee colour, and yet others of a red copper hue, and all were speaking innumerable dialects. There were also some Melanesians from Tupuselei and Gaite who were not unlike the finest type of Fijian, and contrasting with these were the natives of Samarai, nearly all in the service of the various officials, who wore their hair cut in curious geometrical shapes, something like the clipped yew trees to be seen in our gardens.

Some of them smoked a sort of curious long pipe made of bamboo about a yard and a half long, and as thick round as the arm. Tobacco leaves were stuffed in at one extremity and smoked through the other. Maybe this was the origin of the amazing statement made by Captain Cook that from his ship he had seen the natives with a sort of stick in their hand from which issued flames and smoke like that produced by a musket being fired. What the gallant captain had taken as a hostile demonstration was probably nothing else than the natives calmly smoking their pipes as they watched his vessel pass.

There were innumerable canoes on the bay. The natives of this part of New Guinea were skilful mariners, and every year made long voyages, with the help of the favourable monsoon, to the further extremity of the bay of Papua, laden with pottery, which they bartered for sago, their staple food.

Before my departure the *Firecrest* was honoured by visits from the Governor and from Monseigneur de Boismenu, Vicar-Apostolic of Papua, and we had a long talk about the late Reverend Father Bourjade, a renowned aviator during the war, when he made a name for himself by destroying kite balloons. He had met a premature end from fever in this unhealthy climate, and his memory was yet green in this great foreign island, where they were very proud of him.

CHAPTER XVII

FROM PACIFIC TO INDIAN OCEAN

I WEIGHED anchor on May 19th and sailed out of Papua harbour and the lagoon by the Basilisk channel. The trade-wind was by no means settled, and four days after my departure I could still see the reservoir that stands on the hill that dominates Port Moresby. Even when a light breeze sprang up, I always had against me the strong current boring down from the Gulf of Papua. The water had taken on a yellowish tinge and on its surface floated enormous tree trunks which caused me great anxiety. The abundance of life all around was extraordinary; I was continually surrounded by a multitude of fish and a vast number of sea-birds that came to roost at nightfall on the boom. Their cries and squabbles often awakened me, and I had to run up on deck armed with a stick to restore order.

I never tired of studying the habits of the fish. I had already obtained innumerable proofs of their intelligence and their methods of communicating with one another. When there was very little wind I used to amuse myself by skimming a mother-of-pearl bait along the surface of the water. The dolphins soon recognized all the dangers connected with this lure. They shot up to it as quick as lightning, nuzzled it without ever taking it in their mouths, and for hours at a stretch would play with me in this fashion. I was already well aware of this instinct of play amongst the lower creatures. I had seen dolphins catch a flying-fish in their mouths, toss it up into the air with a twist of the head, let it escape and catch it again instantly, playing with their prey like a cat does with a mouse.

When a piece of wood or some other object came floating by the fish would dart away from the *Firecrest* and play around it, while the seabirds would swoop down with sharp screams that sounded like whoops of joy. Of a truth, the life of these creatures seemed one of continual play, thus confirming my theory that playing is one of the primordial instincts of man; that though it is but reasonable that he should work to gain his daily food, it is unwise to make the pursuit of wealth the principal object of existence. Here, also, I found the chief reason for the disappearance of the primitive races as soon as they come into contact with white civilization, which makes existence too dull, and by suppressing the instinct of play, robs them of all interest to life itself.

My course towards the Indian Ocean was barred by the dangerous coral islands and reefs named "The Great Barrier" that stretch across from the eastern coast of Australia to New Guinea. There was only one channel in any way practicable for me, and that was the north-eastern, or Bligh, passage. But there was never a lighthouse to steer by, and all steamers that passed through it were accustomed to anchor for the night.

This was certainly one of the most difficult feats of my cruise, to make my way single-handed through this dangerous passage, studded with cruel rocks. At five o'clock on May 26th an observation of the sun placed me approximately at the entrance of the channel and climbing aloft I was able to make out the buoy at Bramble Cay, ten miles or so away. However, I did not anchor for the night but dared to keep to my southerly course, which I altered during the night to a south-westerly. The *Firecrest* steered herself, and kept a true course, for when morning came the dangerous reefs off Darnley Island were far away on the starboard beam and Stephens Island lay only five miles on the port bow. By this time sailing was delightful in the sheltered waters of the passage dotted with sandy islands covered with coco-nut trees—Campbell, Dalrymple, Keats, Marsden and York. Unfortunately the wind headed me, veering to the south, thus preventing me from making before nightfall to Coco-nut Island, where I had intended anchoring. As I approached a little islet—unnamed on my chart—a sudden squall tore my mainsail and staysail and I had to take them in. It was getting pitchy dark; to leeward were the dangerous Dungeness reefs, while the strength of the

FROM PACIFIC TO INDIAN OCEAN

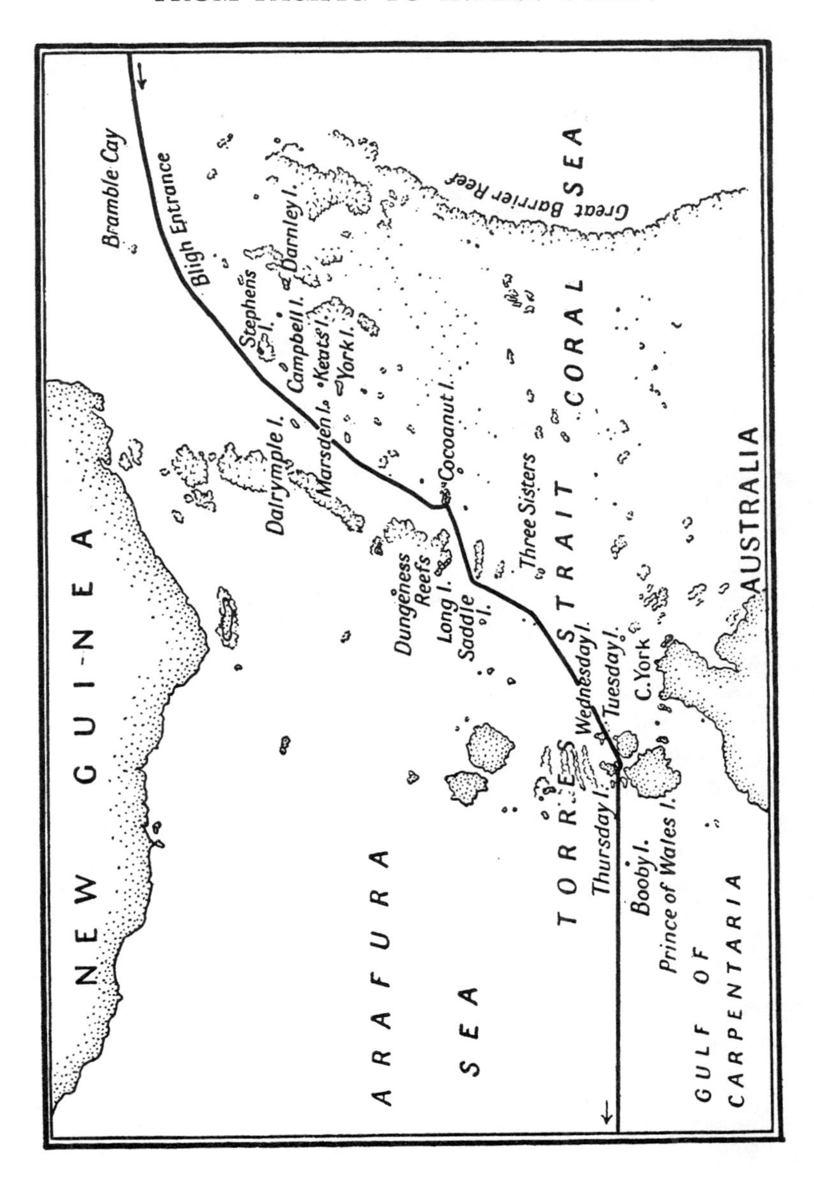

tidal streams was too great to allow me to heave to with a reasonable degree of safety. So I had to drop a hawser and kedge to some sixteen fathoms deep. The squall had caused a heavy swell, and somewhere about midnight the hawser parted. I had not yet repaired the sails, I could not pick up my course again, and there was nothing to do but drop my anchor with sixty fathoms of chain cable, thereafter passing a very comfortless night on account of the terrific wrenches of the swell upon the chain. When day dawned the wind was still fresh, and as soon as I had got the sails repaired I tried to heave the anchor up. With the assistance of running tackle I had just veered about ten fathoms on board when the chain snapped. I was in the narrowest and most reef-infested part of the channel, with no possibility of making Thursday Island before nightfall, and the only safe thing was to run into the shelter of Long Island, where there was plenty of sea room clear from all dangers.

It was at this moment that I saw a sloop manned by natives making towards me from Coco-nut Island. When I hailed them in English and asked if they could lend me an anchor, they offered to pilot me to their own island, some five miles a-weather, where I should find a safe place to lie up for the night. Their sloop was twice the tonnage of the *Firecrest*, and sailed faster in the heavy swell; so they gave me a tow-rope, and several natives came on board. It was the first time I had ever been towed by a sailing boat! The wind was blowing from the south, and the *Firecrest* had two turns of the mainsail rolled. I was keen to show the natives what my boat could do in a brisk breeze and a short sea, so I set up my whole mainsail. The *Firecrest* heeled over until her rail was under water; she buried her nose in the seas that swept the whole length of the deck, but all the same she began to sail closer to the wind than her tug. The natives got frightened and clung to the rigging. Accustomed to larger boats, that sailed without heeling over so much, they expected every instant that the *Firecrest* would capsize, but I knew that her heavy lead keel would stop her heeling over too far.

We soon reached Coco-nut Island, a charming little spot of land on a coral reef covered with coco-nut palms, where I passed the night safely moored to the stern of the sloop *Pamoura*.

Most of the inhabitants, including the chieftain, who rejoiced in the title of consul, came to visit me on board. They were very pleasant and well-mannered folk, black enough in skin, but betraying sure evidence of having at some time crossed with a lighter Polynesian stock. I was surprised to find that an elderly man of about sixty, who had first spoken to me in the beachcomber jargon of the islands, tried to converse with me in French. Observing my astonishment, he told me that he came from Nantes, but had lived for thirty-five years in the Straits. From sheer lack of practice he had practically lost the language of his youth, had never learned the native and could only speak a sort of broken English.

I went ashore to see the chief of the island and try to get an anchor. He would not take money, but lent me an anchor and a hawser which I was to leave for them to collect when I got to Thursday Island. Small as it was, this islet was truly charming and reminded me vividly of my beloved Polynesia. The Frenchman, who quickly began to pick up his own language, took me to his hut and while one of his seven daughters prepared a meal, told me his history. He was known by the nickname of Jimmy Dis-donc, from the Breton sailor habit of using frequently these two words in conversation. He had sailed in his youth before the mast on a sailing ship, and having lost his heart to some of the native belles of the islands, deserted. What stories he had to tell!

As a pearl-diver with machines he remembered the times when rogues of all sorts reigned supreme in the archipelago, when the unscrupulous white men were a law unto themselves. He had never been able to make his fortune—drink and women had been his ruin; but his eyes gleamed strangely when he spoke about his adventures.

"Once upon a time," he told me, "I owned a schooner, but I gave it to a native chief in exchange for his daughter. I never regretted it for a moment, and if it were to be done over again I would do it gladly. Ah, what a beauty she was, mate!"

All sorts of dates and events were muddled up in his memory.

"I once met," he said, "an American sailor who, like you, was sailing round the world all by himself. He was a real Yankee, too—thin, tall, gaunt, bald, with a pointed beard. He gave a lecture at Thursday Island, and showed us lantern slides of his voyage. That must have been ten years ago," said he.

I explained to him that this visitor could have been none other than the famous Captain Slocum in the *Spray*, and that it was at least thirty years ago. "Like enough; probably it *was* thirty years ago," he answered. "Time passes so quickly in the islands!"

Near me was seated his only son, a strikingly handsome young fellow of a copper hue. He held my hand and fixed his brilliant eyes upon me, trying in vain to make out the sense of the words he could not understand.

"Why don't you take Louis with you?" said Jimmy Disdonc. "I have been too long in the country ever to leave it, though I should very much like to see France again. One day I was alongside a French warship in the anchorage at Thursday Island and I had a chat with some of the sailors. They asked me to go on board, but I wasn't such a fool; I knew well enough that once they had me on the ship they would have me put in irons and taken me back to France as a deserter. No, I shan't leave the island, but why don't you take Louis with you? You can show him our country and bring him back when next you come to the Straits."

But I knew too much of the hardships of my ascetic life to inflict them on a companion—even a voluntary one; and I knew, moreover, that it would not be wise to bring into contact with our artificial civilization this child of the wilds who led such a healthy natural existence in his own adorable island.

The principal occupation of the inhabitants of Coco-nut Island was spearing fish on the reef and diving for troca shells. As in Polynesia the fishing was carried out with long spears with several prongs, and the natives were extraordinarily skilful in using these weapons, rarely missing the target even at a distance of seventy feet. They dived for troca, a mother-of-pearl of conical shape, from the sloop which I had met, in depths of five to ten fathoms. They went across to Thursday Island to sell their catch, and the money was banked with the Protector of Natives of Torres Straits, who gave them in exchange food and clothing.

On Tuesday it was blowing half a gale and the natives besought me not to sail. I gave Jimmy Dis-donc some Fiji taros which I thought might grow in the sandy soil of the island. On the morning of Wednesday, June 1st, I weighed anchor and having a beam wind passed near some dangerous islands rejoicing in very picturesque names—Three Sisters, the Nine-pin, the Saddle—indicated on my chart which was one hundred years old. Soon I ran in between Tuesday and Wednesday Islands, which were covered with wild vegetation but where human step seemed never to have trod. At last I reached the channel which forms the anchorage of Port Kennedy and at half-past four in the afternoon dropped anchor in the midst of a flotilla of at least a hundred pearling ketches, and in a six knots tidal stream. In only eight hours and a half I had sailed sixty miles from Coco-nut Island. A really excellent speed for a craft the size of the *Firecrest*. The harbour-master, officers of health and customs people came alongside at once and made me sign innumerable documents, leaving me yet others to be filled up—leaving on my mind a great impression of the volume of Australian red tape.

In contrast to the neighbouring Wednesday Island, which is so wildly beautiful, Thursday Island—or T.I. as it is called locally—proved sandy and very sparsely wooded. The houses and shops were abominably ugly for the most part, built of white deal with corrugated iron roofs. There was, all the same, a certain picturesqueness about the place, with its medley of traders, Chinese, Malays, Filipinos, pearl-divers and builders of junks, even a few Australian aborigines, who worked on the fishing-boats.

Pearl-diving was entirely in the hands of the Japanese who undertook the job and provided divers in suits on a several years' contract. It amazed me that "All White Australia" had granted a coloured nation the right of exploiting one of her greatest sources of wealth! Shortage of labour was, no doubt, the cause of this. There were a few native skin divers, however, who went down without any suits for troca or mother-of-pearl, but their best records were very inferior to what I had seen for myself in the Tuamotu Archipelago. The mother-of-pearl got in Torres Strait is better and more valuable than that found at the Tuamotu islands; on the other hand the proportion of pearls is less.

Thursday Island is part of Queensland. To speak about distant Australia to an inhabitant of Thursday Island is as great an insult as to tell a Corsican, on landing, that you have just come over from France and not from the mainland. The *Firecrest* was in Australian waters, as I was not likely to forget, for they give yachts no privileges and I was obliged to conform to the same formalities at arrival and departure as if mine had been a huge cargo boat. I had to furnish exhaustive lists, in triplicate, of every scrap of food I had on board, and was forced to fill in a vast number of "Nil" forms—lists of passengers, crew, etc. Australian red tape, indeed, is unbelievable, but happily it is largely compensated for—or was in my case anyhow—by the extreme affability and willingness of the officials.

I got some tennis with some excellent Australian players and the *Pilot of Torres Strait*, which claims to be the smallest newspaper in the world, devoted several articles to my exhibitions. In so small a place as T.I. it was inevitable that I should suffer some of the inconveniences of fame; but what did it matter when amongst the usual crowd of jealous detractors I met one sincere friend? W——, an excellent sportsman who would be deeply offended if I were to mention his name. His wife was the grand-niece of the last King of Samoa. He showed me the utmost kindness and insisted on helping me when, in spite of numberless cables, I could not get the firms in Brisbane to send me, in time for my departure, a chain cable and anchors which I had ordered and which I needed badly. He took me for a ride in his motor-canoe to Prince of Wales's Island where, near a vast ant-heap, were the remains of a dugong, or sea cow, caught and cooked by the Australian aborigines.

At last, I had to fill in again the usual endless forms to enable me to depart and when this was done I was rather relieved to get away safely from the frightful anchorage of Thursday Island, with its dangerous tidal streams. One more stage of my cruise round the world had been passed; the Pacific was but a memory, and before me lay the wide Indian Ocean.

CHAPTER XVIII

THE ARAFURA SEA

I SAILED from Port Kennedy at eight o'clock in the morning on June 15th, before a fresh southerly breeze, and by noon Booby Island was in sight. At the same time a motor-boat from T.I. was crossing over with provisions for the lighthouse keepers and the few inhabitants of the place. Breakers were dashing all round the island, and to me it seemed a very difficult place to effect a landing. Booby Island had, in old times, a store depôt, and a letter-box for the convenience of whalers, whose voyages usually lasted several years. Whalers coming out from Europe or America were leaving letters there, and others homeward bound were collecting them. Before leaving the island I exchanged signals with the motor-boat.

Soon after nightfall I observed a total eclipse of the moon. By the morrow I had left astern all the dangers of Torres Straits, and could reckon with satisfaction on the fact that the rest of my way to France would be absolutely clear of reefs.

The surface of the Arafura Sea was covered with a kind of red dust, which had already been observed and remarked upon by Captain Cook and Charles Darwin. Countless little sea-snakes, flashing in bright colours, were wrigging frequently to the surface. At night the water was remarkably phosphorescent and the *Firecrest* left a long shining wake.

During my passage the wind blew from the east and never from the south-east, forcing me to keep on tacking and thus considerably adding to the distance I had to cover. On June 23rd, not far from Cape Wessel, down under the horizon, I passed a steamer, and for some days my track followed the coast-line of Arnheim Land and Northern Australia, but out of sight of land. On July 1st, I sighted the high peaks of Timor, the following day I passed Roti Island, and the day after that, sailing through Semau Straits between Roti and Timor, I ran into the marvellous roadstead of Kupwang, and dropped anchor opposite Fort Concordia, having made a passage of eighteen days.

Kupwang is an old fortified Dutch town, with several block-houses and a rampart along the shore. The Dutch Resident, M. Hamerster, gave me a warm welcome; to my great surprise he seemed to know all about the *Firecrest* and her cruise, but this was explained when he showed me a Dutch edition of the book I had written about my crossing of the Atlantic.

In the old fort proper were to be found all the fascination and glamour of the East that Conrad knows so well how to describe; Malays in *sarongs* and innumerable Chinese at their tiny shops and stores where everything seems to be divided out into minute portions before being sold. There were temples belonging to all sorts of religions, mosques and joss-houses brilliantly lighted, with images and all the attributes of ancestor-worship. The native population consisted of people of many races, some from the island of Roti, others from Savu—men with a lighter colour and considerable resemblance to the Polynesians. There were also a few natives, who had come down from the mountains with their turbans and marvellously made sword blades, and when one of their rajahs passed along the street he was saluted with the utmost respect by all who belonged to his clan.

I sampled Malay cooking, which was highly spiced and concocted for palates hardened to the use of betel-nut. I much preferred the Chinese cuisine. But better than anything, I liked to wander through the streets watching the continuous movement, the colour and the life, until I came to the movable restaurant of some young Mussulman in his fez; there I would stop and eat *sake* or pieces of mutton skewered on a long stick and grilled in the open over red-hot charcoals. To refresh myself I drank delicious palm wine, which street vendors sold in baskets made of one big palm leaf. Often the warm evening air was filled with the plaintive music of the forty-eight-stringed guitars, whose box was likewise made of a big palm leaf.

Thus it was that each stage of my journey brought with it

new sensations and experiences. But however much I might be taken with the fascination and glamour of the East, yet nothing could efface the memory of Polynesia, and now that I was homeward bound it became unspeakably melancholy to be daily leaving it farther behind me.

At the place where I went ashore in my Berthon canoe they were working at low tide, repairing the jetty which had been damaged in a storm. A contractor's foreman supervised the gang of young Malays, whose singular beauty had nothing of the masculine about it. They worked in the water, often far into the night, at pile-driving by means of a curious implement. A great lump of iron was contrived so as to slide up and down between two bamboo trunks, and was raised and dropped in steady rhythm by means of ropes made of twisted coco-nut fibre, divided into numerous ends manipulated by one party of workmen; others held the fragile erection in position and droned out a monotonous chant. The contraption seemed liable to fall apart at any moment, and it was, in fact, constantly in need of mending. The whole business seemed a prodigious waste of effort and energy, but it was a typical example of the methods of work in places where labour can be had for next to nothing.

As the hull of the *Firecrest* needed cleaning, I had her drawn up on the beach at Nanseim, where she was shored up with two magnificent bamboo trunks a foot and a half in girth and immensely strong. The whole length of the shore was peopled by natives from Roti Island, whose dialect of the Malay language contained many words akin to Polynesian languages. Their houses, too, were very similar in appearance to those of Eastern Oceania, which were formerly built of canes and palm leaves, but they were divided into partitions and were floored with a sort of cement. There one seemed to have made use of civilization to render the homes more comfortable. So, at Kupwang, the white men's houses were not roofed with corrugated iron, but with tiles or fibro-cement, which does not conduct heat.

During the three nights of full moon the natives of Nanseim

danced on a clearing by the seashore, holding each other by the hand, stamping up and down with a rhythmical cadence until the moon set. Their legs were wrapped with leaves, and their dances were very similar to those I had seen at Wallis and Coco-nut Islands.

Before I left, the Resident came to tea with me on the *Firecrest*, accompanied by his three daughters. M. van Ginkel, the Assistant Resident, presented me with many souvenirs of the island, including native shawls woven on Savu Island, and bows and arrows from Surambaya. Many attempts, too, were made to persuade me to accept a shipmate for my voyage—a gaudy-coloured parrot, a pretty little ouistiti, a civet or wild cat were all in turn offered and refused, but when a fascinating little Timor pony—so small that it would have been a crime to ride him, and as full of frolic and gambols as a circus pony—put his head on my shoulder, I swore he was the one I should have liked to take with me had there been room for him on the *Firecrest*.

In the evening of July 15th, after three days of calm, I weighed anchor and hoisting my head-sails, drifted gently out into the night. Two days later I sighted the island of Savu and coasted along its northern shore. It seemed to me as attractive as it had to Captain Cook, when, in the course of his first voyage, he put in there to recover some of his crew from scurvy. Savu was noted throughout the islands for the beauty of its women, but I could not put in, for I wanted to get across the Indian Ocean to the African coast before the cyclone season set in.

The following day I sighted Sumbawa, and through the night sailed across a phosphorescent sea, leaving behind me a glittering wake in which were sporting schools of dolphins (*delphinus delphini*). I had decided to sight Christmas Island in order to rate my chronometers; one of them had been temporarily repaired by a Chinese watchmaker at Timor, and in the Arafura Sea I had not been satisfied with the going of the other. I wanted to check them and work out new temperature curves, so that I should not miss making land at the very low atoll of the Cocos.

At first the trades were very gentle, easterly and north-easterly, but never south-easterly, so I had plenty of leisure during the first part of my passage to revise my notes on the voyage. Red-tailed phætons often circled round me at a great height. On August 1st, I sighted Christmas Island and found that the error of my chronometers was exactly what I had calculated.

Hitherto I had met with nothing but fair weather, but on the morrow the wind freshened and the sea became rough. Squalls and showers succeeded one another constantly and the sky was continually overcast. The entries in my log read :

> *Monday, April 8th.*—Squalls and rain all night. Rain, cloudy. Am anxious about the proximity of the Cocos and on account of the bad visibility which prevented my taking observations for thirty hours. Notice that the stay of my staysail is in bad condition. At 10 o'clock a high wind that attained the force of a squall. At 16 o'clock I was obliged to run before it under a close-reefed jib, waves very high, wind east-north-east. During the night a lunar sight taken under bad conditions gave me the exact position I had expected.

At daylight on Tuesday, August 9th, a solar line of position put me twenty-four miles from Keeling Island, and at ten o'clock in the morning I had the satisfaction of seeing, on the horizon, the tops of its palm trees. Once again I felt the thrill of delight I had experienced when sighting the atolls of Polynesia. I sailed along the islands lying on the outer reef and off Direction Island, where I saw people standing near one of the wireless aerial masts watching me. As I tacked into the entrance channel to Port Refuge a sailing canoe, manned by some Englishmen of the Cable Company, came out to meet me, and I dropped anchor near Dymoke Shoal. At high tide, towed by a launch, I entered farther in, almost touching the shelves of coral on either side, and at last dropped anchor in green transparent water near the little jetty of Direction Island, after a passage of twenty-five days.

The staff of the Eastern Extension Cable Company gave me a hearty welcome. Isolated on Direction Island, in the midst of a luxuriant though not very varied vegetation, they were established as only the British know how to establish themselves in the colonies, with excellent mess quarters, a library, billiards and several tennis courts. A wireless mast erected in place of that pulled down by the landing party of the *Emden* bore an inscription commemorating the event, and on North Keeling, fifteen miles away, a few scraps of old iron were all that remained of the once famous corsair.

Five miles south of Direction Island, on the edge of the lagoon, is a little island known locally as Home Island, on which live some five hundred natives of Malay ascendance.

Some days after my arrival I crossed the lagoon in my Berthon boat and was received by the hereditary owner, Mr. J. S. Clunies Ross, a descendant of Captain John Clunies Ross, who settled in the Cocos in 1816. He lived in a large house built in the Scottish style by his father, very comfortable, and arranged to accommodate a large number of visitors. He took me to inspect his shipbuilding yard, which was his principal hobby. He had built several little motor-launches and numerous sailing canoes. Double-ended and V-bottomed, they had remarkable sailing powers. The Malays on the Cocos Islands were certainly skilful shipwrights. There was in the yard a three-masted schooner, about sixty feet long and drawing very little water, with a double skin, which was the prettiest built craft I saw in my voyage. Mr. J. S. Clunies Ross was, in fact, the absolute monarch of the Cocos Islands. The copra harvest, which constituted the entire wealth of the island, belonged solely to him. No money was allowed to circulate, and he gave the Malays whatever seemed best to him in exchange for their labour. The island seemed to me a sort of a paradise. The roads were tidy, the huts clean and picturesque. The natives were small in stature but of pleasant features, looked healthy, and lived in clean and comfortable huts. I could not help comparing this place with our French atolls in Polynesia, where, although the islands were indisputably wealthier, the inhabitants were totally destitute, as the traders grew wealthy at their expense and sent the money out of the country. In the happy Cocos Islands there were no traders, either in material goods or in things spiritual. The dream I had indulged in when I was in Polynesia began to take on more definite form, and I saw myself as being one day the owner of an uninhabited atoll which I would people with Polynesians of my own selection, where no money would circulate and where my subjects would spend a happy life in practising sports and cultivating the arts.

At Keeling Island I had some good games of tennis and though the Cable Company champion beat me the first day, I soon had my revenge. On Friday evenings the Governor kept open house and twice I spent an excellent evening with him and some of my friends of the Cable Company, making the acquaintance of the Malay cuisine and thoroughly enjoying turtle fillets cooked with saffron, after their own special manner.

During my visit I often crossed the lagoon to Home Island in my Berthon boat and played football with Clunies Ross's staff and the Malays, who were playing a pretty game. I also competed once in the yacht races which were run every week off Direction Island, but the boat I sailed was easily beaten.

When the *Firecrest* had been fitted with a new steel-wire stay, and I had replenished my stocks of rice, biscuit and paraffin oil, as well as refilled the water-tanks, I was ready for the long voyage that lay before me. There could be no question of paying for my provisions, as no money circulated in the whole island. I left the charming atoll with regret, bearing with me the pleasantest memories of the welcome I had received from the English Cable Company and from the owner of the island.

My next port of call was Rodriguez Island, two thousand miles distant and encircled by a chain of reefs that made access to it difficult. Unable to get proper charts and having only pilot books to rely upon, I had cabled across to Rodriguez for the bearings and distances of the main landmarks on the island,

and the information I had thus obtained, coupled with my nautical directions, enabled me to make a rough sketch chart.

After a farewell lunch at the Cable Station I weighed anchor at five o'clock in the afternoon of August 21st, hoisted three jibs and the trysail, and leaving Horsburgh Island astern, the darkness soon hid the little atoll from view.

CHAPTER XIX

ACROSS THE INDIAN OCEAN

THE Cocos Islands lie in latitude 12° south, and my next calling port, Rodriguez, in latitude 19° 30′; between them stretched more than two thousand miles of the Indian Ocean. This long passage began with variable winds from the north-north-west, and even from the south-west, which was remarkable for the southern hemisphere winter; then came the trade-winds east-north-easterly, and blowing up with a rough sea. Having almost a stern wind I had to follow a zigzag course in order that the *Firecrest* could steer herself. It was a curious thing that throughout my passage of the Indian Ocean the south-east trade-wind never once blew from that quarter.

Everything got very damp during the run and various parts of my rigging broke, amongst other things one of the bowsprit stays and one of the shroud rigging screws.

On September 8th the wind became very variable, the sea rose and for some days the weather was bad, though it soon cleared up again and light breezes alternating with calms set in as before. As I got farther south I began to feel the cold. My diet was very monotonous too, for at Cocos Islands I had been able to get very few vegetables, and had to content myself almost entirely with rice.

At last, at daylight on September 21st, I sighted Rodriguez Island. Thanks to the bearings I had received by cable I had no difficulty in clearing the north-eastern passage of the reef. When I was fairly in the roadstead of Port Mathurin two open boats sailed out to meet me, one of them flying the British flag. The outer roadstead, about a mile from the shore, was reached from Port Mathurin, a little village standing on a spit of land between two streams, by a creek opening through an inner coral reef, of which I had no chart. So I hove to and waited for the official cutter, but they signalled me to follow them into the narrow creek, which, to my utter amazement, suddenly became very shallow; at the same moment they shouted to me to drop my anchor.

The wind was astern and the *Firecrest* was making about four knots; I had no room to bring to in the wind, so as to slacken my speed before dropping the anchor. To lower my mainsail single-handed with a following wind was a tough job, especially as I had to be at the tiller every instant to steer clear of the coral edges on either side of the channel, which was scarcely sixty feet across. I succeeded, however, in half lowering the sail, dropped anchor and had almost checked the *Firecrest's* way when I felt her touching the coral bottom. At the same instant the officials from the cutter came on board, as well as a great number of natives who crowded the deck and offered me assistance of which I had no need. Despite my remonstrance I was unable to clear the deck, and it took us more than an hour and a half to get afloat and anchor up again in a good place in the channel. I could have done the work myself in a few minutes.

The British Resident, who had come on board, was a Mauritian of French descent, and the natives spoke a Creole French full of all sorts of obsolete words. The pilot, who insisted upon directing all operations, was a black, and constantly interrupted his work to tell me that he was a Frenchman, and to ask news of one of his ancestors named Leveque, who lived in Brittany, which he imagined to be a country similar in size to his own Rodriguez. When I asked him why he had let me run so far into this narrow channel, he appeared very surprised to learn that a cutter drawing so much water as the *Firecrest*, and built with a fine stream line, could not stop her way as easily as a small shallow boat without a keel. And thus it was that the only time I tried to enter a harbour without a chart and trusted myself to a pilot, I very nearly suffered serious damage.

At last the decks were cleared of my importunate guests and I was able to receive the Englishmen from the Cable Station, who had come to meet me in the other cutter and were waiting to invite me up to their mess. There, after a refreshing bath and a good lunch, they showed me the chart of the inner anchorage, and I saw that it would have been utterly impossible to have got farther into the narrow channel in which I had run aground, and that only my own promptitude in handling the boat had saved her from tearing herself open on the coral edges with which the channel was bordered. Now the whole affair lives in my memory as resembling somewhat the entry of a clown into the ring, with all those actors who took part in the play without being asked.

The Cable Company people of Rodriguez gave me as friendly a welcome as I had received at Cocos. The Mauritian Resident, M. Noel, asked me to dinner and came with his wife to pay me a visit on board my boat.

The population of the island is descended from Breton and Norman sailors, crossed with African blacks. It formerly belonged to the French East India Company. It is at Port Mathurin that a British fleet of seventy frigates and troop transports assembled before sailing to besiege the Isle of France, now Mauritius. A year before my arrival the survivors of the *Trevessa* had landed there, after their ship had been lost in the Indian Ocean, thirteen hundred miles to the southward. After suffering great hardships, during which two men succumbed, Captain Foster and eighteen sailors succeeded in making the island after twenty-one days in the long boat.

I was also invited to lunch at the Mission Station, which stands high up on the mountain-side, where I was received by two Fathers who gave me a kind welcome and took me to see their garden, of which they seemed very proud. They lived in the utmost poverty and simplicity, in marked contrast to the gilded opulence of certain missions in the Pacific.

After a very agreeable stay of one week—during which time I by no means forgot to play tennis, any more than I omitted to renew my stock of sweet potatoes, China tea, which I got from a Chinese shopkeeper, as well as some Chinese sauce, which I found an excellent condiment for my rice—I set sail for Réunion, a short trip of four hundred miles—a mere trifle compared with the huge distances that I had before me on my return voyage by way of the Cape.

After eight days, throughout which the light breezes and calms held, I sighted Mauritius through the haze on the morning of October 7th. It was not without something of a thrill that I saw the peaks of this island that for more than a century had been known as the Isle of France, and where, on my charts, the principal places still retained charming old French names—Piton de la Riviere, Cap Malheureux, Petite Riviere, Curepipe, Passe des Citronniers, Riviere des Pamplemousses, which reminded me of Bernardin de Saint Pierre and his famous novel *Paul et Virginie*. On the morrow the mountain-tops of Réunion appeared above the clouds, more than nine thousand feet in height. But the breeze was very light and it was not until the evening of October 9th that I got near the island. At daylight the following morning I ran along the northern coast, passing off the town of Saint-Denis before a good steady wind. I thought I was as good as in Port des Galets, the only one in the island that afforded a safe shelter, but when I ran towards the coast and Cape Bernard was in line with the wireless mast of Saint-Denis, I was suddenly becalmed and a strong current bore me away. So it went on the whole of the day, and I never got nearer than two miles off the lighthouse of Les Galets, for the mountains kept the wind from my sails and the current took me back.

I could see two large steamers in the roadstead, as well as tugs and lighters that came out from the harbour between the two breakwaters, against which the rollers were crashing with a roll of thunder. If I had had enough food on board I would not have waited to put in, but would have sailed off for Madagascar and Durban. That evening a steamer, *La Ville d'Arras*, passed close to me and her passengers cheered loud and long. All night I drifted here and there with the currents and the tide, and by daybreak I was a bit nearer the coast, but still becalmed. By this time, however, I had been sighted from the shore, and at seven o'clock in the morning a tug came out from Port des Galets, and the harbour-master, who was on board, offered to tow me into the inner harbour, which I was glad to accept, for there was still no wind. Behind the tug I passed through the narrow entrance between broken seas. On the breakwaters and quays were gathered a number of the inhabitants, for *La Ville d'Arras* had wirelessed my arrival, and they were waiting for me.

As soon as possible the harbour-master came to welcome me, accompanied by various of the customs and health officials, and handed me a telegram of congratulation and welcome from the governor. I was delighted and surprised, for I was little used to such a reception in French possessions; at Tahiti it had apparently been considered better, in high official circles, to ignore my presence in the port. When I asked by telephone which day I might come and pay respects to the governor to thank him for his telegram, they told me I need not trouble, as he was already on the way from his residence, nearly twenty miles' distance, to welcome me in person. So I had nothing to do but hastily tidy up the boat and wait to receive my distinguished visitor.

M. Repiquet came to see me accompanied by his aide-de-camp, and evinced the greatest interest. With the utmost kindness he fell in with my wish to avoid anything of an official reception, and asked me up to a quiet lunch with him in a couple of days' time. He also put the dockyard at my disposal for any repairs I wanted done. During his visit a considerable crowd began to assemble along the quays where they stood watching me with curiosity. I managed to escape for a while, long enough to get a bath and lunch with the port doctor, and then the telegrams began to pour in—from the syndicated press, from sporting associations, from the British Consul, as well as numbers of private persons.

Soon after this the train came in from Saint-Denis with a load of passengers consumed with curiosity; and, what I dreaded much more, a host of newspaper reporters. But when they knew my repugnance to being interviewed they exhibited the greatest courtesy and left me alone. Everybody wanted to invite me and show hospitality; the press and the sporting folk were anxious to show me the island, and several months' stay would not have sufficed to do all that was planned for me. So I kept to my determination of refusing every invitation and insisted on my intention of getting the *Firecrest* ready for sea, employing every single moment of leisure in keeping myself fit by sport and exercise.

I set to work at once in shifting the various parts of the steel-wire rigging and other iron work which had become rusty and needed renewing. The hull of the *Firecrest* was always in good condition and only the metal-work had suffered from the corrosive damp of the tropics. The repair shops of the C.P.R. (Railways and Port of Réunion) had some excellent smiths who undertook also to make me an anchor, for in the whole island there was nothing that could be of any use for sailing boats.

On the morrow I was able to take a little rest and pay my visit to the governor. In the morning his principal secretary came for me in a car. The road was very picturesque and ran along the mountain-side with terrific hills and continual hairpin bends. We crossed various gorges with picturesque names, and after a run of some twenty miles or more, though the distance as the crow flies could not have been half that, we arrived at the top of a mountain nearly six thousand feet high, with the town of Saint-Denis lying far below at our feet—an immense stretch of horizon before us and a superb view of the whole coast of Réunion. When we got near the town by a long zigzagging descent, a crowd of cars came out to meet us, and the whole population seemed to have collected in the streets, where they stared at me with open curiosity.

What surprised me and attracted my attention immediately was the enormous number of sun-helmets. Everyone had got one, even the tiniest children seemed to have come into the world thus protected. Naturally I was in my usual condition of being hatless, and this was the cause of great amazement. Fear of the sun seemed almost an obsession at Réunion, yet the sun was neither more nor less dangerous there than elsewhere.

After stopping to look at the monument to Roland Garros, for Saint-Denis was the birthplace of this man who was one of the first to fly like a bird, and had been a hero of my college days, we entered a house where I met Monseigneur de Beaumont, bishop of the island, the British Consul, the mayor of Saint-Denis and various other notables of the town. At this juncture I had to sign my name on the roll at the town hall.

In the course of an agreeable lunch with M. and Madame Repiquet, I was able to chat with my host about my beloved Wallis Island, which he knew very well, having previously been governor of New Caledonia. In the afternoon I played a singles at tennis with M. Branlat, who had been one of the great French Rugby players in prehistoric days. To my great surprise the courts were good and in excellent condition. A great crowd assembled to watch me play. When evening came I had the novel experience of returning to Port des Galets by a special train made up of the director's saloon, in which I travelled with the managing director of the Réunion Railway and Port. The track went through a long tunnel and was in itself a monument of skill and ingenuity. I had refused all invitations, as is my invariable custom, as I did not want to be away from the *Firecrest* for the night; and so closed this pleasant day, which will always be impressed on my memory by the kindness shown me by the inhabitants. In no civilized country had I been so fêted and honoured. It was the same during the whole of my stay in the island, where I could always reckon on an enthusiastic reception by the crowd.

As a general rule I rarely went away from Port des Galets and the *Firecrest*, for the work being done on her required constant supervision. If I went to Saint-Denis and took advantage of the car the governor had placed at my disposal, it was only to play tennis or football. The president of the Olympic Club made me an honorary member and I was delighted to mix with the young people and spend a care-free life in the world of sport. The football ground was rather uneven, however, and very slippery, and this made the game difficult.

To my regret I had to refuse all private invitations, as well as the requests of various local associations that I should go and visit them. The pupils of the Lycée, however, who were in the Olympic or the Patriotic football teams, came on a visit to me one day on the *Firecrest*, and we all went away together on the little railway that carried us far away from the drabness of Port des Galets and its somewhat arid setting. We passed through Saint Paul, one of the largest towns on the island, from which the sea was reached by way of a long lake, and it seemed to me that it would have been a much better site than Port des Galets for an artificial harbour. At last we reached the beach at Saint Gilles, opposite the coral reefs, where we spent a glorious day, happy to be alive in the sunshine.

To my great regret I had no time to visit the island and the high mountains that go to make its chief beauty. The sea coast, indeed, could not be compared to that of the Polynesian islands.

I likewise had to refuse pressing invitations from the island of Mauritius, where they wished to receive me and demonstrate that the island was still French, even after a hundred years of British dominion. It would have taken me too long to beat up against the trade-wind and current for the hundred miles that separate Réunion from Mauritius; and I could not make up my mind to leave the *Firecrest* and take passage in a Messageries Maritimes steamer. Indeed, I only left my own boat to go and play football or tennis, or to see the races, where Annam princes were riding against Malagasy jockeys. Wherever I went, however, I met with the same cordial reception from a people that remain passionately French, though so far from the old country.

After a stay of five weeks my repairs were completed. The town council insisted on paying the bills and this was a parting gesture of my memorable stay at Réunion. The governor came and paid me a final visit on board, and sent me a telegram as I was on the point of sailing. Towed out by the port tug, of which Captain Lahaye had taken command, and escorted by a motor-launch, I cleared the bar once again on November 18th. Although I had kept the hour of my departure secret, several friends came to see me off, and they seemed even more moved than myself when I cast off the tow-rope. In a short time I was once more alone on the ocean, heaving along in a steady swell.

CHAPTER XX

THE INDIAN OCEAN IS CROSSED

On the day following my departure from Réunion the trade-wind became quite fresh and at the same time a strong sea began to run across the wind. This was the result of a cyclone which had taken place between Mauritius and Réunion, as I heard later from a letter received at Durban. I was very keen to visit Madagascar, but the anchorage of Saint Lucia, on the east coast, was the only place which could have afforded me comparative safety. As the cyclone season had begun I was forced to give up my plans as well as a projected visit to the primitive people of the Antanos and the Machikoros, for bad weather made landing on the eastern coast dangerous. This was a very rough passage. It would be tedious to quote at length from my log, which contains nothing but references to gales and high seas. I give, however, one or two extracts :

26th Nov.—Strong sea. Wind very fresh. Position at noon 25° 18′ south, 48° 18′ east, gale at about 3 p.m., heavy sea, waves breaking on the deck all night.

27th Nov.—Weather moderating, wind 8 Beaufort, rough sea. The fog prevents me from sighting the high peaks of Madagascar which are within range of visibility.

Tuesday, 29th.—5 p.m. Wind increasing to a gale, lower the mainsail, then to the bowsprit to take in the jib-topsail. Strong swell and choppy sea produced by contrary currents. Wind veers to the south and increases. All night a cross sea breaking on deck, wind three quarters astern, sea two quarters ahead, reminding me of the sea of the Gulf Stream.

Wednesday, 30th.—Wind increases in the evening and veers to the east, the waves break viciously on board, the wind shows a tendency to moderate during the night.

After this period of bad weather there came several days of calm. I had reached latitude 26° south having left the zone of the trade-winds and reached the tropical calms which the English call the "horse latitudes."

I experienced ten days of calm during which I never felt weary. At sea there is always something new and unexpected and the clearness of the sky gave me plenty of opportunity for making observations. Thus, on December 4th I sighted a whale about a mile off in the wind and the next day at about 2 a.m. I saw a comet in the sky. The observation of a total eclipse of the moon on December 8th gave me an opportunity of making an approximate calculation of the error of my chronometers.

The calm weather soon gave way to slight breezes which allowed me to draw near to the African coast, but there I met with strong gales from the west, which came upon me with great force. Here is a description extracted from my log of one of these blows :

> 4*th Dec.*—4 p.m. Wind very fresh, heavy sea, threatening sunset followed by a fall in the wind. At 11.40 p.m. on deck, not a breath of air, but suddenly a number of flashes of lightning visible in the west. Hastily go to the bowsprit to take in the jib. The blow comes with great fury, and my first jib is torn away before I can lower it. Very heavy rain. I run at first southwards under the storm-jib alone, then hove to under the trysail on the port tack. At 11 o'clock a high gale from the south-west, strong sea, very *cool* during the following night. On the morning of 13th Dec. I sighted the African coast, rather nearer to me than it should have been, a strong current having carried me towards land during the night.

I was about two hundred miles from Durban, but it took me several days to reach that port, for I encountered nothing but a succession of calms and gales. In addition, the current bore strongly to the north in contradiction to the information given on my charts. On December 15th the currents were so strong and the sea so rough that I had to keep a sharp look-out during the night, for I was once again on the track taken by steamers.

On the evening of the 16th I noticed the reflection in the clouds of the lights of Durban, and an observation of the moon, taken at four o'clock on the following morning, gave me my position as twenty miles from Durban.

At seven o'clock I sighted the Bluff, which, according to humorists, is what strikes most the traveller coming to Natal. With a following wind I soon entered the straight channel just as an enormous tug with the pilot on board came out to look for me. Without any assistance, however, I had already dropped anchor in a good position in the harbour after a rough passage of twenty-nine days, during which, apart from a torn jib, my rigging had not suffered the least damage. Scarcely had I dropped anchor than the harbour-master came on board and took me to a mooring-buoy specially fitted with cord fenders and intended for Sir Alan Cobham's flying-boat, which they were expecting to arrive. I remained there during part of my stay.

Very shortly afterwards, the Secretary and several members of the Royal Natal Yacht Club called upon me and I was made an honorary member of the Club for the duration of my stay. The Bay of Durban was an admirable place for the regattas which were held there each week. The yachts most in favour were flat-bottomed craft, capable of very high speed, and carried two rudders and two centre-boards. It seemed to me, however, that they were not so fast as the surf-boats of the Society Islands, the Fijis and New Guinea. Each year Mr. George Goodrich and the Commodore of the Yacht Club, Rupert Ellis-Brown, raced in English waters, where they had been very successful. Several of my countrymen came on board to see me and they invited me to a dinner on Christmas Eve at one of the best hotels in Durban. I must confess, however, that I was wholly out of my element after a long year's solitude. Indescribable uproar filled a room where a number of merry-makers were packed round tiny tables. All of them seemed to be making heroic efforts to amuse themselves with childish toys, false noses, paper hats and crude, stupid carnival jokes. The food was the usual succession of made-up dishes favoured by the big restaurants, and compared disadvantageously with the carefully prepared and elaborate meals of certain primitive people with whom I had been in contact. The orchestra was blaring and discordant; more seductive and more original music could have been made by Tahitian children playing the drum or a few bamboo pipes.

Perhaps I shall be inaccurately represented as an enemy of Civilization. But is this really Civilization? I can enjoy a good dinner as well as anyone, a dinner with tasty and carefully prepared dishes, in the company of intelligent and interesting guests or listening to the music of an orchestra playing in a remote room subdued and well-chosen music. But this is something which is unobtainable in the present society life in which I was once again forced to participate and follow the absurd customs. I was unable to get fresh fruit in the restaurants and was always offered tinned fruit, that I never take, although in the streets fresh fruit was cheap and plentiful. Wireless sets, also, were to me a source of annoyance rather than of pleasure, as I could go nowhere without hearing them. In point of fact, it seemed to me that when the modern man has left his work, all he is interested in doing is making a noise to try and forget.

No doubt I am expected to express my enthusiasm for the beauty of that town of which the South Africans are so proud. Durban is certainly clean and well laid out, and its situation on the bay is incomparable, but the environs of the harbour are spoilt by timber yards and factory chimneys, and the view of the sea from the whole length of the promenade along the bay has been hidden by wooden bathing buildings. Perhaps nature has not been as much spoiled there as at Eastbourne, Brighton and some of the seaside resorts on our own side of the Channel, or certainly less than at Atlantic City; nevertheless one has followed the traditional way of building and little use has been made of the resources of modern science to preserve the dignity and beauty of the scenery.

There was anchored in the harbour, not far from the *Fire-*

crest, a pretty and sturdy little British ketch of one hundred and twenty tons, flying the burgee of the Royal Yacht Club of Singapore, and carrying the name *Black Swan* on her counter; she had arrived from Australia, bound for France via the Cape of Good Hope. Of course the newspapers, invariably inaccurate when dealing with maritime affairs, were full of reports of a voyage round the world when the yacht was not even covering a third of the distance. During my stay there was frequent intercourse between the *Firecrest* and the *Black Swan* and her sympathetic owner, Mr. Wearne.

When I had to travel in the town and was not inclined to go afoot, I enjoyed taking a rickshaw, which is a light conveyance on two wheels, drawn by a Zulu native with horns on his head, white socks soap-painted on his legs, and who shook little bells like a playful horse. It was a vehicle, in my own opinion, very superior to the motor-car and I was always pleased to travel slowly and put a curb on the over-speedy life of present times.

During my call I was naturally very busy in putting the rigging of the *Firecrest* in good order, in preparation for the rough passage round the Cape, where I expected to meet with rough weather. What time I had to spare I passed in playing tennis or in going for motor rides with Mr. and Mrs. Machy, countrymen of mine with whom I had become acquainted. The South African veld attracted me more than the town, with its high hills and scenery, which is an endless repetition as far as the eye can reach. In the country one frequently met native villages and Zulus with a broad and engaging smile, and of magnificent physique, wearing woven cotton drawers of simple design.

In the town of Durban, which is predominantly Anglo-Saxon, the distinction between the white and black races was most carefully guarded, and as a result there were very few half-castes.

During my stay I had the privilege of attending a large dance given in honour of the English cricket team, which had come to play a series of matches against South Africa, and so I could admire the beauty of movement and the marvellous physical beauty of a black race which had courageously defended itself against the invaders.

It rained frequently while I was at Durban, and I had really very little opportunity of playing tennis. Before leaving, however, I took part with a friend of mine from Bloemfontein, in an exhibition doubles against the two best local players. To my great surprise, despite my lack of practice, I played very satisfactorily, and we easily won our match. Our adversaries, although rated highly at Durban, were not in the same class as the best South African players. The local partisanship was remarkable, and I have carefully preserved the newspapers bearing reports of our own match as a delightful example of one-sidedness. This, indeed, is one of the most striking things about South Africa, and the sensitiveness of the South Africans to everything which has a bearing on their country is extraordinary. I suppose the same applies to every young nation. But America must first be visited in order to realize how young a country is South Africa.

When I called at the port offices, previous to my departure, I was presented with an account for port dues. At all other places warships and yachts are generally exempted from these charges. I paid the bill, but when I observed that South Africa was the only country which I had encountered on my voyage where I had been asked to make such a payment and that I should be pleased to keep the account as a souvenir, the officials appeared to be very annoyed and said that they would inform the Government at Johannesburg.

On Tuesday, January 24th, having had a new spindle placed in one of my chronometers, I left Durban harbour, tugged by the harbour-master's launch. I had kept my departure secret so as to avoid the journalists.

CHAPTER XXI

THE CAPE OF GOOD HOPE

LEAVING Port Natal on January 24th, towed out by the harbour-master's launch, there was a light head-wind and it was quite choppy in the narrow channel. Several of my friends had come to the end of the jetty to wave me good-bye. The launch left me a few cable lengths outside the harbour; I hoisted the sails and almost at once the breeze dropped! All that evening and the next day the *Firecrest* lay becalmed, rolling heavily in the swell and drifting southwards with the current. On the following day came a strong breeze from the north-east, which had followed the calm of the previous day, while the barometer had fallen to 745 mm. In the evening a strong gale got up, and I was obliged to take in all my canvas and lie to under the staysail alone.

I was obliged to heave to for close on forty-eight hours. The cross current, in conjunction with the wind, made the sea very rough and the waves began to beat in despite the tarpaulin hoods which I had drawn over the skylights. This was the worst weather I had met with in the *Firecrest* with the exception of the hurricanes in the vicinity of the Bermudas. As a matter of fact, on my arrival at the Cape, there was a letter waiting for me from a friend of mine who had been travelling by car along the coast between East London and Port Elizabeth. He said he had been very uneasy about me, for he himself had been forced to stop over in his journey for several hours by reason of the clouds of dust, blown up by the gale. The wind moderated a little on January 28th, and I was able to sail on my course again. My wind charts foretold for this season a large proportion of favourable winds. As usual, it was otherwise, and during the whole of my passage I met with nothing but calms and head-gales, which followed one another on an average every forty-eight hours. However, I made satisfactory progress, keeping about sixty miles distant off the coast and helped by the strong current up to my arrival at the Agulhas shoals on February 5th, when I got out of the current. The next day a strong gale blew from the west, veering almost at once to the south-west, and I sailed close-hauled under the trysail and storm-jib for most of the time.

The following day land was in sight a little to the west of Cape Agulhas, and I saw that I had drifted northwards during the night. The sea was rough and the waves were a good thirty feet high. A trawler, the *Richard Campbell*, circled about me and tried to make signals. I gained then a good idea of the size of the waves, for at times she disappeared completely in the trough and the screw raced almost entirely out of the water. I satisfied myself with taking several photographs and she sailed away. Wind and sea gradually increased and reached their height during the night; then, climbing to the top of the mast, I was able to judge the height of the waves, which rose somewhere about forty-five feet. The log-book has the following entries :

Thursday, 9th Feb.—Calm, several boats in sight. During the night I sighted the Agulhas light.

Friday, 10th Feb.—Nearly dead calm, then a light breeze from the west. Am in sight of Cape Agulhas, about five miles from the coast. In the afternoon the breeze freshened and the sea ran high. A red sunset points to wind on the morrow.

Saturday, 11th.—Westerly wind, three boats in sight at three a.m., at six-thirty high wind from the north-west. At nine o'clock a gale. I take in the torn jib and mend it. I roll in five turns of the mainsail. Strong sea. At noon the wind veers to the west. Position at noon : 35° 8′ south, 19° 13′ west. 2 p.m. A large wave turned the *Firecrest* on its side, wetting the canvas right up to the top, very rough sea. Waves breaking everywhere. I roll in seven turns in the mainsail.

Sunday, 12th.—Wind lessens and veers to the south. A calm

day with a strong swell. One of my primus stoves becomes unsoldered and I repair it. In the evening a good breeze from the south-east. Cold.

On the Monday, the 13th, an observation of the moon taken before daylight gave my latitude as 35° 1′ S. I believed that to be inaccurate, for my charts indicated a northerly current, and I had sailed north during the night. However, I was hanging about all the afternoon and only sighted Cape Hangclip at noon. My lunar sight and calculations had not betrayed me after all. I had had a current of almost two knots against me, bearing me to the south. At last, at four o'clock in the afternoon, I doubled the Cape of Good Hope and took in all my canvas at night time, allowing myself to drift on the northerly current. There were innumerable seabirds, and all night long I heard the plaintive cry of the seals while the current carried me towards the coast in the direction of Chapman Bay. The next day there was a light breeze, and I hugged the coast, lost in admiration of the incomparable mass of those majestic heights, recalling to my mind the marvellous verses which Camoens has left of them.

The breeze held light, and I only just doubled Green Point and reached the entrance to the docks by five in the evening. I had been observed at the signalling station and one of the harbour officials came out to meet me and piloted me to my appointed place in Victoria Dock. This was on February 11th, after a rough crossing of three weeks, during which I had met with nothing but calms, contrary gales and a spell of bad weather, very unusual for this season. However, the *Firecrest* had got no serious damage, and I grinned to read in a Cape newspaper the account of the interviews with the passengers of a large mail-boat which had arrived the same day as myself. They were complaining of having met with a terrific storm.

The *Firecrest* was berthed in docks for a month in the thick of the smoke and the horrible coal dust which the south-easter blows about. The Commodore of the Royal Yacht Club and some of its members called upon me. At the Cape there were several cruising yachts, unlike Durban, where they only indulged in racing, and the members of the Club were highly interested in the *Firecrest* and the plans for my dream-boat which I had nearly completed.

On arriving I made arrangements with a private dockyard to dry-dock the *Firecrest*. I found that her hull was very foul and I had to change several of the copper sheathing plates and replace them with muntz metal, the only metal to be had there. The wooden stock of the rudder under the bronze fastenings was completely eaten away by worms, and I was forced to shift the bronze part.

The *Firecrest* was nine days on the slips waiting for a favourable tide so that she could be floated off, but the port authorities were kind enough to ask only the fees payable for the customary four days' overhauling.

On my arrival I had received a warrant from the Government reimbursing me for what I had paid for port dues at Durban and exempting me from all charges for my call at the Cape.

While the *Firecrest* was in dry dock I completely overhauled the rigging and gave her several coats of paint. Mr. Bruce, of Winifred, Harvard and Bruce, an American acrobat who was performing in one theatre at the Cape, often used to come and chat to me about yachting in San Francisco Bay, and took pride in helping to give the last coat.

One day, as I was undressed in my working togs, scraping the paint off the *Firecrest*, an English sailor came to ask me to go, just as I was, on board the sloop-of-war *Wallflower*, whose officers invited me to lunch with them.

Much to my surprise, the bill from the dockyard was very moderate. This was the first time in my voyage that I had received fair treatment from a private firm. Normally I had always been exploited, possibly because all sorts of ridiculous rumours were circulating about important prizes and sensational bets I was supposed to have received or made.

Cape Town is built at the foot of Table Mountain in a magnificent setting, a curious town with little æsthetic attraction. When Table Mountain is covered with its cloth of clouds, the south-east wind blows in squalls that raise vast clouds of dust and rubbish of all sorts that sweep along the streets. The predominating Boer element makes the Cape a very different town from the essentially British Durban. In Natal the Zulus are of pure descent, and a splendid race they are, but at the Cape there are only unkempt and rag-wearing half-breeds and tramps steadily deteriorating in physique.

I was soon ready to sail, and having refused with much regret an invitation cabled from my friend, Jean Borotra, from Australia to remain as one of the French touring tennis team in South Africa, I took to the open sea again on March 17th. As one of my friends wanted to make a film of my departure I accepted the offer of the harbour-master's launch to tow me from the very crowded docks. I wanted to carry out all the operations of getting under sail by myself and I had intended making use of the launch merely to keep me from making sternway while I raised the anchor; but everyone wanted to lend a hand and help me to hoist sail. There were some quite fresh gusts from the south-east and the *Firecrest* was soon bowling along at her fastest speed of eight knots, and instead of towing me the launch started to be towed herself! So I had to cast off the tow-rope and land two involuntary passengers at the entrance of the harbour, under shelter of the jetty.

In consequence, the film I was so anxious to get, showing me working the boat all by myself, was certainly a failure.

The fresh north-westerly breeze at the mouth of the harbour dropped almost immediately and gave place to a dead calm as I ran into a thick bank of fog. The breeze blew up again at about 2 p.m. and dispersed the mist so that I sighted Robbin Island; then a thick pall of fog closed round me once again and I had to set my course by compass only, and I was not feeling too confident so near land with the strong currents from the coast. All went well, however, and by nightfall I had left astern the lights of Robbin Island as well as the dangers of the coast.

The Cape and St. Helena are distant from each other, as the crow flies, about two thousand miles. At the beginning of my passage the breeze was patchy and I encountered several gales and storms. It was not until March 30th, in latitude 27°, that I fell in with the trade-winds, which were accompanied by a decided rise in the temperature. Thence onwards my voyage was uneventful and at dawn, on April 19th, I sighted the peaks of St. Helena about thirty miles off. I went round the north-east side of the island, which seemed arid and desolate, and when I reached the other side I only received the breeze in squalls that blew down through the mountain passes. At 3 p.m. I dropped anchor in James Bay, off the picturesque town of Jamestown, which is set in a deep valley between two mountains, thirty-three days out from the Cape.

St. Helena had all those inconveniences which are inseparable from an island frequented by tourists, for as soon as I had landed I was surrounded by picture-postcard vendors and souvenir merchants. The inhabitants, of all colours and types, descended, for the most part, from intermarriage between British colonists and sailors and the African slaves who used formerly to work in the island. They seemed to me honest and interesting; of pleasant features, but rather small in appearance. The children were strangely more under-developed than one would expect of those of a tropical country.

The deep and narrow valley of Jamestown was fertile and its vegetation in strong contrast to the reddish-brown aridity of the rock that surrounded it. One day I rode through the island on horseback. My road followed the side of the mountain and the construction must have involved a considerable amount of work. In the higher regions the vegetation was decidedly European in character and the cottages were similar to those to be seen in England. On arriving on the ridge between the two slopes of the mountain, on the highest point of the islands, I felt the cool strong breath of the trade-winds, and at this height of barely 2,000 feet it was cold and damp. At my feet stretched the fertile vale of Longwood, and, lower still, at the bottom of a ravine, was the tomb of Napoleon. I must confess that not for one moment did I dream of visiting the house at Longwood. I cannot bear guides and places frequented by tourists. I contented myself with pacing slowly and reverently, in solitary meditation, along those paths which the imprisoned Emperor had been so fond of, and then I went back to my boat.

A mail steamer put in at St. Helena during my stay and landed a number of tourists. When evening came I took a trip in my little Berthon boat round the steamer about two miles from land and the officers asked me on board to dinner. At 10 p.m. when the boat was about to sail and I climbed down to my own little craft the passengers cheered me loudly and sang an excellent imitation of the Marseillaise. Mr. Harvey, the master of the *Glengoon Castle,* paid a long visit to the *Firecrest* and was very interested in my instruments and methods of navigation.

I took part in a football match between the English garrison and the natives of St. Helena, and on April 27th I returned on board and raised anchor, bound for Ascension Island, only eight hundred miles away. The trade-winds were light and invariably blew from astern, forcing me to make frequent changes of course, so that it was fourteen days before I sighted the high peaks of Ascension. As I ran in, the island seemed to be singularly black, arid and jagged; yet I always felt the same thrill of delight in discerning new mountain heights and bays. By two o'clock in the afternoon I was well off the north-east point of the island when a cutter came to meet me from the Eastern Cable station in English Bay. At this moment between two peaks I caught sight of the summit of Green Mountain, an oasis in the clouds that shrouded the arid and rough heights of the island. Along the west coast I was sheltered from the trade-winds and the current was carrying me out, but one of the motor-boats of the Cable Company came out and piloted me to moorings off the jetty of Fort Thornton, facing the houses of Georgetown.

Ascension Island was for a number of years a British naval station and it was classed as the *Stone* frigate of His Majesty's Navy. At the present time the island is administered by the British Cable Company and is inhabited by its officials and their servants brought from St. Helena. When I landed in my Berthon a number of the inhabitants collected on the jetty to give me an enthusiastic welcome. I had already much appreciated the reception accorded to me by the Cable Company officials at Cocos Island and Rodriguez, but my reception at Ascension surpassed these.

C. F. Burrell, the genial Mess Secretary, at once took me under his wing and rendered my stay most agreeable. The Cable Company officials were very comfortably settled with an excellent mess, libraries, billiard tables, golf-links, tennis courts, cricket and hockey fields. On account of the staff reductions brought about by the use of new machinery for relaying and transmitting, they were too few to indulge in team sports among themselves, so they had taught the natives from St. Helena, who were their servants in work time and frequently their adversaries on the playing fields. They did a great service to these people by instructing them in their methods of physical exercise, of hygiene and of hydrotherapy. Such a system put into force in our French islands of the Pacific would be of the utmost value and almost the only way of saving the natives from physical degeneration and decrease in numbers.

During my stay I was able to play tennis on a fine cement court, but the strength of the trade-winds made the playing conditions very uneven. I was, however, able to play football quite frequently and this was my favourite sport during my voyage because it gave me more rough exercise than tennis.

A few days after my arrival we set out afoot on an excursion to the top of Green Mountain. The road, which wound in and out among the scorias, must have cost the sailors an immense amount of labour. An aqueduct brought water from the top of the mountain and there were tanks in various places. Not being accustomed to mountain expeditions I was very tired when we reached the cottage which was the rest house of the Cable Company more than two thousand feet high. It was very cold and moist up there and the vegetation was entirely European. There was a small wood and the ground was covered with moss which oozed moisture. There was also a farm, a kitchen garden and some European cattle. By the time we got there it was almost dark, and after a refreshing bath I was able to enjoy the strange pleasure of warming myself in front of a wood fire in the tropics at a latitude of seven degrees south of the Equator.

That night, yielding to Burrell's persuasions, I did not sleep on the *Firecrest* and spent a pleasant evening in good company. At dawn on the following day I discovered that the bare surface of the island was made up of cinders, scorias and lava. There were some forty craters with curious shapes and picturesque names such as the Devil's Riding-schools. Far below, in the distance, was the anchorage of Georgetown, and, a tiny speck in the water, the *Firecrest* moored to her buoy.

The swell was always very strong at Clarence Bay, and visitors who came on board were usually much inconvenienced by it and eager to get back to dry land as quickly as possible. Also there was a phenomenon common to several islands isolated in the middle of the ocean known as rollers. High waves are formed, a mile or two out at sea, often for no apparent reason in calm weather, and roll in to break with great fury on the stairs at the foot of the jetty. Under these conditions, landing was very difficult. However, I nearly always managed to leap on to the landing stairs and to hoist my Berthon out of the water at the same time. In fact, despite the pressure of friends who begged me to sleep on shore, I always returned on board ship except for one night when the sea was too rough.

It was the day that the packet boat called from St. Helena and South Africa and visitors were forbidden to board her. It was very interesting to watch the loading up of the large sea-turtles, whose breeding, together with the shipping of guano, were the only industries of the island. These immense creatures, often weighing as much as half a ton apiece, were brought in lorries and then by means of ropes passed under their fins they were hoisted in the air by a crane and lowered into lighters.

Another of the attractions of Ascension was fishing in the bay where all sorts of fish were to be had of all shapes and sizes. I often observed, close to the *Firecrest*, the presence of *balistes buniva,* which is provided with a sound-producing apparatus like a drum that vibrates as it shakes its pectoral fin. A similar fish, the *balistes vetula,* is very brilliantly coloured. One day, one of my friends fishing from a lighter moored nearer the *Firecrest*, caught on his hook an enormous shark nearly three-quarters of a ton in weight. I fired several shots at him from my rifle without producing much effect as we passed a rope with a running bowline round his tail. But before we could get him on board three of his ferocious companions, attracted by the blood, began shyly to attack him, then to tear him in pieces. From this I had visible evidence that the amazing stories which travellers tell of the extraordinary vitality of these animals are not exaggerated. His stomach and intestines were eaten until there remained only his tail, the spinal column, a little flesh round the head, and a few viscera. Incredible as it may seem, even then the large brute was not dead, opening and shutting his eyes and seemingly showing no discomfort at being torn to shreds. Nor was it until we had severed his spinal column so as to get his head on board that all traces of life disappeared.

And so passed, all too quickly, my short stay at Ascension. I spent my time in the best of good company and I was very sorry to be unable to prolong it, particularly as I had been obliged to spend several months in larger places where I did not enjoy my stay. Indeed, the reception given to me by the Englishmen of the Cable Company at Ascension will remain as one of the pleasantest memories of my voyage. So thoroughly did they exert themselves to make me feel at home that at a farewell dinner given to several of their comrades leaving for England when numerous toasts were proposed, I almost had the impression of being myself a member of the Company which I left so regretfully.

On the morning of May 26th, I set sail with a light breeze. The previous evening I had dined with the Superintendent of the Company and the Bishop of the Islands of St. Helena, Ascension and Tristan da Cunha.

CHAPTER XXII

THE SOUTH ATLANTIC

THE long passage from Ascension to the Cape Verde Islands was going to be particularly difficult. I was in the zone of the south-easterly trade-winds, but St. Vincent, my destination, was in the north-easterly. Between these two zones lay an area subject to storms and calms. Moreover, the Cape Verde Islands lay in a current of more than a knot which was flowing against me. The proper route for sailing ships bound for Europe is in consequence well to the west of these islands towards the Azores, but at the speed I could sail the passage would have taken too long, for I was afraid of running short of water.

The south-easterly trade-winds were very light, but aided now and again by a favourable light current I crossed the line on Tuesday, June 5th, after having spent three years in southern latitudes. I was surrounded by numbers of fish and sea-birds. Frequently in my crossing I had noticed on deck little cephalopodes and had thought they had been washed up there by the sea. But one day, to my great surprise, I noticed that they shot up from the surface literally flying, and were carried along by the breeze. That same night I saw the Pole Star, for the first time for three years. I had a light breeze from the south lasting up to June 11th, when the current bore to the north-west, absolutely contrary to the direction marked on the British Admiralty Charts. On that day I completely lost the trade-winds in 5° of latitude north and entered the terrible zone of the doldrums, where I met nothing but torrential rains, calm, thunder and lightning. I found myself upon the steamship lane and, an extraordinary thing for me, scarcely a day passed without my seeing one, though they took no notice of me. I had constantly to take in or hoist my sails, and the wear and tear caused by the moist heat on the rigging was very great.

On June 18th, in a dead calm, I was surrounded by several hundred cetaceans of the blackfish variety possessing an enormous back fin shaped like a sabre and an almost square head. They stood in the water absolutely vertically, turning over to look at the horizon and to study me with their little eyes. This movement, which is called "pitch-poling," has been wrongly stated by certain authors as peculiar to the cachalot. On the 21st I was followed for a long time by a shark and an enormous ray. This ray, which seemed over thirty feet in width, appeared to me to be more dangerous than the squall which it accompanied.

In 10°, light breezes came from the north, but an adverse current hindered my progress. It was not until July 3rd that I began to feel the north-east trade-winds. On that day I sighted land a little before noon. It was the Isle of Brava and I ascertained that my chronometers had gone slow, probably affected by the moist heat of the doldrums.

The adverse current ran at a speed of four knots between noon and 10 p.m., when I was able to determine my latitude by means of a star passing across the meridan. On July 6th, the island of St. Antonio and St. Vincent hove in sight, but outside of the channel which separates them, I lost the breeze. On the following day a north-easterly breeze blew up into a gale and by sunset the *Firecrest* was heeled completely on her beam ends, so that the sea entered the skylights. The wind remained very fresh and irregular and in the channel I had to tack endlessly from one isle to another against a current of three knots, which made progress very slow. Being so near land I could not leave the tiller.

On Monday, July 9th, the wind fell and by night-time became a light breeze. I had just stood off from the coast near St. Vincent, the opposite shore being five miles away, and I thought it was safe to snatch a short rest. I had been asleep hardly two hours when a light shock awakened me. I guessed at once before leaping on deck what had happened. I had touched a coral reef only a few yards from the shore of St. Antonio. It was almost unbelievable, but the fact was obvious.

There was only a slight breath of air and a strong cross-current had forced me on to the shore. In a few seconds the *Firecrest* was aground, the top of the mast almost touching the cliff, and I could have leapt ashore without getting my feet wet. As it was midnight and the tide was already beginning to ebb, there was nothing to do but to go out in the Berthon and drop an

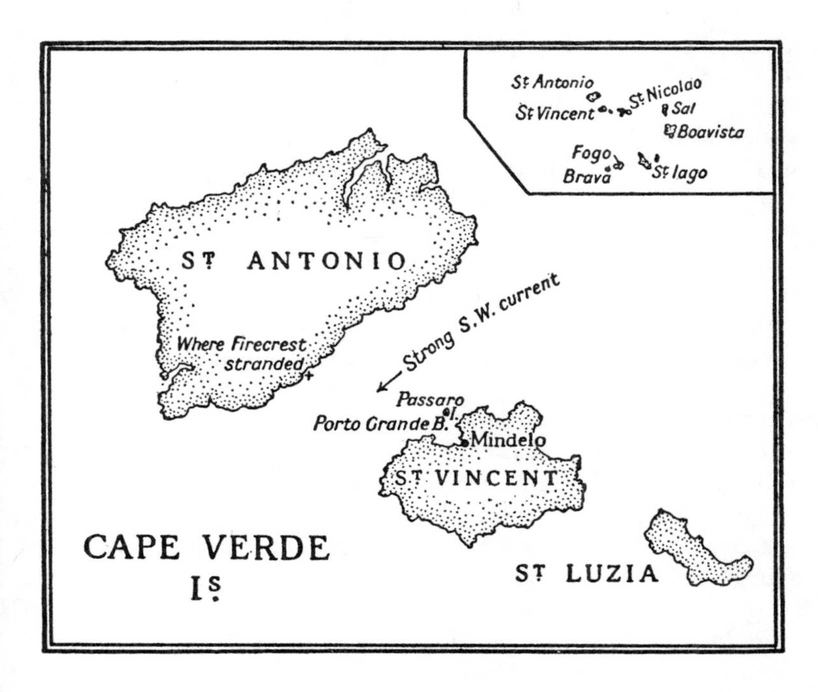

anchor. It was bad luck, but I had to accept the inevitable, which probably meant the total loss of the *Firecrest* if a strong gale blew up. I had no reason to reproach myself for any error in navigation, but I had taken a risk in lying to so close to land with the tiller lashed and would have to take the consequences. Having negotiated the dangerous Tuamotus Archipelago and Torres Straits, it was a little vexing to run aground in a sheltered sound. But one runs great risks in making a voyage single-handed! Steamers run aground even when keeping a constant look-out, and I could not be absolutely certain that if I had not slept I should have been able to make headway against the strong current which had cast me on to the shore. In a similar way Captain Cook, one of the greatest navigators of all time, and possessing specially strong cutters to tow his vessel, had been unable to overcome a current which had thrown him on to a coral reef in the Bay of Tautira at Tahiti.

For the rest of the night waves broke over the *Firecrest*, but without shifting her or causing the least damage. At dawn the tide was low and I climbed the cliff. The surrounding country seemed absolutely deserted and bare. A chain of high mountains stretched in front of me with a large pass between two of them, near which was a little white house. This was two or three miles away. Of vegetation there was none, only sand and stones. Nevertheless about five miles away to the north-east I saw a little village in the midst of a patch of grass. I hoped I should find there some means of getting to St. Vincent and of procuring a tug before a high sea shattered the *Firecrest*. At first I placed on the cliff a flag at the top of a mast rigged up with oars to attract attention; then I made the *Firecrest* fast with several anchors. I hoped that someone would come along so that I could send him to the village, not wishing to leave the boat myself. But there was no sign of life, and I might as well have been cast away on a desert island. Yet in a neighbouring ravine I struck the newly made footsteps of a man, a child and a dog. At last at 11 a.m. I decided to leave the *Firecrest*, and I ran towards the village. This was a difficult cross-country journey over uneven and broken land, across sand-dunes, under a leaden sun. Half running, half walking, I soon arrived at the village without feeling the least fatigued, although I had had no rest for four days. The first person that I met was a negro dressed in nothing but a sun helmet. I tried him with English and with Spanish, but without success; and then, mustering all my resources, I said a few words of Latin and to my great surprise obtained some result. Little did I ever imagine that the Latin tags learnt at school would be of the slightest use. Two sailing boats were moored off the village.

There was the means of my obtaining help. I was in a tremendous hurry, but everybody wanted to stop and talk to me. At last I was taken to the mayor, who spoke a few words of French, and then there arrived a native captain belonging to the islands who spoke English with a strong American accent, for he had emigrated to New Bedford and was a naturalized American. To him I was able to explain my situation. After a long palaver which seemed to me interminable, as the Creole's slowness sorely tried my patience, arrangements were made for someone to telephone the capital, which was situated on the other declivity, and get them to send a wireless message to the neighbouring island of St. Vincent explaining my situation and asking for help. At once an order was sent by the mayor for a guard to be mounted on my boat and everybody showed the greatest kindness. After a hasty meal I left in a rowing boat with the captain, Manuel Chantre, and several natives for the *Firecrest*, which I found intact but a little nearer the shore and with her hull on a spur of rock. Water had begun to trickle in, so I carried on shore various articles which were valuable. Until night time I worked in the water, making her fast with additional anchors.

Leaving the *Firecrest* in charge of the police, I returned to the village. I gave a cinema entertainment to those who had accompanied me, and had a good night's rest; then, as there was no reply to my wireless messsage, I got on board the *Santa Cruz*, a sailing boat of forty tons and, after three hours' sailing, reached Porto-Grande. The harbour launch passed close to us and on seeing my signals ran alongside and I jumped across to her. The harbour-master was aboard and told me, in excellent French, that he had only just received my wireless message and that he was coming to my assistance. We therefore went aboard the *Infante Don Henrique*, and, having pointed out to Captain Bela the position of the *Firecrest*, we set off immediately, for there was no time to lose if we were to get the *Firecrest* off before high tide. Seated at a good lunch I was able to recount my misfortunes, for this was a very different kind of a boat to what I was accustomed, with officers and numerous crew. The *Firecrest* hove in sight at the end of an hour and the *Infante Don Henrique* dropped anchor. The harbour-master, Captain Bela and I went on shore and to my delight I found that my boat had suffered no damage during the night. A long, stout hawser was passed ashore from the tug and made fast to the mast of the *Firecrest*, passing under the keel, while the weight of several natives whom I had placed in the masting prevented the leaden keel from straightening the boat. The cable began to wind round the windlass of the *Infante Don Henrique* and a loud cracking noise was heard as the *Firecrest* began to slide off. This came from a piece of rock which had torn a hole in her side. In a short time she was floating in deep water. The sea rushed in the gap that had been made a little below the water line. Having temporarily stopped the leak with matting, a crew with buckets was left on board to keep her afloat, while the *Infante Don Henrique* tugged against the strong swell at a speed of ten knots, to make Porto-Grande as quickly as possible. This was certainly not the sort of arrival I had hoped to make, but the *Firecrest* was safe again. A powerful pump was placed on board and a crew kept at work all night. A large and variously coloured crowd lined up along the wharf and watched my arrival with interest and curiosity.

Next day I made arrangements with a Portuguese firm and the *Firecrest* was put on the slips. Four side planks had been stove in and had to be renewed. It was a small job, but unfortunately our resources were limited, and for the repairs I was obliged to use white wood full of knots and of a poor quality.

The harbour-master, Daniel Duarte Silva, was very helpful towards me, and so was his brother-in-law, Señor Antonio Sarmento de Vasconcellos y Castro, the French Consul at St. Vincent. I was thus able to discover the intimate relationship between France and Portugal and how far French culture had influenced the latter. Daniel Duarte Silva, grand nephew of a celebrated Portuguese chemist, who was a naturalized Frenchman and a friend of Berthelot and Sainte-Claire Deville, showed his friendship and sympathy for me in a thousand different ways.

Two new sails were made for me, one by the harbour sailors, the other on board the *Infante Don Henrique.* The interior repairs to the *Firecrest* took me several weeks, but on August 14th I put to sea again, wishing to make France before the cold weather set in. After a short stay at the island of St. Antonio, to look once again at the memorable scene of my running ashore, I followed a north-north-westerly course, but the *Firecrest* leaked badly. I had to pump constantly, and after five days I turned back to Porto-Grande, which I reached on August 25th. Once again the *Firecrest* was put on the slips, and this time superintending everything myself, I was able to make her quite seaworthy. It was, however, too late now to reach France before winter, and I decided to put in to the Cape Verde Islands and finish this book.

Thus for the first time the *Firecrest* came back. No doubt this was prudent and wise, but was that really the reason for doing as I did? When I come to analyse my intentions I know that it was not; that primarily I put back because I dreaded to see my cruise coming to an end; a dread that had grown steadily on me ever since I left the Pacific. Above all, I was faced with the thought that on my arrival in France the *Firecrest* would have to be laid up. By returning to the Cape Verde Islands I gained a short respite in these sunny climes, and by returning to France the next spring I should save having to lay up my boat.

But how readily would I have braved all dangers and difficulties, pumping day and night lightheartedly, if my objective had been new tropical isles and not France, where I expected an enthusiastic reception, and a fame that was bound to curtail my liberty. I knew that in the Cape Verde Islands I could find the peace which I desired, so that I could work upon my book, for I had not written, so to speak, a single word for two years.

CHAPTER XXIII

HOME

THE harbour of Porto-Grande is an immense bay surrounded by high and barren mountains. Towards the north it has the effect of being quite closed in by the towering peaks of the island of St. Antonio. To the west the jagged mountain heights are like truncated steeples, minarets and towers, and take strange and fantastic shapes which, according to the nationality of the imaginative traveller, resemble Napoleon or Washington, though my acute sailor eyes could not perceive in them any similarity to anything in particular. As far as the sight could reach, in an extraordinary transparent atmosphere, nothing was to be seen but brown land and rocks, without the slightest vestige of verdure. When the figure of a native appeared silhouetted on one of the mountains it seemed magnified out of all proportions, perhaps because there was no grass to conceal so much as his feet.

St. Vincent seemed even more barren and arid than Ascension, my last stopping place, where the crowning height, known as Green Mountain, was a veritable oasis of verdure.

Two days after my arrival I played some exhibition tennis at a place which boasted absolutely the only tree on the island, if one can except a few coco-nut trees planted along the shore. Near this tennis court was a wooden figure battered by the weather, which was once the figurehead of the famous clipper *Donald McKay*, and represented one of the ancestors of the genial American designer of the same name, who, in his day, laid the lines of the fastest clippers that ever sailed the seven seas.

Close at hand was the city of Mindelo, with its innumerable jetties from which lighters were ceaselessly carrying coal to and from the yards of the great English companies. This seemed to be, indeed, a land of coal. All around the *Firecrest* lay numbers of lighters at anchor awaiting the vessels that were constantly putting in to Cape Verde to coal. Coal was everywhere; a thick film of it lay on the surface of the sea; the squalls that every now and then dragged the anchored ships, even in this safe anchorage, were laden with a dense dust that clung to the ropes and spars of the *Firecrest*.

The island was peopled with folk of all colours. Some dirty, ragged natives on the quays, half black and half white, were shoving trolleys laden with coal, which they emptied into the lighters. Here, once again, the picturesque and hygienic loin-cloth of Polynesia would have been much more suitable to work under the tropical sun than the cast-off clothing of white civilization.

Little negro children, stark naked, ran about the shore, continually plunging into the water to get stray lumps of coal out of the sand; these they carefully collected in bags. In very truth, with the exception of the traders, the whole population lived on nothing but coal and the ships that called in to fill their bunkers, for the island itself produced nothing. Every scrap of food, every drop of water even, was brought from neighbouring and more fertile islands by a large fleet of small cutters and schooners, with ungainly hulls and rigging in poor shape, and heavily laden with fruit and animals of all sorts. There were also, at the same time, some bigger excellent American-built schooners in the island trade.

The people of this island had never been used to getting a living except from visitors and passing seamen, and they considered all strangers as wealthy people who had been sent to them by Providence to be plucked. And yet, in spite of a greed which had become almost hereditary and instinctive, I met from the inhabitants a certain generosity and a vast kind-heartedness that would have been unknown among people more endowed with wealth and apparently more civilized. We soon became good friends, and whenever I went ashore I was sure to be surrounded by a great crowd of children who followed me whithersoever I went.

I have said that I put in to the island to work on my book,

but my courage failed me; my hands, too, were so hardened and rough with working at sea that they were very unwieldy at the pen. This enforced inactivity made me very uneasy; I thought with longing of the great spaces, and reflected sadly that my cruise was nearly finished, that my course now lay for France, that my liberty and dominion of the seas was almost over, and the bondage of celebrity was awaiting me.

The month of September came and went; the month of October passed; and yet I did not write a line, but just raked together a few notes and memories of the Marquesas and Tahiti, though time had scarcely dimmed the memory of them at all, so that my recollections were still too vivid for me to condense them to writing. From time to time I played tennis at the English Cable Company, or with my friend Daniel Duarte Silva, a keen sportsman; but nothing really gripped my interest. I played more from a sense of duty, and to keep fit. I lived in memories, in regrets for the marvellous tropical islands of the Pacific, with many a thought, too, of the dreary days that must pass ere I could replace my old *Firecrest* with the ship of my dreams, and voyage once again to the southern seas.

Towards the end of October a three-funnelled warship put in, flying French colours. She was the *Edgar Quinet* training ship. I was welcomed on board by Captain Darland, who had formerly acted as intermediary between my friend Albarran and the Minister of Marine, Georges Leygues, when the *Cassiopée* had been sent to the aid of the *Firecrest* after her disaster on Wallis Island. I was received very hospitably in the officers' mess, and this was the prelude to four days of excellent comradeship with Lieutenants Meyer, Hourcade, Fontaine, and the other officers of the wardroom, who, living less than myself in actual contact with salt water, were none the less full of zeal and love for their profession.

The next day I had the pleasure of playing football with the snotties and sailors of the *Edgar Quinet* against one of the best teams of St. Vincent. Neither side scored a goal. If, despite all my exertions, I was unable to lead the warship's team to victory, at least I had the satisfaction of not beating my good friend Silva, who kept goal for the Portuguese side.

I also had to give a lecture on my cruise to the cadets of the *Edgar Quinet*, but the strain of recounting my adventures told so heavily on me that I made up my mind never to speak again in public. However, I have the pleasantest memories of those budding young officers, of their great interest in all my doings, and of their charming hospitality when I was invited to lunch at one of their messes. Among those young folk, in very truth the hope of the French navy, I felt perfectly at ease, perhaps because my own heart is youthful within me, so that among men of my own generation I always feel a youngster among old fellows. These lads showed me the utmost attention. Before my departure they insisted on my accepting warm sea-clothes and blankets, and although I never like taking help, the kindly spirit in which the gifts were offered would have made it ungracious in me to refuse them. The *Edgar Quinet* sailed shortly afterwards, leaving me with a pleasant sensation as of having set foot for a brief moment on a moving corner of French soil, and of finding a warm welcome there.

One warship succeeded another in the immense harbour of Porto-Grande. Among them was the *Raleigh*, of the United States Navy. After a game of tennis with Admiral Dayton I dined with him, the captain and Mrs. Sands, Acting British Consul. The world is indeed a small place, for to my great surprise I was received on board by Captain Jacobs, second in command, who was port captain at Cristobal, Colon, where I passed through the Panama Canal. There is some sort of bond linking together sailors all the world over, and once again I found myself enjoying the same cordial hospitality that I had experienced in Samoa, and on the *Rochester* in the harbour of Balboa.

Shortly afterwards came in the French cruiser *Antares*, practically a sister ship to the *Cassiopée*. She was from the Antilles, and arrived just in time for me to take the officers to the New Year's Eve dance given by the officials of the Cable Company. The figures "1928" were inscribed in electrically illuminated letters on one wall of the ballroom; at midnight they flicked out and were instantaneously replaced by "1929," to the accompaniment of loud cheers.

With the Swedish training ship *Fylgia* my relations were less agreeable, for on her arrival at midnight one of her launches cut in two the *Firecrest*'s bowsprit. Luckily I had my anchor lights showing. On the morrow I made a formal complaint, whereupon the captain of the *Fylgia* sent his carpenters on board and having the luck to find several good lengths of American spruce, the damage was repaired in a few hours; for the Scandinavian carpenters knew their job better than any craftsmen I ever saw during the whole course of my cruise; they were, in fact, just such skilful fellows as used to be met with in the olden days of wooden ships.

While one after another vessels were putting in to coal, I wrestled with myself, and little by little the manuscript of my book began to grow. At the middle of December I had scarcely made a start, but by the end of the following month it was nearly finished. I practically gave up tennis, and only played football to keep myself fit. There were several good clubs in the island, and as the natives from their earliest youth were in the habit of knocking about with bare feet, they were clever players. Unfortunately they did not play often enough for my liking, and usually more than a month elapsed between their matches, which prevented my keeping up my form.

At last, towards the beginning of February, the manuscript was finished. It was the greatest joy in the world to get going once again on the minutest fitting out of my boat; for common sailor as I had become, writing had been a real labour, while I revelled in splicing and rigging the boat. Entirely by myself—for I would allow no one to help me—I got the *Firecrest* ready for the last stage of her voyage.

I hoped to be able to get away from the Cape Verde Islands in the early spring, and thus be able to take advantage of the strong winter trades as far as the Azores, where I expected to fall in with the brave westerly winds that blow steadily towards the coast of France until the month of June. I could see myself back in time for the French Tennis championship, for Wimbledon, and in time, perhaps, to take part myself, after a few days' training. But ill-luck dogged me. The mainsail I had got at New York, long since scorched by the tropic sun, was by this time quite useless. At the end of October I had sent minute and precise instruction to my friend Pierre du Pacquier, at Havre, to get me another. The new sail was duly dispatched from the Havre on December 8th, but it was lost, for the Portuguese vessel on which it had been put foundered off Porto, with the entire cargo. A second sail, ordered almost immediately, was delayed in transit, and did not reach me until two months after it had left Havre.

Except for this the *Firecrest* was ready for sea, and I waited impatiently. At last, towards the end of April, to my great delight, the sail arrived, and, thanks to the courtesy of the Portuguese customs authorities, was delivered to me at once. All my instructions had been carried out to the letter, and it fitted perfectly. So the *Firecrest* was hauled ashore once more, and her copper sheathing cleaned and repaired. At long last everything was ready, and I began to look forward with delight to some months' navigation, free from all the cares and worries that are ever inseparable from life ashore.

Before sailing I was lucky enough to get a game of football. I played centre-forward against the team of the English cruiser *Durban*. On the eve of my departure I played for the Mindelense in a final match. This club, in which were several men of colour, was not considered the best in the island from a social point of view, but it undoubtedly had the best sporting spirit, was playing the best game, and it was the one in which I felt most at home. To commemorate my visit I offered a cup to be played for by the two best teams in the island—a cup that had been my first tennis trophy, won in my childhood at Dinard. I had the luck to kick the winning goal.

On Monday, May 6th, my chronometers were regulated, and having taken on board some biscuits, rice, and potatoes, and a new binnacle with which a trader on the island had presented me, I had the joy of weighing anchor at ten o'clock in the morning. The harbour-master, Daniel Duarte Silva, and the French Consul, Señor Sarmiento de Vasconcellos y Castro, came on board. Spreading all my canvas, I glided out before a freshening breeze, saluted by the sirens of all the ships in port, and escorted by numbers of staunch friends from the Mindelense Football Club. A little sloop of the same tonnage as the *Firecrest* put out at the same time. Crowds of people thronged the beach to watch my departure and wave farewell. The wind increased, the *Firecrest* heeled over before it until her rail was completely under water, and I left the little sloop far astern, amid ejaculations of amazement from the onlookers, who were quite unused to seeing boats sail on with such an angle of heel as my small old narrow English cutter.

Near Bird Island my escort left, and my friends bade me farewell with three times three cheers. I had made up my mind to make a northerly course through the straits that separate St. Antonio from St. Vincent. The breeze grew fresher, and I took in two rolls of my mainsail. Near St. Antonio the trade-wind blew up into something of a gale. I tried to tack against wind and current, but the *Firecrest* laboured too heavily, and as the wind continued to grow stronger I lowered the mainsail altogether and hoisted the trysail, wishing to get down into the straits before the north-easterly wind. I had some difficulty in lowering the mainsail, for it was new and hard to manage. As I passed off the village of Corvoeiros I saw all the inhabitants out on the cliffs waving to me, and a cutter came out with some of the young natives on board who had helped me when I drove ashore there eight months previously. Not to disappoint them, I ran in and dropped the anchor. I had to get to work at once, and noted with uneasiness that the *Firecrest* had shipped a lot of water. I had to change various blocks which were not working too well. It was already late in the evening, so I decided to pass the night anchored there, and start off again the following morning. In the meantime the mayor of the village paid me a visit, bringing with him a supply of provisions and a dinner already cooked. Early the following day I set sail, still beating against the wind, and making northward up the straits. The breeze, which had dropped during the night, freshened with dawn, and I had to work up against the same strong current that had brought me to disaster eight months before. It seemed, in fact, as though I was not to get away from these islands. When I spread all my canvas I made headway against the current, but on the other hand the *Firecrest* shipped too much water; if I reduced my sail I hardly made any way at all. I could easily have gone down the straits southward, but I wished to test my boat and see if she was really leaking seriously. I was at the pump day and night, and had to keep a sharp look-out on the dangerous coast. At last, at seven o'clock on Friday, May 10th, not having been able to double the northern point of St. Antonio against the violent and contrary current, I decided to make for the south. For the last time I passed the dreary and barren site of my memorable mishap, and spent the whole night becalmed off the delightful bay of Tarrafal, where the tank ships go to load up water to carry across to St. Vincent. By the morrow the topmost peaks of St. Antonio had vanished from sight; I was once again alone on the vast ocean, and Cape Verde Islands were no more than a single memory in the midst of many, many others.

During my fight against the wind and currents of the straits I noticed with satisfaction that steamers steered clear of me as soon as they saw the bright white lamp which I now used in place of the regulation side-lights. I had on board provisions for more than three months, and it was my intention to make straight for France if the winds were not too contrary. But here again I was not very fortunate. The trade-winds in the North Atlantic vary between north-east and north; with an easterly wind I should have been able to make a fairly northerly course, and my passage would have been rapid. As a matter of fact the winds were almost always more to the north than to the east, and, keeping going constantly on the starboard tack, I was carried out into the middle of the Atlantic.

On May 14th, eleven days after my departure, I discovered

I was suffering from a catarrhal conjunctivitis. I was now in for fifteen days of great discomfort. There was a fresh wind and a choppy sea, and my eyelids continually stuck together by constant suppuration, and yet all the time I was obliged to work hard in the midst of spray. To complete my misfortunes the turnbuckle of the bobstay snapped, and while waiting until the weather should be fair enough to enable me to mend it properly, I had to scramble about in the water and rig up a jury tackle which was constantly wearing through and breaking. At the same time I had to work hard at the pumps to keep the boat afloat.

At ten o'clock on the morning of May 26th, in 32° 36′ W. longitude and 29° 31′ latitude, I crossed the course of my outward voyage and thus completed the circle of the voyage round the world. This gave me, however, no more than a relative satisfaction, for I had nothing to look forward to and everything to dread at my return to civilized life. Already the Southern Cross, last sign of my beloved southern hemisphere, was far down on the horizon; every evening the Pole Star mounted higher and higher in the heavens, and once again I began to see northern constellations which I had almost forgotten.

The trade-winds grew feebler and soon I entered the zone of tropical calms, where light and variable breezes, with occasional squalls, kept me constantly on the alert. I made very little headway, and I decided to put into the Azores to water and take in fruit, as well as to get a new bolt to replace the one which had been broken. On Monday, June 10th, I knew I was somewhere near Horta, in the Azores. It was raining and visibility was very bad; as evening came on I tried in vain to pierce the mist and get a glimpse of the land, which I knew to be very near. In the night the light from Cape Comfreda appeared less than a mile distant. I had once again made an excellent landfall. All night I drifted slowly along the south-eastern coast, so that at daybreak I might double the Cape of Castello Branco, a rock of curious form. The greenness of the island slopes and the cultivated fields that stretched across the hills were a veritable contrast with what had greeted my eyes at the last two ports of call, Ascension and St. Vincent. The north-west wind soon dropped into a calm, and I was peacefully waiting for it to spring up again when three motor-launches came out from Horta and were so kindly insistent upon giving me a tow that I had to accept for fear of offending them. Passing the peninsula of Caia and Hell's Caldron, an extinct crater opening to the sea, I soon found myself in the picturesque harbour of Horta, thirty-five days after my departure from Porto-Grande. From the Portuguese authorities I received the kindly welcome to which I had grown accustomed at the Cape Verde Islands. The captain of the port brought out some sailors and moored me up to a large buoy within the harbour; then the French Consul paid me a visit and took me to lunch, offering me the utmost hospitality, though here, as elsewhere, I declined to leave the *Firecrest* at night. The governor of the island put at my disposal the workshops of the Fayal Supply Company for any small repairs in the rigging that I might need, and offered me the use of his motor-launch to go to and from the shore when I required it, though I preferred to use my canvas Berthon boat, which had met with some rough usage and was only just seaworthy.

Despite the incessant work invariably occasioned by putting into a port, I was able to win several games of tennis against the best players of the island. I also accepted the hospitality of the Eastern Telegraph Company, and enjoyed the same friendly and sporting relations with its staff which I had encountered at previous ports of call. To my great surprise I found there Mr. J. M. Mansfield, who had been the first to come aboard the *Firecrest* after her perilous passage through the dangerous reefs of Rodriguez Island, in the midst of the Indian Ocean, fifteen thousand miles away.

Several interesting boats were in the harbour. There was *Terre Neuve*, on her way back from fishing, and a friendly crew of Breton fishermen, with whom the solitary sailor of the *Firecrest* would have liked to have become better acquainted had their visit not been so short. Then came the cruiser *Vasco da Gama,* whose officers paid a visit to the *Firecrest* and took me back with them to lunch. This vessel held the record for being the oldest warship afloat. Finally there was the steamer *Providence,* of the Fabre Line, whose captain and officers pressed me to accept all sorts of provisions, though I would take nothing from them but fruit, remaining constant to my vegetarian diet while at sea. From the *Providence* I learned that in France I was supposed to have been lost, on account of the report some fanciful steamer captain had made, and they told me that the Navy had sent out many ships in search of me.

After six days in port I was once more ready to start. Captain Pinto, of the Portuguese Merchant Navy, came on board and gave me several charts and navigation tables, which he had helped to make. At one o'clock in the afternoon of Tuesday, June 18th, I left Fayal in a dead calm, towed out by the two launches of the coaling companies who fought out the honour of escorting me. Another launch followed, having on board her the French consul and several of my friends from the English Cable Company. When they left me at nightfall just out of the channel between Fayal and Pico, I was close to the lighthouse of Cape Ribeinha, beneath the verdant hills of the island. The calm lasted all that night, and by daybreak the current had borne me into the strait again. This had been seen at Horta, however, and the launches which had towed me out the previous evening came back and carried me out of the strait and beyond the tidal current. At last a light breeze sprang up, and I was able to bear away, looking back with admiration at the perfect configuration of Pico, with its majestic peak encircled with clouds. During the night I passed the island of Graciosa—a well merited name—and by daybreak was once more alone between sky and sea.

I reckoned on a rapid passage with strong winds, but once more the forecasts of my charts, so far as winds were concerned, were far from realized. Light easterly breezes followed one another during the next days. Contrary to my previous experience, I often came across steamers and, one night—it was June 24th—the insistence with which one of them made for the *Firecrest* and circled round her made me think that she was looking for some fallen aviator. I was to learn later that she was probably in search of Franco, the Spanish airman.

At last the wind shifted to the west. Then came several days of heavy weather, though this was nothing for the *Firecrest*; during this time I was passed by several British steamers, who signalled me very courteously. Then the wind shifted again to the north-east, and I made very little way. My diet was pleasantly varied by some delicious grapefruit the *Providence* had given me. As the end of my voyage grew nearer a great sadness took possession of me; the cruise was soon to end, and with it the happiest period of my life; in a very brief time I should be cruelly deprived of the freedom I loved to dearly.

The passage which I had thought to make in some twenty days turned out to be very long, for easterly head-winds succeeded one another; in fact, I doubt if aviators could ever find atmospheric conditions more favourable for crossing the Atlantic from east to west than they were in June, 1929. I realized that I could not hope to arrive in time for the tennis tournament at Wimbledon; in fact, the approach of what many would have thought to be the ultimate goal of my travels left me calm, for I knew that it would simply be one port of call amongst many others; so I occupied my rare moments of leisure in reading the old Portuguese verse of Luis de Camoens.

On Tuesday, July 16th, the steamer *Michigan* of the French Line came alongside the *Firecrest* and insisted on speaking to me. I took advantage of this to send a message to my friend Pierre du Pacquier and to verify my chronometers which, to my great surprise, had not lost one second. I refused all provisions and would accept nothing but a parcel of newspapers, where I knew I should learn all about the tennis results. Although the sea was so calm I was not without apprehension at finding myself so close under the great steel wall of the steamer's side, and I remembered the damage I had suffered in 1923 from a similarly close proximity to the Greek ship. However much I liked the people of the *Michigan*, it was with the utmost pleasure that I saw her steam away, and while my boat steered herself I opened the newspapers to see what Borotra and Lacoste had been doing in the finals of the French Tennis Championship.

On July 20th I entered the Channel, midway between the English and French coasts, neither of which I wished to sight, for I trusted to the accuracy of my sun and star observations. Out of sight of land I knew also I should meet fewer steamers, yet in these narrow waters is to be found the most traffic in the world, and the risk of collision was so great that I had to keep watch day and night. On the evening of the 22nd, steering herself, the *Firecrest* passed very near a trawler off Start Point. Then followed two days of calm and fog. On the 24th I found myself becalmed upon a sea of glass and in a bank of dense fog, with no more than fifty yards' visibility. I knew I was between Portland Bill and the Casquets, if anything, nearer the English coast. How I cursed the loss of my fog-horn which the damp of the tropics had long ago made so useless that I had thrown it overboard. Towards two o'clock in the afternoon the fog lifted, and a trawler steamed round the *Firecrest*—on her stern I was able to read the name *Mistinguette*. The crew recognized me at once and asked permission to come alongside, so the master, Maze, and Aubry, the engineer, came on the *Firecrest*. In my turn I was asked on board their boat, so to give these fine fellows pleasure I went and thoroughly enjoyed the meal they had prepared for me, though nothing really came up to the simple frugal diet I was accustomed to on the *Firecrest*. After this the whole crew of the *Mistinguette* visited my boat by turns, and together we drank several bottles of Spanish cider, which had been given me by the French Consul at Cape Verde. I was offered a fog-horn, but when it came to parting company the skipper of the *Mistinguette* insisted, with much earnestness, that I should let him tow me as far as Cherbourg. I let him do so, for, to tell the truth, I was by no means sorry to be carried clear of the fog, and the constant strain which had forced me to keep watch night and day. Besides, by this tow I should be able to keep my promise to go and watch Jean Borotra play for the Davis Cup which was to start the following morning. It was nearly four o'clock when I was taken in tow, and by nightfall I saw the harbour lights—the first lights I had seen since leaving the Azores. At eleven o'clock we were caught once again in a dense fog, and steamed in to Cherbourg harbour at reduced speed. The *Mistinguette* moored close to the cruiser *Mulhouse*, with the *Firecrest* in tow; the fishermen turned their searchlight on me and sounded the siren several times, but nobody paid any attention to us.

After yet another night passed without any sleep, but in talking in the saloon of the *Mistinguette*, we cast off again at four o'clock in the morning. The fog had lifted and as we passed under the stern of the *Mulhouse* I hailed the officer of the watch and asked him to send a message, announcing my arrival, to my friend Pierre du Pacquier at Havre. Then the *Mistinguette*, which was going out fishing again, towed me to sea into the wind, in a choppy and boisterous sea. When I was far enough out to be able to double Barfleur I cast off the tow-rope and shouted farewell to my friends. As I hoisted the sails a fresh breeze sprang up from the north-east, accompanied by a heavy swell. At the time a smart little English cutter passed by me, whose crew of young amateurs took me for a fisherman and asked how far they were from Cherbourg. At ten o'clock I passed the lighthouse and semaphore of Barfleur. I was borne along by the strong tide, and I signalled across to them the code number of the *Firecrest*—O Z Y U. The wind was almost dead ahead, and I was obliged to keep on tacking in a rough sea. There was no possibility of my being able to arrive before the morrow, for I had been carried towards Port en Bessin and the mouth of the Seine, and the tide was already on the turn. All that day I hauled the wind, constantly keeping in sight a great three-master that I had scarcely lost from view since my entrance into the Channel. Wind and tide made the sea very high and the *Firecrest* continually buried her bow in great waves. Towards evening I had to take in my mainsail and hoist the storm-sail. The following morning, at daybreak, I was three miles to the north of Port en Bessin. The breeze had shifted a little to the north and was now almost dead against my making Havre. Towards eleven o'clock in the morning a pilot boat from Caen ran up close to the *Firecrest*, the skipper and another man came on board and seemed to think that my narrow-built cutter was much more difficult to sail than their large twenty-five-ton boat. At last, towards afternoon, the sloop-of-war *Ailette*, which had been searching for me since the previous evening, ran alongside and offered me a tow, which I accepted, for it would have been utterly impossible for me to enter Havre under sail against the strong easterly wind that was blowing. I lowered my sails and furled them at once, two young sailors coming on board to help me. The simple, kindly friendship they evinced will ever remain one of the pleasantest memories of my return. Harbour was near and I had not had a wink of sleep for ninety-six hours. Very soon I saw the entrance betwen the breakwaters; the pilot boats, as well as vessels of all sorts, in the harbour, saluted me. Finally I saw my great friends, Pierre du Pacquier and "Coco" Gentien, on a motor life-boat. Our emotion at meeting again was so profound that for some minutes we were unable to speak.

My best of all friends, Pierre Albarran, was not there, but I knew that I should find him among the crowd which had assembled on the quay, whose reception I was going to face entirely for his sake.

And thus, after more than seven hundred entire days spent at sea, after more than forty thousand sea-miles traversed, after incessant struggles against elements, I brought home my old, worn and battered *Firecrest*, into a French port to carry out the promise made to him, my best friend, by wireless sent from the liner *Paris* after our separation in August, 1924:

You must not be sad, for one day I shall come back.

ALAIN GERBAULT.

Yacht Firecrest, *Havre*,
September 6th, 1929.